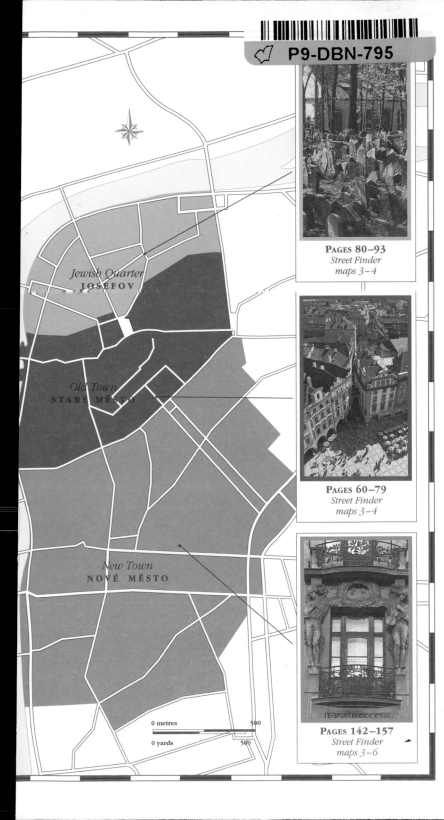

Jewish Quarter
JOSEFOV

Old Town
STARÉ MĚSTO

New Town
NOVÉ MĚSTO

0 metres   500

0 yards   500

PAGES 80–93
*Street Finder
maps 3–4*

PAGES 60–79
*Street Finder
maps 3–4*

PAGES 142–157
*Street Finder
maps 3–6*

EYEWITNESS TRAVEL GUIDES

PRAGUE

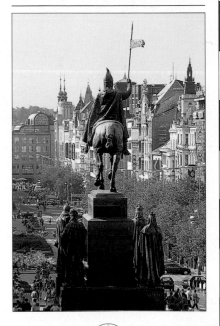

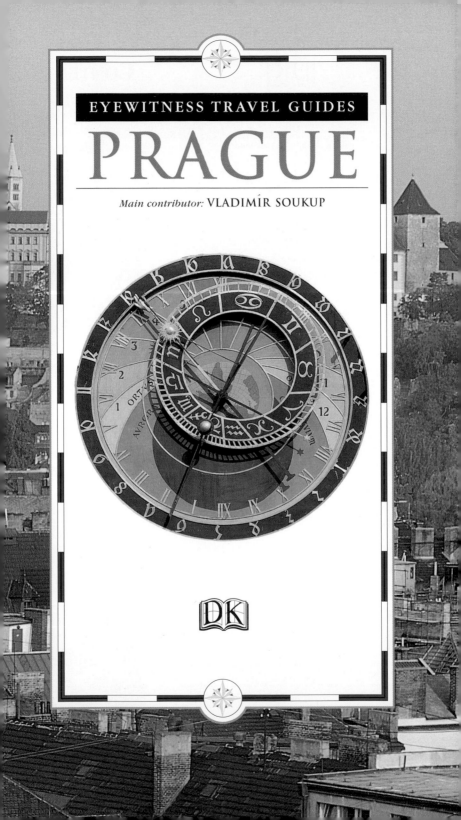

LONDON, NEW YORK,
MELBOURNE, MUNICH AND DELHI
www.dk.com

PROJECT EDITOR Heather Jones
ART EDITOR Lisa Kosky
EDITORS Ferdie McDonald, Carey Combe
US EDITOR Mary Ann Bruchac Lynch
DESIGNERS Louise Parsons, Nicki Rawson

CONTRIBUTORS
Petr David, Vladimír Dobrovodský, Nicholas Lowry,
Polly Phillimore, Joy Turner-Kaděčková

PHOTOGRAPHERS
Jiří Doležal, Jiří Kopřiva, Vladimír Kozlík, František Přeučil,
Milan Posselt, Stanislav Tereba, Peter Wilson

ILLUSTRATORS
Gillie Newman, Chris Orr, Otakar Pok, Jaroslav Staněk

This book was produced with the assistance of
Olympia Publishing House, Prague.

Reproduced by Colourscan, Singapore
Printed and bound in China by Toppan Printing Co., (Shenzhen Ltd)

First American Edition, 1994
05 06 07 08 09 10 9 8 7 6 5 4 3 2 1

Published in the United States by DK Publishing, Inc.,
375 Hudson Street, New York, New York 10014

**Reprinted with revisions 1996, 1997, 2001, 2002, 2003,
2004, 2005**

Copyright © 1994, 2005 Dorling Kindersley Limited, London

Published in Great Britain by Dorling Kindersley Limited.

ISSN 1542-1554
ISBN 0-7894-9422-1

FLOORS ARE REFERRED TO THROUGHOUT IN ACCORDANCE WITH EUROPEAN USAGE;
IE THE "FIRST FLOOR" IS THE FLOOR ABOVE GROUND LEVEL.

**The information in this
Dorling Kindersley Travel Guide is checked annually.**
Every effort has been made to ensure that this book is as up-to-date
as possible at the time of going to press. Some details, however,
such as telephone numbers, opening hours, prices, gallery hanging
arrangements and travel information are liable to change. The
publishers cannot accept responsibility for any consequences arising
from the use of this book, nor for any material on third party
websites, and cannot guarantee that any website address in this
book will be a suitable source of travel information. We value the
views and suggestions of our readers very highly. Please write to:
Publisher, DK Eyewitness Travel Guides,
Dorling Kindersley, 80 Strand, London WC2R 0RL, Great Britain.

CONTENTS

HOW TO USE
THIS GUIDE 6

Rudolph II (1576–1612)

INTRODUCING
PRAGUE

PUTTING PRAGUE
ON THE MAP *10*

THE HISTORY OF
PRAGUE *16*

PRAGUE AT A GLANCE *36*

PRAGUE THROUGH
THE YEAR *50*

A RIVER VIEW OF
PRAGUE *54*

Outdoor café tables

Wallenstein Palace and Garden in the Little Quarter

Church of Our Lady before Týn

Czech beer-bottle top

Fiacre, Old Town Square

Baroque façades of houses at the eastern end of Old Town Square

HOW TO USE THIS GUIDE

Planning the day's itinerary in Prague

THIS EYEWITNESS Travel Guide helps you get the most from your stay in Prague with the minimum of difficulty. The opening section, *Introducing Prague*, locates the city geographically, sets modern Prague in its historical context and describes events through the entire year. *Prague at a Glance* is an overview of the city's main attractions, including a feature on the River Vltava. Section two, *Prague Area by Area*, starts on page 58. This is the main sightseeing section, which covers all the important sights, with photographs, maps and drawings. It also includes day trips from Prague and four guided walks around the city.

Carefully researched tips for hotels, restaurants, shops and markets, cafés and bars, entertainment and sports are found in *Travellers' Needs*. The last section, the *Survival Guide*, contains useful practical advice on all you need to know, from making a telephone call to using the public transport system.

FINDING YOUR WAY AROUND THE SIGHTSEEING SECTION

Each of the five sightseeing areas in the city is colour-coded for easy reference. Every chapter opens with an introduction to the part of Prague it covers, describing its history and character, followed by a Street-by-Street map illustrating the heart of the area. Finding your way around each chapter is made simple by the numbering system used throughout. The most important sights are covered in detail in two or more full pages.

Each area has colour-coded thumb tabs.

Locator map

A locator map shows where you are in relation to other areas in the city centre.

A suggested route takes in the most interesting and attractive streets in the area.

1 Introduction to the area
For easy reference, the sights in each area are numbered and plotted on an area map. To help the visitor, this map also shows metro stations, tram stops, river boat boarding points and parking areas. The area's key sights are listed by category: Churches; Museums and Galleries; Historic Streets and Squares; Palaces; and Parks and Gardens.

The area shaded pink is shown in greater detail on the Street-by-Street map on the following pages.

2 Street-by-Street map
This gives a bird's eye view of the most important parts of each sightseeing area. The numbering of the sights ties in with the area map and the fuller descriptions on the pages that follow.

The list of star sights recommends the places that no visitor should miss.

PRAGUE AREA MAP

THE COLOURED AREAS shown on this map *(see inside front cover)* are the five main sightseeing areas – each covered in a full chapter in *Prague Area by Area (pp58–157)*. They are highlighted on other maps throughout the book. In *Prague at a Glance (pp36–57)*, for example, they help locate the top sights. They are also used to show some of the top restaurants in *Travellers' Needs (pp192–3)* and to plot the routes of the river trip *(p54)* and the four guided walks *(p170)*.

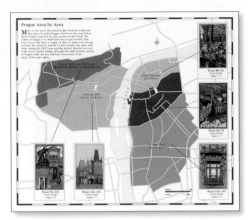

Numbers refer to each sight's position on the area map and its place in the chapter.

Practical information lists all the information you need to visit every sight, including a map reference to the *Street Finder (pp244–9)*.

Façades of important buildings are often shown to help you recognize them quickly.

The visitors' checklist provides all the practical information needed to plan your visit.

3 Detailed information on each sight

All the important sights in Prague are described individually. They are listed in order, following the numbering on the area map. Practical information on opening hours, telephone numbers, admission charges and facilities available is given for each sight. The key to the symbols used can be found on the back flap.

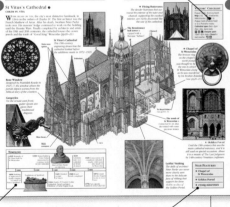

A timeline charts the key events in the history of the building.

4 Prague's major sights

Historic buildings are dissected to reveal their interiors; and museums and galleries have colour-coded floorplans to help you find important exhibits.

Stars indicate the features no visitor should miss.

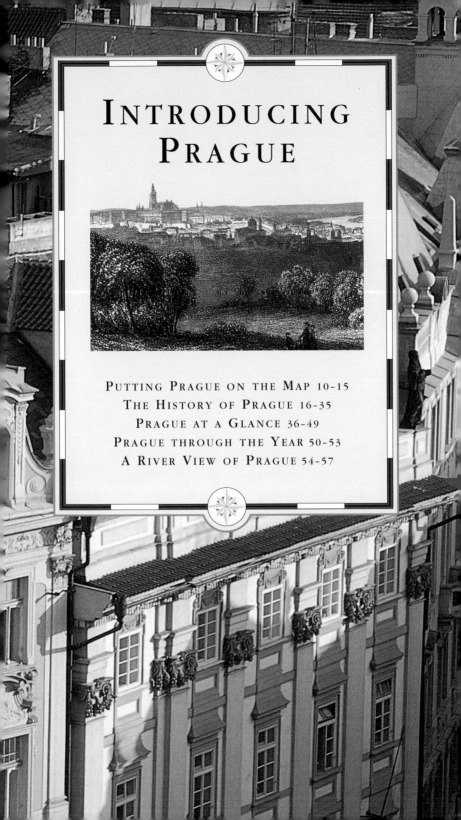

INTRODUCING
PRAGUE

Putting Prague on the Map

Prague HAS A POPULATION of just over 1 million and covers 500 sq km (200 sq miles) at its outer limits. It is the capital of the recently-formed Czech Republic and head of the region of Bohemia. Prague's geographical position at the centre of Europe makes it a convenient base from which to visit both the Bohemian countryside and many other major cities, such as Nuremberg, Vienna, Bratislava and Budapest.

View looking southwest over the Vltava

Europe

The Czech Republic, right at the heart of continental Europe, is completely landlocked. Prague, the capital, has one airport and road and rail links to neighbouring countries.

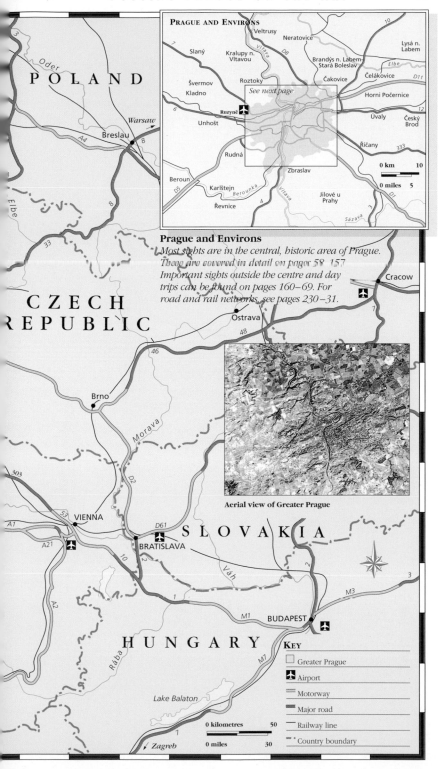

Prague and Environs

Most sights are in the central, historic area of Prague. These are covered in detail on pages 58–157. Important sights outside the centre and day trips can be found on pages 160–69. For road and rail networks, see pages 230–31.

PRAGUE AND ENVIRONS

See next page

0 km   10

0 miles   5

Aerial view of Greater Prague

POLAND

Warsaw

Breslau

CZECH REPUBLIC

Ostrava

Brno

Cracow

VIENNA

BRATISLAVA

SLOVAKIA

HUNGARY

BUDAPEST

Lake Balaton

Zagreb

KEY

☐ Greater Prague

✈ Airport

═ Motorway

▬ Major road

── Railway line

– · Country boundary

0 kilometres   50

0 miles   30

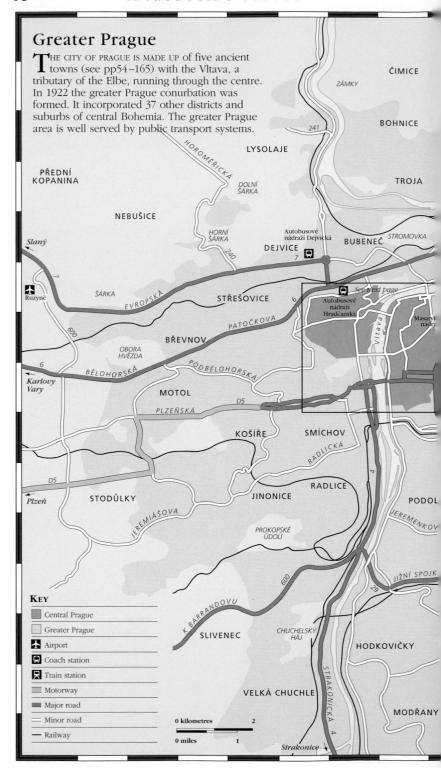

Greater Prague

THE CITY OF PRAGUE IS MADE UP of five ancient towns (see pp54–165) with the Vltava, a tributary of the Elbe, running through the centre. In 1922 the greater Prague conurbation was formed. It incorporated 37 other districts and suburbs of central Bohemia. The greater Prague area is well served by public transport systems.

ČIMICE

ZÁMKY

241

BOHNICE

LYSOLAJE

PŘEDNÍ KOPANINA

HOROMĚŘICKÁ

DOLNÍ ŠÁRKA

TROJA

NEBUŠICE

HORNÍ ŠÁRKA

240

Slaný

Autobusové nádraží Dejvická

DEJVICE 🚌
7

BUBENEČ

STROMOVKA

See next page

🚌

ŠÁRKA

EVROPSKÁ

STŘEŠOVICE

6

Autobusové nádraží Hradčanská

Masaryl nádr.

Vltava

✈ Ruzyně

PATOČKOVA

BŘEVNOV

600

OBORA HVĚZDA

BĚLOHORSKÁ

PODBĚLOHORSKÁ

6

Karlovy Vary

MOTOL

D5

PLZEŇSKÁ

KOŠÍŘE

SMÍCHOV

RADLICKÁ

4

D5

Plzeň

STODŮLKY

JEREMIÁŠOVA

JINONICE

RADLICE

PODOL

JEREMENKOV

PROKOPSKÉ ÚDOLÍ

600

JIŽNÍ SPOJK

29

KEY

K BARRANDOVU

SLIVENEC

CHUCHELSKÝ HÁJ

HODKOVIČKY

STRAKONICKÁ 4

VELKÁ CHUCHLE

MODŘANY

🟦	Central Prague
⬜	Greater Prague
✈	Airport
🚌	Coach station
🚉	Train station
▬	Motorway
▬	Major road
—	Minor road
▬	Railway

0 kilometres 2

0 miles 1

Strakonice

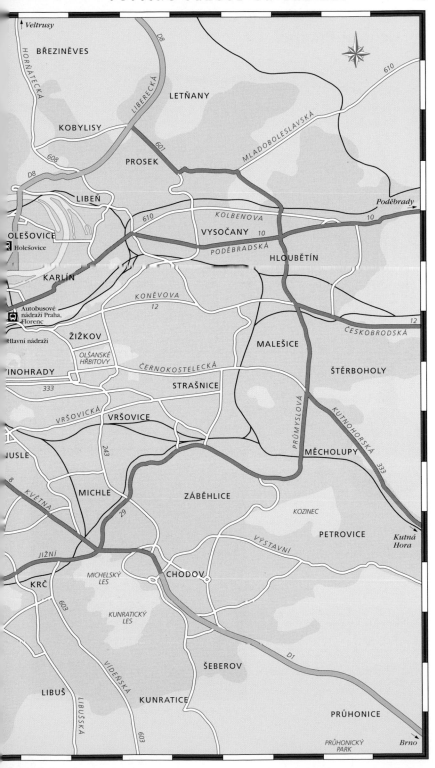

↑ *Veltrusy*

BŘEZINĚVES

HORŇATECKÁ

D8

LIBERECKÁ

LETŇANY

KOBYLISY

608

601

D8

PROSEK

MLADOBOLESLAVSKÁ

610

LIBEŇ

610

KOLBENOVA

Poděbrady

OLEŠOVICE

Holešovice

VYSOČANY

10

10

PODĚBRADSKÁ

HLOUBĚTÍN

KARLÍN

KONĚVOVA

12

Autobusové
nádraží Praha,
Florenc

ČESKOBRODSKÁ

12

Hlavní nádraží

ŽIŽKOV

OLŠANSKÉ
HŘBITOVY

ČERNOKOSTELECKÁ

MALEŠICE

ŠTĚRBOHOLY

INOHRADY

333

STRAŠNICE

VRŠOVICKÁ

VRŠOVICE

243

PRŮMYSLOVÁ

KUTNOHORSKÁ

333

MĚCHOLUPY

USLE

8

KVĚTNÁ

MICHLE

29

ZÁBĚHLICE

KOZINEC

PETROVICE

*Kutná
Hora*

JIŽNÍ

VÝSTAVNÍ

KRČ

603

MICHELSKÝ
LES

CHODOV

KUNRATICKÝ
LES

VIDEŇSKÁ

ŠEBEROV

D1

LIBUŠ

LIBUŠSKÁ

KUNRATICE

603

PRŮHONICE

PRŮHONICKÝ
PARK

Brno

Central Prague

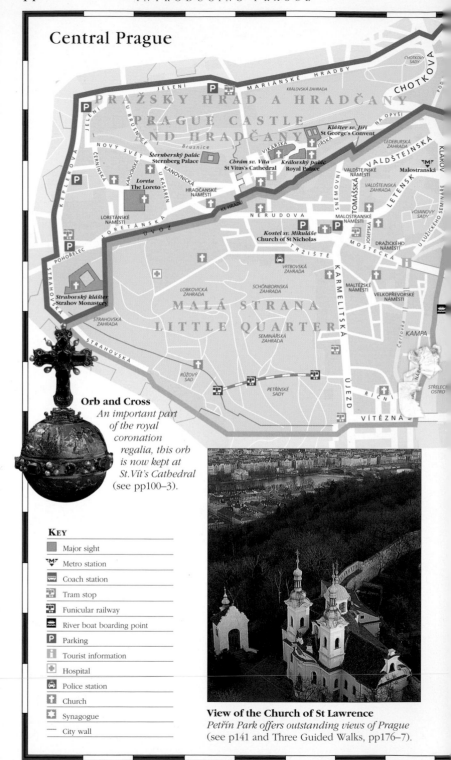

Orb and Cross
An important part of the royal coronation regalia, this orb is now kept at St.Vít's Cathedral (see pp100–3).

KEY

▮	Major sight
ᴹ	Metro station
🚍	Coach station
🚋	Tram stop
🚋	Funicular railway
⛴	River boat boarding point
P	Parking
ℹ	Tourist information
✚	Hospital
🚓	Police station
✝	Church
✡	Synagogue
—	City wall

View of the Church of St Lawrence
Petřín Park offers outstanding views of Prague (see p141 and Three Guided Walks, pp176–7).

Painted House Façade
The Old Town has many Renaissance and Baroque houses. Some have colourful mural paintings like this one in Old Town Square (see pp66–9).

Art Nouveau Statue
The New Town has many examples of Art Nouveau architecture (see pp148–9).

THE HISTORY OF PRAGUE

PRAGUE'S POSITION at the crossroads of Europe has made it a magnet for foreign traders since pre-recorded times. By the early 10th century it had developed into a thriving town with a large market place (the Old Town Square) and two citadels (Prague Castle and Vyšehrad), from where its first rulers, the Přemyslids, conducted their many family feuds. These were often bloody: in 935, Prince Wenceslas was savagely murdered by his brother Boleslav. Wenceslas was later canonized and became Bohemia's best-known patron saint.

During the Middle Ages Prague enjoyed a golden age, especially during the reign of the Holy Roman Emperor, Charles IV. Under the auspices of this wise and cultured king, Prague grew into a magnificent city, larger than Paris or London. Charles instigated the founding and building of many institutions, including the first University of Central Europe in Prague. The University's first Czech rector was Jan Hus, the reforming preacher whose execution for alleged heresy in 1415 led to the Hussite wars. The radical wing of the Hussites, the Taborites, were finally defeated at the

Prague coat of arms

Battle of Lipany in 1434. During the 16th century, after a succession of weak kings, the Austrian Habsburgs took over, beginning a rule that would last for almost 400 years. One of the more enlightened of all the Habsburg Emperors was Rudolph II. He brought the spirit of the Renaissance to Prague through his love of the arts and sciences. Soon after his death, in 1618, Prague was the setting for the Protestant revolt which led to the 30 Years' War. Its aftermath brought a serious decline in the fortunes of a city that would revive only in the 18th century. Prague's many fine Baroque churches and palaces date from this time.

The 19th century saw a period of national revival and the burgeoning of civic pride. The great public monuments – the National Museum, the National Theatre and Rudolfinum – were built. But a foreign power still ruled the city, and it was not until 1918 that Prague became the capital of an independent Republic. World War II brought occupation by the German army, followed by four decades of Communism. After the "Velvet Revolution" of 1989, Prague is today on the threshold of a new era.

View of Prague Castle and Little Quarter, 1493

◁ *St Wenceslas and St Vitus*, by Bartholomaeus Spränger, about 1600

Rulers of Prague

THREE GREAT DYNASTIES have shaped the history of Prague: the Přemyslids, the Luxemburgs and the Habsburgs. According to Slavonic legend, the Přemyslids were founded by Princess Libuše *(see p21)*. Her line included St Wenceslas and Přemysl Otakar II, whose death on the battlefield at Marchfeld paved the way for the Luxemburgs. This family produced one of Prague's greatest rulers, Charles IV, who was King of Bohemia and Holy Roman Emperor *(see pp24–5)*. In 1526, the city came under the control of the Austrian House of Habsburg whose rule lasted 400 years, until 28 October 1918, when Czechoslovakia gained its independence. Since then there has been a succession of presidents.

The mythical Princess Libuše

1346–78 Charles IV

1453– Ladisla Posthumu

1310–46 John of Luxemburg

1140–72 Vladislav I

935–72 Boleslav I

1305–6 Wenceslas III

1230–53 Wenceslas I

1278–1305 Wenceslas II

1034–55 Břetislav I

900	1000	1100	1200	1300	1400
PŘEMYSLIDS				**LUXEMBURGS**	
900	1000	1100	1200	1300	1400

972–99 Boleslav II

1061–92 Vratislav II

921–35 St Wenceslas

1173–9 Soběslav II

1197–1230 Přemysl Otakar I

1253–78 Přemysl Otakar II

1378–1419 Wenceslas IV

1419–37 Sigismund

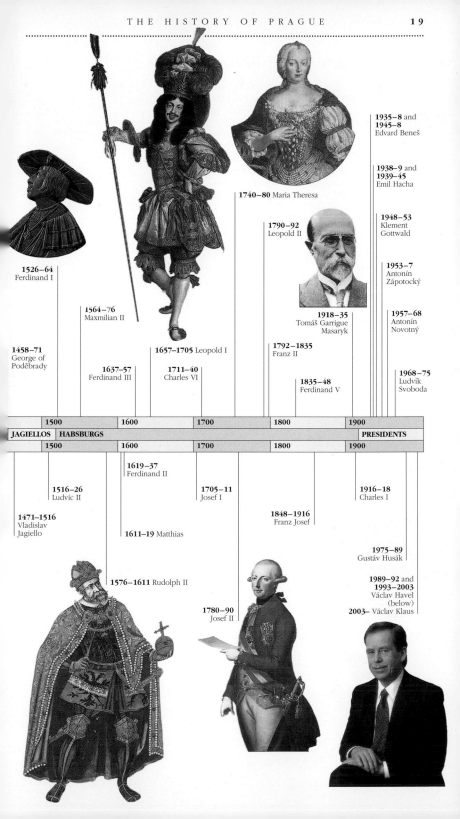

1935–8 and
1945–8
Edvard Beneš

1938–9 and
1939–45
Emil Hacha

1740–80 Maria Theresa

1790–92
Leopold II

1948–53
Klement
Gottwald

1953–7
Antonín
Zápotocký

1526–64
Ferdinand I

1564–76
Maxmilian II

1957–68
Antonín
Novotný

1918–35
Tomáš Garrigue
Masaryk

1657–1705 Leopold I

1792–1835
Franz II

1458–71
George of
Poděbrady

1637–57
Ferdinand III

1711–40
Charles VI

1835–48
Ferdinand V

1968–75
Ludvík
Svoboda

1500	1600	1700	1800	1900

JAGIELLOS   HABSBURGS   **PRESIDENTS**

1500	1600	1700	1800	1900

1619–37
Ferdinand II

1516–26
Ludvíc II

1705–11
Josef I

1916–18
Charles I

1471–1516
Vladislav
Jagiello

1848–1916
Franz Josef

1611–19 Matthias

1975–89
Gustáv Husák

1989–92 and
1993–2003
Václav Havel
(below)
2003– Václav Klaus

1576–1611 Rudolph II

1780–90
Josef II

Prague under the Přemyslids

9th-century earring

E ARLY CELTIC TRIBES, from 500 BC, were the first inhabitants of the area around the Vltava valley. The Germanic Marcomans arrived in 9–6 BC, and gradually the Celts left. The first Slavic tribes came to Bohemia in about 500 AD. Struggles for supremacy led to the emergence of a ruling dynasty, the Přemyslids, around 800 AD. They built two fortified settlements: the first at Prague Castle (see pp94–110), the second at Vyšehrad, a rocky headland on the right bank of the Vltava (see pp178–9). These remained the seats of Czech princes for hundreds of years. One prince crucial to the emerging Czech State was the pious Wenceslas. He enjoyed only a brief reign but left an important legacy in the founding of St Vitus's rotunda (see p102).

EXTENT OF THE CITY
◾ 1000 AD ☐ Today

Boleslav's henchman raises his sword to strike the fatal blow.

St Cyril and St Methodius
Originally Greeks from Salonica, these two brothers brought Christianity to Moravia in about 863. They baptized early Přemyslid, Bořivoj, and his wife Ludmilla, grand mother of St Wenceslas.

Second assassin grapples with the Prince's companion.

Early Coin
Silver coins like this denar were minted in the royal mint of Vyšehrad during Boleslav II's reign from 967–99.

Wild Boar Figurine
Celtic tribes made small talismans of the wild animals that they hunted for food in the forested areas around Prague.

TIMELINE

Bronze head of a Celtic goddess

623–658 Bohemia is part of an empire formed by Frankish merchant, Samo

600 AD | **700**

M500 BC
Celts in Bohemia. Joined by Germanic Marcomans in 1st century AD

6th century
Slavs settle alongside Germanic tribes in Bohemia

8th century
Tribe of Czechs settle in central Bohemia

Vyšehrad acropolis – first Czech settlement on the right bank of the Vltava

Sword and Helmet
St Wenceslas was buried in the southern apse of the rotunda of St Vitus. His sword and helmet were preserved as relics and today form part of the Cathedral's treasure.

Wenceslas seeks sanctuary.

A monk closes the door against Wenceslas.

PRINCESS LIBUŠE

The legendary founder of the Přemyslids was Princess Libuše, head of a West Slavic tribe. She took notice of the discord among her clansmen, and succeeded her father to become the first woman ruler. Choosing a humble plough-man (*Přemysl-Oráč*) as consort and ruler, she began a dynasty that was to last 400 years.

Princess Libuše foresaw the glory of Prague in a vision

Rotunda of St Vitus
Founded by Wenceslas in the early 10th century, the rotunda became a place of pilgrimage after the saint's death in 929. It stood where St Wenceslas Chapel is today.

Roman-arched windows

ASSASSINATION OF PRINCE WENCESLAS

Curving stone walls

In 929, the young Wenceslas was murdered on the orders of his brother, Boleslav. This manuscript illustration of 1006 shows the moment when the assassins caught up with the prince as he was about to enter the church for the morning mass.

00
ynasty of
ˇemyslids
unded

Early Christian breast cross

921 Wenceslas becomes Prince of Bohemia

870 Prague Castle founded

993 Bishop Adalbert Vojtěch founds monastery at Břevnov

00 | **900** | **1000**

863 St Cyril and St Methodius bring Christianity to Moravia

929 Wenceslas dies

920 Founding of St George's Basilica at Prague Castle

Bishop Adalbert's bejewelled glove

Early Medieval Prague

EXTENT OF THE CITY

☐ *1230*   ☐ *Today*

PRAGUE CASTLE STEADILY grew in importance from the beginning of the 9th century onwards. Prone to frequent fires, its wooden buildings were gradually replaced by stone and the area developed into a sturdy Romanesque fortress with a palace and religious buildings. Clustered around the original outer bailey was an area inhabited by skilled craftsmen and German merchants, encouraged to come and stay in Prague by Vladislav II and, later, Přemysl Otakar II. This came to be known as the "Little Quarter" and achieved town status in 1257. It was joined to the Old Town by a bridge, known as the Judith Bridge.

Initial letter D from the Vyšehrad Codex

PRAGUE CASTLE IN 1230
Sited on a high ridge, the Romanesque fortress had protective stone walls and easily-guarded gates.

St George's Convent and Basilica *(see pp106–9 and p98)*

The Prince's Palace grew into the Royal Palace *(see pp104–5)*.

The White Tower gave access from the west.

Entrance from Old Town

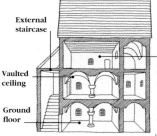

Decorative Comb
This ornate, bone, fine-toothed comb was one of the relics of St Adalbert.

Site of Hradčany Square

External staircase

Vaulted ceiling

Ground floor

Living room

Romanesque Stone House
These three-storeyed houses were based around a very simple floor plan.

St Vitus's Basilica and Chapter House *(see pp100–3)*

Stone houses were built on what is now Nerudova Street in the Little Quarter *(see p130)*.

TIMELINE

St Adalbert with a martyr's palm frond

1040 St Adalbert's remains brought to Prague	**1092–1110** Reign of Bretislav II	**1110** Small German settlement in Prague	**1140** Strahov Monastery founded
	1091 Old Town marketplace first mentioned by travellers		
1050		**1100**	**115**
1070 Vyšehrad becomes temporary seat of Czech princes	**1091** Great fire at Prague Castle	**1110–20** Reign of Bořivoj II	
1085 Vratislav I becomes first King of Bohemia		**1135** Seat of Czech princes moves from Vyšehrad to Prague Castle	

Romanesque stone head from Judith Bridge Tower

St Agnes of Bohemia
Sister of Wenceslas I, this devout woman built a convent for the order of the Poor Clares (the female counterparts of the Franciscans) (see pp92–3). She was not canonized until 1989.

WHERE TO SEE ROMANESQUE PRAGUE

Remains can be seen in the crypt of St Vitus's *(pp100–3)*, the basements of the Palace of the Lords of Kunštát *(p78)* and the Royal Palace *(pp104–5)*.

St George's Basilica
The vaulting in the crypt dates from the 12th century (p98).

St Martin's Rotunda
This well-preserved building is in Vyšehrad (p179).

The Black Tower was the exit to Bohemia's second town, Kutná Hora *(see p168).*

Vratislav II
The Vyšehrad Codex, an illuminated selection from the gospels, was made to mark Vratislav's coronation in 1061.

Little Quarter Square

Little Quarter Coat of Arms
Vladislav II's portrait was incorporated into this 16th-century miniature painting.

Přemysl Otakar II
The last great Přemyslid king was killed in battle after trying to carve out a huge empire.

1233 Founding of St Agnes's Convent

1182 Romanesque construction of Prague Castle completed

1200

1212 Přemysl Otakar I receives the Sicilian Golden Bull, confirming the sovereignty of Bohemian kings

1158 Judith Bridge built *(see pp136–9)*

Sicilian Golden Bull

1257 Little Quarter receives town status

1258–68 Strahov Monastery rebuilt in Gothic style after fire

1250

1290

1278 Přemysl Otakar II dies at Marchfeld

Prague's Golden Age

I N THE LATE MIDDLE AGES, Prague attained the height of its glory. The Holy Roman Emperor Charles IV chose Prague as his Imperial residence and set out to make the city the most magnificent in Europe. He founded a university (the Carolinum) and built many fine churches and monasteries in the Gothic style. Of major importance were his town-planning schemes, such

Gift from Pope Urban V in 1368

as the reconstruction of Prague Castle, the building of a new stone bridge to replace the Judith Bridge, and the foundation of a new quarter, the New Town. A devout Catholic, he owned a large collection of relics which were kept, along with the Crown Jewels, at Karlstein Castle *(see pp168–9)*.

EXTENT OF THE CITY

▨ 1350	☐ Today

Charles IV wears the Imperial crown, set with sapphires, rubies and pearls.

St Wenceslas Chapel
Proud of his direct descent from the Přemyslids, Charles had this shrine to St Wenceslas built in St Vitus's Cathedral (see pp100–3).

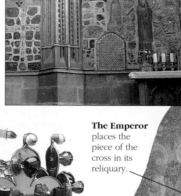

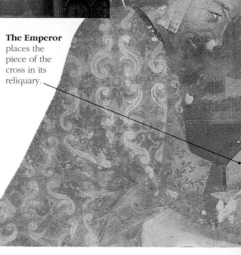

The Emperor places the piece of the cross in its reliquary.

St Wenceslas Crown
Worn by Charles at his coronation in 1347, the Bohemian crown was based on early Přemyslid insignia.

TIMELINE

1280 Old-New Synagogue completed in Gothic style

Town Hall, Old Town Square

1333 Charles IV makes Prague his home

1344 Elevation of Prague bishopric to archbishopric

1305	1320	1335

Portal of Old-New Synagogue

1306 Přemyslid dynasty ends

1310 John of Luxemburg occupies Prague

1338 John of Luxemburg gives permission to Old Town to build a town hall

Votive panel showing Charles, Archbishop Jan Očko and Bohemia's patron saints

St Vitus by Master Theodoric

This is one of a series of paintings of saints by the great Bohemian artist for the Holy Rood Chapel at Karlstein Castle (c1365).

University Seal, 1348
The seal depicts the Emperor offering the foundation documents to St Wenceslas.

A jewelled reliquary cross was made to house the new relic.

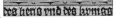

Building the New Town

This manuscript records Charles IV supervising the building of the New Town during the 14th century.

CHARLES IV AND HIS RELICS

Charles collected holy relics from all over the Empire. In about 1357 he received a part of Christ's cross from the Dauphin. This mural in Karlstein Castle is thought to be the best likeness of the Emperor.

WHERE TO SEE GOTHIC PRAGUE

Prague's rich Gothic legacy includes three of its best-known sights – St Vitus's Cathedral (pp100–3), Charles Bridge (pp136–9) and the Old-New Synagogue (pp88–9). Another very important building from Charles IV's reign is the Carolinum (p65). Churches that have retained most of their original Gothic features include the Church of Our Lady before Týn (p70).

Carolinum
This fine oriel window was part of the university (p65).

Old Town Bridge Tower
The sculptural decoration is by Peter Parler (p139).

1348 Charles IV founds Charles University

1357 Charles Bridge begun

Sculpture of young Wenceslas IV by Peter Parler in St Vitus's Cathedral

1378 Reign of Wenceslas IV begins

1391 Bethlehem Chapel founded

1350	1365	1380	1395

1361 Wenceslas IV born, oldest son of Charles

1378 Charles dies

1348 Charles IV founds Prague New Town

Bethlehem Chapel

Hussite Prague

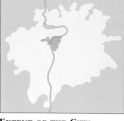

George of Poděbrady

IN THE EARLY 15TH CENTURY, Europe shook in fear of an incredible fighting force -- the Hussites, followers of the reformist cleric, Jan Hus. Despite simple weapons, they achieved legendary military successes against the Emperor's Catholic crusades, due largely to their religious fervour and to the discipline of their brilliant leader, Jan Žižka, who invented mobile artillery. The Hussites split into two camps, the moderate "Utraquists" *(see p75)* and the radical "Taborites" who were finally defeated at the Battle of Lipany in 1434, paving the way for the moderate Hussite king, George of Poděbrady.

EXTENT OF THE CITY
■ 1500   □ Today

Nobles' Letter of Protest
Several hundred seals of the Bohemian nobility were affixed to a letter protesting about the execution of Jan Hus.

GOD'S WARRIORS
The early-16th-century Codex of Jena illustrated the Hussite successes. Here the Hussites, who included artisans and barons, are shown singing their hymn, with their blind leader, Jan Žižka.

Jan Žižka

The priest held a gilded monstrance.

War Machine
For maximum effect, farm waggons were tied together to form a shield. A chilling array of weapons were unleashed including crossbows, flails and an early form of howitzer.

TIMELINE

1402–13 Jan Hus preaches at Bethlehem Chapel *(see p75)*

1415 Jan Hus burned at the stake at Constance

1419 Defenestration of councillors from New Town Hall

1434 Battle of Lipany

The Taborites made lethal weapons from simple farm tools

1400	1420	1440

1410 Jan Hus excommunicated. Building of Old Town Clock

1424 Jan Žižka dies

1420 Hussites victorious under Jan Žižka at Vitkov and Vyšehrad

1448 Prague conquered by troops of George of Poděbrady

Jan Hus preaching

The chalice, symbol of the Utraquists

Satan Dressed as the Pope
Lurid images satirizing the corruption of the church were painted on placards and carried through the streets.

The banner was decorated with the Hussite chalice.

A variety of farm implements were used as makeshift weapons by the peasants.

Hussite Shield
Wooden shields like this one that bears the arms of the city of Prague, were used to fill any gaps in the waggon fortress's tight formation.

The peasant army marched behind Jan Žižka.

REFORMER, JAN HUS

Born to poor parents in a small Bohemian town, Jan Hus became one of the most important religious thinkers of his day. His objections to the Catholic Church's corrupt practices, opulent style and wealth were shared by many Czechs – nobles and peasants alike. His reformist preaching in Prague's Bethlehem Chapel earned him a huge following, noticed by the Roman Papacy, and Hus was excommunicated. In 1412 Wenceslas IV, brother of the Emperor Sigismund, asked him to leave Prague. In October 1414, Hus decided to defend his teaching at the Council of Constance. Even though he had the Emperor's safe conduct, he was put in prison. The following year he was declared a heretic and burned at the stake.

Jan Hus at the Stake in 1415
After suffering death at the hands of the Church on 6 July 1415, Jan Hus became a revered martyr of the Czech people.

1458 Coronation of George of Poděbrady *(see p172)*

1485 Hussite uprising in Prague

1492–1502 Vladislav Hall built

1460   1480   1500

Chalice on the outside of the Týn Church denotes the Hussite cause

1487 First book printed in Prague

1485 King Vladislav Jagiello begins to rebuild Royal Palace at Prague Castle

Vladislav Jagiello

The Renaissance and Rudolph II

Renaissance tankard

WITH THE ACCESSION of the Habsburgs, the Renaissance reached Prague. Art and architecture were dominated by the Italians who enjoyed the patronage of the Imperial court, especially that of Rudolph II. The eccentric Rudolph often neglected politics, preferring to indulge his passions for collecting and science. His court was a haven for artists, astrologers, astronomers and alchemists, but his erratic rule led to revolts and an attempt by his brother Matthias to usurp him. In the course of the Thirty Years' War *(see pp30–31)* many works of art from Rudolph's collection were looted.

EXTENT OF THE CITY

◻ 1550   ◻ Today

Rudolph II
A connoisseur of the bizarre, Rudolph was delighted by this vegetable portrait by Giuseppe Arcimboldo (1590).

Fish pond

Dalibor Tower

Belvedere

Pergola

Orchard

Formal flower beds

Lion House

Rabbi Löw
A revered Jewish sage, he was said to have invented an artificial man (see pp88–9).

Mosaic Desk Top
Renaissance table tops with Florentine themes of fountains and gardens were made at Rudolph's court in semi-precious stones.

TIMELINE

Vladislav Hall

Ferdinand I

Charter for manglers and dyers

1502 Vladislav Hall built

1526 Habsburg rule begins with Ferdinand I

1541 Great fire in Little Quarter, the Castle and Hradčany

1556 Ferdinand I invites Jesuits to Prague

1520	1540	1560

1538–63 Belvedere built

1547 Unsuccessful uprising of towns of Prague against Ferdinand I

Sense of Sight
Jan Brueghel's allegorical painting shows the extent of Rudolph II's huge collection – from globes to paintings, jewels and scientific instruments.

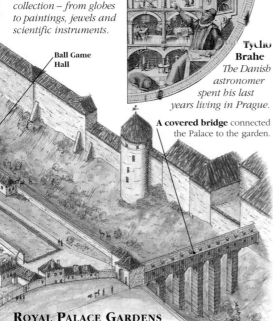

Ball Game Hall

Tycho Brahe
The Danish astronomer spent his last years living in Prague.

A covered bridge connected the Palace to the garden.

ROYAL PALACE GARDENS
No longer a medieval fortress, Prague Castle and its gardens were given over to the pleasure of the King. Here Rudolph enjoyed ball games, exotic plants and his menagerie.

WHERE TO SEE RENAISSANCE PRAGUE

The Royal Garden *(p111)* preserves much of the spirit of Renaissance Prague. Paintings and objects from Rudolph's collections can be seen in the Sternberg Palace *(pp112–15)*, the Picture Gallery of Prague Castle *(p98)* and the Museum of Decorative Arts *(p84)*.

At the Two Golden Bears
Built in 1590, the house is famous for its symmetrical, carved doorway, one of the most graceful in Prague (p71).

Belvedere
The palace is decorated with stone reliefs by Italian architect, Paolo della Stella (p110).

Ball Game Hall
Beautiful Renaissance sgraffito covers the façade of this building in the Royal Garden, but it has been heavily restored (p111).

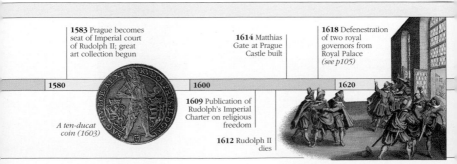

1583 Prague becomes seat of Imperial court of Rudolph II; great art collection begun

1614 Matthias Gate at Prague Castle built

1618 Defenestration of two royal governors from Royal Palace *(see p105)*

1580

1600

1620

A ten-ducat coin (1603)

1609 Publication of Rudolph's Imperial Charter on religious freedom

1612 Rudolph II dies

Baroque Prague

I N 1619 THE CZECH NOBLES deposed Habsburg Emperor
Ferdinand II as King of Bohemia and elected instead
Frederick of the Palatinate. The following year they paid
for their defiance at the Battle of the White Mountain,
the beginning of the Thirty Years' War. There followed
a period of persecution of all non-Catholics, accompanied
by the Germanization of the country's institutions. The
leaders in the fight against Protestantism were the Jesuits
and one of their most powerful weapons was the
restoration of their churches in Prague in the Baroque
style. Many new churches
also adopted this style.

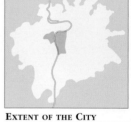

EXTENT OF THE CITY

◼ *1750* ▢ *Today*

A sculpture of Atlas
(1722) adorns the
top of the tower.

Mirror Chapel

Church of St Nicholas
*This outstanding High
Baroque church in the
Little Quarter was the
work of the great
Dientzenhofers*
(see pp128–9).

**Grape
Courtyard**

**Measuring
the World**
*Some monasteries were
seats of learning. Strahov (see
pp120–21) had two libraries built,
decorated with Baroque painting. This
fresco detail is in the Philosophical Hall.*

**Holy Saviour
Church**

TIMELINE

1620 Battle of the White Mountain	*Old Town coat of arms – embellished with the Imperial eagle and 12 flags in recognition of the defence of the city against the Swedes*		**1706–14** Decoration of Charles Bridge with statues
1627 Beginning of Counter-Reformation committee in Prague			

1625	1645	1665	1685	1705

| **1621** Execution in Old Town Square of 27 Protestant leaders | **1634** Wallenstein killed by Irish mercenaries | **1648** Swedes occupy Prague Castle. Treaty of Westphalia and end of Thirty Years' War | | **1704–53** Building of Church of St Nicholas in the Little Quarter |
| | **1631** Saxon occupation of Prague | | **1676–8** New bastions built to fortify Vyšehrad | |

Battle of the White Mountain
In 1620 the Czech army was defeated by Habsburg troops at Bílá Hora (White Mountain), a hill northwest of Prague (see p163). After the battle, Bohemia became a de facto province of Austria.

Observatory Tower

St Clement's Church gave its name to the whole complex.

Italian Chapel

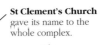

Monstrance
Baroque monstrances – used to display the communion host – became increasingly elaborate and ornate (see pp116–17).

CLEMENTINUM
The Jesuits exercised enormous power over education. Between 1653 and 1723 they built this College. It was the largest complex of buildings after Prague Castle and included three churches, smaller chapels, libraries, lecture halls and an observatory.

WHERE TO SEE BAROQUE PRAGUE
The Baroque is everywhere in Prague. Almost all the churches were built or remodelled in Baroque style, the finest being St Nicholas *(pp128–9)*. There are also the grand palaces and smaller houses of the Little Quarter *(pp122–41)*, the façades in the Old Town *(pp60–79)*, and statues on churches, street corners and along the parapets of Charles Bridge.

Nerudova Street
At the Golden Cup, No. 16, has preserved its typical Baroque house sign (p130).

Charles Bridge
This statue of St Francis Borgia by Ferdinand Brokof was added in 1710 (pp136–9).

1740 Accession of Empress Maria Theresa

Maria Theresa

1748 Bohemian Chancellery loses last vestiges of power

1773 Jesuit Order dissolved

1784 Four towns of Prague united to form a single city

Mozart at Bertramka (p160)

1725	1745	1765	1785

1757 Prague besieged by Prussians

1782 Convents and monasteries closed

1787 Mozart stays at Bertramka preparing for the premiere of *Don Giovanni* at the Estates Theatre *(see p65)*

The National Revival in Prague

T HE 19TH CENTURY was one of the most glorious periods in the history of Prague. Austrian rule relaxed, allowing the Czech nation to rediscover its own history and culture. Silent for so long, Czech was re-established as an official language. Civic pride was rekindled with the building of the capital's great showpieces, such as the National Theatre, which utilized the talents of Czech architects and artists.

Emperor Franz Josef

EXTENT OF THE CITY

■ 1890　　□ Today

The Jewish Quarter and New Town underwent extensive redevelopment and, with the introduction of public transport, Prague grew beyond its ancient limits.

Days of the year

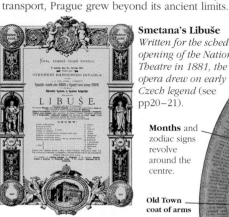

Smetana's Libuše
Written for the scheduled opening of the National Theatre in 1881, the opera drew on early Czech legend (see pp20–21).

Months and zodiac signs revolve around the centre.

Old Town coat of arms

Rudolfinum
A major concert venue beside the Vltava, the building (see p84) is richly decorated with symbols of the art of music.

OLD TOWN CLOCK TOWER CALENDAR
In 1866, the revolving dial on Prague's most enduring landmark was replaced by a new one by celebrated artist, Josef Mánes. His studies of Bohemian peasant life are incorporated into pictures symbolizing the months of the year.

TIMELINE

1805 Czechs, Austrians and Russians defeated by Napoleon at Battle of Slavkov (Austerlitz)

1833 Englishman Edward Thomas begins production of steam engines

1818 National Museum founded

Restored clock from the east face of the Town Hall Tower

1848 Uprising of people of Prague against Austrian troops

1800	1820	1840	180

1815 First public demonstration of a vehicle driven by a steam engine

1838–45 Old Town Hall undergoes reconstruction

The battle of Slavkov

1845 First train arrives in Prague

186 Foundatio stone fo Nationa Theatre laic

Expo 95 Poster
Vojtěch Hynais designed this poster for the ethnographic exhibition of folk culture in 1895. In the Art Nouveau style, it reflected the new appreciation of regional traditions.

WHERE TO SEE THE NATIONAL REVIVAL

Many of Prague's remarkable monuments, the National Museum for example, were built around this period. One fine example of Art Nouveau architecture is the Municipal House *(p64)*, where the Mayor's Room has murals by Mucha. The Rudolfinum *(p84)* and the National Theatre *(pp156–7)* have gloriously-decorated interiors by great artists of the day. The Prague Museum has many objects from the late 19th and early 20th centuries as well as the original painting for Mánes' Old Town Clock.

December   Sagittarius

Municipal House
Allegories of civic virtues painted by Alfons Mucha adorn this Art Nouveau interior.

Jewish Quarter
From 1897 onwards, the slum housing of the ghetto was replaced with new apartment blocks.

National Museum
The Neo-Renaissance façade dominates the skyline (p147).

National Theatre
The décor has murals by Czech artists, including Aleš (pp156–7).

National Theatre

1883 Re-opening of the National Theatre

1891 Jubilee Exhibition

1896 Proper city transport of electric trams starts

1912 Municipal House opens

1914 World War I begins

1916 Emperor Franz Josef dies

1880   1900

1884–91 Building of the National Museum

1897–1917 Slums of Jewish Ghetto cleared

1881 Newly opened National Theatre destroyed by fire, then rebuilt

1883 First public lighting with electric lamps

Early electric trams

The satirical novel Good Soldier Švejk (see p154) explored the futility of war and the inept Austrian military

Prague after Independence

J‍UST 20 YEARS AFTER its foundation, the Czechoslovak Republic was helplessly caught up in the political manoeuvring that preceded Nazi domination of Europe. Prague emerged from World War II almost unscathed by bombings, no longer part of a Nazi protectorate but of a Socialist republic. Any resistance was brutally suppressed. Ultimately, the intellectuals spoke out, demanding observance of civil rights. Denial of such rights led these dissidents to unite and prepare for the "Velvet Revolution". In the end, it was a playwright, Václav Havel, who stepped onto the balcony of Prague Castle to lead the country at the start of a long and often difficult return to independence.

Letná Park metronome

1920 Avant-garde left-wing artists form Devětsil movement in Prague's Union Café

1935 Edvard Beneš succeeds Masaryk as President. Nazi-funded Sudeten German Party, led by Konrad Henlein, makes election gains

1938 Munich Agreement hands over parts of Republic to Hitler. Beneš flees country

Edvard Beneš

1945 Soviet Red Army enter Prague on 9 May to rapturous welcome, following four days of uprisings. In October, provisional National Assembly set up under Beneš

1952 Most famous of many show trials under Gottwald, Slánský Trial sends 11 senior politicians to gallows as Trotskyites and traitors

1918	1930	1940	1950

1918	1930	1940	1950

1924 Death of Franz Kafka, author of *The Trial*

1932 Traditional gymnastic rally or *slet* takes place at Strahov stadium

1942 Tyrannical "Protector" for only eight months, Reinhard Heydrich assassinated by Czech resistance

1955 Largest statue of Stalin in the world unveiled in Letná Park, overlooking city

1958 Premiere of innovative animated film, *The Invention of Destruction* directed by Karel Zeman

1948 Communist Party assumes power under Klement Gottwald; announces 89% support in May elections

PRAHA 1932
IX·SLET
VŠESOKOLSKÝ
NA OSLAVU STÝCH NAROZENIN DR MIROSLAVA TYRŠE
ZA ÚČASTI SVAZŮ - SLOVANSKÉ SOKOLSTVO -

1918 Foundation of Czechoslovak Republic. Tomáš Masaryk first democratically-elected President

1939 German troops march into Prague; city declared capital of Nazi Protectorate of Bohemia and Moravia. Emil Hácha president under the German protectorate

VYNÁLEZ ZKÁZY

POZDRAV

TOMÁŠI G. MASARYKOVI

Welcome Home poster, to mark the president's return on 21 December 1918

1989 The "Velvet Revolution": growing civil discontent prompts demonstrations and strikes. Havel unites opposition groups to form Civic Forum. Temporary Government promises free elections; President Husák resigns and Václav Havel is sworn in by popular demand

1966 Jiří Menzel's *Closely Observed Trains* wins Oscar for Best Foreign Film, drawing the world's attention to Czech cinema

1968 Alexander Dubček elected to post of First Secretary

1990 First democratic elections for 60 years produce 99% turnout, with 60% of vote going to alliance of Civic Forum and People Against Violence

1992 The splitting of Czechoslovakia

1999 Czech Republic joins NATO

1962 Statue of Stalin in Letná Park demolished (replaced, in 1991, by a giant metro-nome)

1979 Playwright Václav Havel founds Committee for the Defence of the Unjustly Persecuted and is sent to prison

2002 Prague suffers its worst flooding in 150 years.

2004 Czech Republic joins the EU

960	1970	1985	2000

960	1970	1985	2000

960 Czechoslovak ocialist Republic ČSSR) proclaimed

1969 Jan Palach burns to death in protest at Soviet occupation

2001 The biggest street protests since the end of communism force Jiri Hodac to resign as director-general of state television

1967 First Secretary and President, Antonín Novotný, imprisons dissident writers

1977 Human rights manifesto Charter 77 drawn up after arrest of band, Plastic People

1968 Moderate Alexander Dubček adopts the programme of liberal reforms known as "Prague Spring". On 21 August, Warsaw Pact occupies Czechoslovakia and over 100 protesters are killed as troops enter Prague

1984 Jaroslav Seifert, signatory of Charter 77, wins Nobel Prize for Literature but cannot collect prize in person

1989 Canonization of St Agnes of Bohemia (*see pp92–3*) takes place on 4 November. Vatican commissions painting by dissident Prague-born artist Gustav Makarius Tauc for the occasion. Czech legend that miraculous events will accompany her elevation to sainthood prove correct when "Velvet Revolution" begins on 17 November

The coat of arms of the president of the Czech Republic has the inscription "truth victorious" and the arms for Bohemia (top left, bottom right), *Moravia* (top right) *and Silesia* (bottom left)

1993 Prague is once again declared capital of Czech Republic

PRAGUE AT A GLANCE

THERE ARE ALMOST 150 places of interest described in the *Area by Area* section of this book. A broad range of sights is covered: from the ancient Royal Palace, which was the site of the Defenestration of 1618 *(see p105)*, to cubist houses built in the Jewish Quarter in the 1920s *(see p91)*; from the peaceful oasis of Petřín Park *(see p141)*, to the bustle of Wenceslas Square *(see pp144–5)*. To help you make the most of your stay, the following 12 pages are a time-saving guide to the best Prague has to offer visitors. Museums and galleries, churches and synagogues, palaces and gardens all have their own sections. Each sight has a cross reference to its own full entry. Below are the attractions that no visitor should miss.

PRAGUE'S TOP TEN SIGHTS

Old Town Square
See pp66–9

National Theatre
See pp156–7.

Church of St Nicholas
See pp128–9.

Charles Bridge
See pp136–9.

Old Town Hall
See pp72–4.

St Vitus's Cathedral
See pp100–3.

Wallenstein Palace and Garden *See p126.*

Old Jewish Cemetery
See pp86–7.

Prague Castle
See p96–7.

St Agnes's Convent
See pp92–3.

◁ Mucha's allegory of Vigilance in the Mayor's Room in the Municipal House *(see p64)*

Prague's Best: Museums and Galleries

With more than 20 museums and almost 100 galleries and exhibition halls, Prague is a city of unexpected and rare delights. Here, religious masterpieces of the Middle Ages vie with the more recent opulence of Art Nouveau and the giants of modern art. New galleries have opened since 1989 with many more temporary exhibitions. There are museums devoted to the history of the state, the city of Prague and its people, many of them housed in buildings that are historical landmarks and works of art in themselves. This map gives some of the highlights, with a detailed overview on pages 40–41.

St George's Convent
Among the fine Bohemian Baroque art on display is this portrait of Italian gemcutter Dionysius Miseroni and his family by Karel Škréta.

Sternberg Palace
The collection of European art here is outstanding, represented in works such as The Feast of the Rosary *by Albrecht Dürer (1506).*

Prague Castle and Hradčany

The Loreto
The offerings of devout local aristocrats form the basis of this collection of religious decorative art. In 1721 this jewel-encrusted, tree-shaped monstrance was given to the treasury by Countess Wallenstein.

Little Quarter

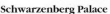

Smetana Museum
The life and work of this 19th-century Czech composer are remembered beside the river that inspired one of his most famous pieces – the Vltava.

VLTAVA

Schwarzenberg Palace
The ornate Renaissance palace forms a handsome backdrop to the Museum of Military History's displays of weaponry and memorabilia.

Museum of Decorative Arts
Five centuries of arts and crafts are represented here, with particularly impressive collections of Bohemian glass, graphic art and furniture. This carved and painted chest dates from 1612.

St Agnes of Bohemia Convent
This collection includes the 14th-century Resurrection of Christ by the Master of the Třeboň Altar.

Maisel Synagogue
One of the most important collections of Judaica in the world is housed in the Maisel Synagogue and other buildings of the State Jewish Museum. The displays include religious artefacts, furnishings and books. This illuminated page is from the manuscript of the Pesach Haggadah of 1728.

Jewish Quarter

Old Town

0 metres	500
0 yards	500

National Museum
The vast skeleton of a whale dominates the other exhibits in one of seven grand halls devoted to zoology. The museum's other displays include fine collections of minerals and meteorites.

New Town

Dvořák Museum
This viola, which belonged to the influential 19th-century Czech composer, is among the personal effects and musical scores on display in the charming Michna Summer Palace.

Exploring the Museums and Galleries

Carved figure on façade of the Museum of Decorative Arts

THE CITY'S MUSEUMS give a fascinating insight into the history of the Czechs and of Prague's Jewish population. Also a revelation to visitors unfamiliar with the culture is the art of the Gothic and Baroque periods and of the 19th-century Czech National Revival. The major museums and galleries are cramped for space, but plans are under way to put more of their collections on show in the near future.

14th-century *Madonna Aracoeli*, St Vitus Treasure, Prague Castle

CZECH PAINTING AND SCULPTURE

THE MOST IMPORTANT and wide-ranging collection in Prague is that of the National Gallery. Its holdings of Czech art are shown at three venues: medieval art at **St Agnes's Convent;** works dating from the 16th to 18th centuries at **St George's Convent**; and 19th to 20th-century art at the Trades Fair Palace.

The **Picture Gallery of Prague Castle** is a reminder of Emperor Rudolph II's once-great collection. Alongside the paintings are documents

Commerce by Otto Gutfreund (1923), Trades Fair Palace

and other evidence of just how splendid the original collection must have been.

For the best of the Castle's Bohemian art, you must visit the Renaissance and Baroque works at St George's Convent. These include examples by Baroque masters Karel Škréta and Petr Brandl. Also within the Castle but currently without a permanent display space is the St Vitus Treasure, a collection of religious pieces including a Madonna from the School of Master Theodoric.

Centuries of Czech sculpture are housed in the Lapidarium at the **Exhibition Ground**. Among its exhibits is statuary formerly found on the Charles Bridge, and the Marian pillar that used to stand in the Old Town Square.

The collection at the **St Agnes of Bohemia Convent** includes Bohemian and central European Gothic painting and sculpture, including panels painted for Charles IV by Master Theodoric. Works by 19th- and 20th-century Prague artists can be seen at the Prague Gallery. Its branches include the Baroque **Troja Palace**, where the architecture makes a great backdrop. Exhibitions are drawn from the gallery's collection of 3,000 paintings, 1,000 statues and 4,000 prints.

The superb Centre for Modern and Contemporary Art at **Trades Fair Palace** represents almost every 19th- and 20th-century artistic movement. Romanticism and Art Nouveau are both represented, as are the understandably popular 1920s figures of Otto Gutfreund. The

development of such ground-breaking groups as Osma, Devětsil, Skupina 42 and the 12.15 group is also strikingly well documented.

EUROPEAN PAINTING AND SCULPTURE

PRAGUE ALSO OFFERS visitors an opportunity to view an exceptional range of masterpieces by Europe's finest artists from antiquity to the 18th century, at **Sternberg Palace**.

The most treasured work in the collection is the *Feast of the Rosary* by Albrecht Dürer, but other equally delightful works include many by 17th-century Dutch masters such as Rubens and Rembrandt.

The Centre for Modern and Contemporary Art at **Trades Fair Palace** has an outstanding collection of Picassos and some fine Rodin bronzes, as well as examples of work from almost every Impressionist, Post-Impressionist and Fauvist. Three notable self-portraits are those of Paul Gauguin (*Bonjour Monsieur Gauguin*, 1889), Henri Rousseau (1890) and Pablo Picasso (1907). Modern German and Austrian painting is also on show, with works by Gustav Klimt and Egon Schiele. The *Dance of Life*, by Norwegian Edvard Munch, is considered greatly influential upon Czech avant-garde art.

The other main venue for European art is the **Picture Gallery of Prague Castle**, which focuses on European painters of the 16th to 18th centuries. As well as Titian's superb *The Toilet of a Young Lady*, there are also works in the collection by Rubens and Tintoretto.

MUSIC

TWO CZECH composers merit their own museums, as does Prague's much-loved visitor, Mozart. The **Smetana Museum**, **Dvořák Museum** and **Mozart Museum** all contain personal memorabilia, musical scores and correspondence. In the summer, concerts are held on the terrace of the Mozart Museum.

The Museum of Musical Instruments, at Újezd 40, Prague 1 (257 53 34 59), has many rare and historic instruments, and a number of scores by composers such as Josef Haydn.

HISTORY

THE HISTORICAL collections of the **National Museum** are held at the main Wenceslas Square building, and at Prague Castle. The artefacts at Prague Castle are housed in the **Lobkowicz Palace** and focus on Czech life and culture. The **Prague Museum** centres on the history of the city, with period rooms, historical prints

Bohemian Baroque glass goblet (1730), Museum of Decorative Arts

and a model of Prague in the 19th century, made of paper and wood by the lithographer Antonín Langweil.

A branch of the museum at Výtoň, on the banks of the Vltava, depicts the way of life of a former settlement. Another at Vyšehrad records the history of this royal seat.

The exquisite Renaissance building of **Schwarzenberg Palace** is a fine setting for the battle charts, weaponry, uniforms and regalia of the Museum of Military History, housed here since 1945.

The Jewish Museum is made up of various sites in the Jewish Quarter, including the **High Synagogue**, **Maisel Synagogue** and the **Old Jewish Cemetery**. Among its collections are holy artefacts taken from other Jewish communities and brought to Prague by the Nazis as part of a chilling plan for a museum of "an extinct race". Another moving display is of drawings made by children who were imprisoned in the Terezín concentration camp.

DECORATIVE ARTS

WITH GLASSWARE spanning centuries, from medieval to modern, porcelain and pewterware, furniture and textiles, books and posters, the **Museum of Decorative Arts** in the Jewish Quarter is one of Prague's best, but only a small selection of its holdings is on show. Look out for specialized temporary exhibitions mounted either at the museum itself or at other venues in Prague.

Many other museums have examples of the decorative arts, ranging from grandiose monstrances – including one with 6,222 diamonds – in the treasury of **The Loreto** to simple everyday furnishings in the **Prague Museum**. There is also a fascinating collection of pre-Columbian artefacts from Central America in the **Náprstek Museum**.

16th-century astrolabe from the National Technical Museum

SCIENCE AND TECHNOLOGY

A VAST EXHIBITION hall holds the transport section of the **National Technical Museum**. Ranks of vintage cars, motorcycles and steam engines fill the space, and over them hang examples of early flying machines. Other sections trace the progress of sciences such as electronics. Visitors can even tour a reconstruction of a coal mine. As befits the city where Tycho Brahe and Johannes Kepler studied the stars, there is a fascinating astronomy exhibition.

Prague's Best: Churches and Synagogues

THE RELIGIOUS BUILDINGS of Prague vividly record the city's changing architectural styles, and many are treasure houses of religious art. But they also reflect Prague's times of religious and political strife, the lives of its people, its setbacks and growth as a city. This map features highlights of their architecture and art, with a more detailed overview on pages 44–5.

St George's Basilica
St George, sword raised to slay the dragon, is portrayed in this late-Gothic relief, set above the doorway of the magnificent early Renaissance south portal.

St Vitus's Cathedral
The jewel of the cathedral is the Chapel of St Wenceslas. Its walls are decorated with semi-precious stones, gilding and frescoes. Elizabeth of Pomerania, the fourth and last wife of Charles IV, is shown at prayer in the fresco above the Gothic altar.

Prague Castle and Hradčany

The Loreto
This shrine to the Virgin Mary has been a place of pilgrimage since 1626. Each hour, its Baroque clock tower chimes a hymn on the carillon of 27 bells.

Little Quarter

V L T A V A

Church of St Thomas
The skeleton of the martyr St Just rests in a glass coffin below a Crucifixion by Antonín Stevens, one of several superb works of religious art in this church.

Church of St Nicholas
In the heart of the Little Quarter, this is Prague's finest example of High Baroque. The dome over the high altar is so lofty that early worshippers feared it would collapse.

Church of Our Lady before Týn

Set back behind a row of arcaded buildings, the many-spired twin towers of the church dominate the eastern end of Old Town Square. The Gothic, Renaissance and Baroque features of the interior create striking contrasts.

Old-New Synagogue

Prague's oldest synagogue dates from the 13th century. Its Gothic main portal is carved with a vine which bears twelve bunches of grapes symbolizing the tribes of Israel.

Jewish Quarter

Old Town

Church of St James

Consecrated in 1374, this church was restored to new Baroque glory after a fire in 1689. Typical of its grandeur is this 18th-century monument to chancellor Jan Vratislav of Mitrovice. Fine acoustics and a superb organ make the church a popular venue for concerts.

Slavonic Monastery Emauzy

These cloisters hold a series of precious frescoes from three Gothic masters depicting scenes from the Old and New Testaments.

New Town

0 metres	500
0 yards	500

Church of St Peter and St Paul

Remodelled many times since the 11th century, the design of this church is now 1890s Neo-Gothic. This striking relief of the Last Judgment marks the main entrance.

Exploring Churches and Synagogues

R ELIGIOUS BUILDING began in Prague in the 9th century,
reaching its zenith during the reign of Charles IV

(see pp24–5). The remains of an 11th-century
synagogue have been found, but during the
19th-century clearance of the overcrowded
Jewish ghetto three synagogues were lost.
Many churches were damaged during the
Hussite rebellions *(see pp26–7)*. The
political regime of the 20th century also
took its toll, but now churches and
synagogues have been reclaimed and
restored, with many open to visitors.

**Altar, Capuchin
Monastery**

ROMANESQUE

T HREE REASONABLY well-
preserved Romanesque
rotundas, dating from the
11th and 12th centuries, still
exist in Prague. The oldest is
the **St Martin's Rotunda**; the
others are the rotundas of the
Holy Rood and of St Longinus.
All three are tiny, with naves
only 6 m (20 ft) in diameter.

By far the best-preserved
and most important Roman-
esque church is **St George's
Basilica**, founded in 920 by

**11th-century Romanesque
Rotunda of St Martin in Vyšehrad**

Prince Vratislav I. Extensive
reconstruction was carried out
after a fire in 1142, but its
chancel, with some exquisite
frescoes on its vaulting, is a
Late-Romanesque gem.

The **Strahov Monastery**,
founded in 1142 by Prince
Vladislav II *(see pp22–3)*, has
retained its Romanesque core
in spite of fire, wars and
extensive renovation.

GOTHIC

G OTHIC ARCHITECTURE, with
its ribbed vaulting, flying
buttresses and pointed arches,
reached Bohemia in about
1230 and was soon adopted
into religious architecture.

The first religious building
in Gothic style was the **St
Agnes of Bohemia Convent**,
founded in 1233 by Wenceslas
I's sister, Agnes. Prague's oldest synagogue, the **Old-New
Synagogue**, built in 1270, is
rather different in style to the
churches but is still a superb
example of Early-Gothic.

The best example of Prague
Gothic is **St Vitus's Cathedral**.
Its fine tracery and towering

**High, Gothic windows at the east
end of St Vitus's Cathedral**

nave epitomize the style.
Other notable Gothic churches
are **Our Lady before Týn**
and **Our Lady of the Snows**.

Important for its historical
significance is the reconstructed Gothic **Bethlehem
Chapel** where Jan Hus *(see
p27)* preached for 10 years.

The superb Gothic frescoes
found in abundance at the
Slavonic Monastery Emauzy,
were badly damaged in World
War II, but have been restored.

RENAISSANCE

I N THE 1530s the influence of
Italian artists living in Prague
sparked the city's Renaissance
movement. The style is more
clearly seen in secular than
religious building. The Late-
Renaissance period, under
Rudolph II (1576–1611), offers
the best remaining examples.

DOMES AND SPIRES

The domes and spires of Prague's churches are
the city's main landmarks, as the view from the
many vantage points will confirm. You will see a
variety of spires, towers and domes: Gothic and
Neo-Gothic soar skywards, while Baroque often
have rounded cupolas and onion domes. The
modern top of the 14th-century Slavonic Monastery, added after the church was struck in a
World War II air raid, is a rare example of
modernist religious architecture in Prague. Its
sweeping, intersecting twin spires are a bold
reinterpretation of Gothic themes, and a striking
addition to the city's skyline.

Gothic   *Baroque*

**Church of Our Lady
before Týn (1350–1511)**

**Church of St Nicholas in the
Little Quarter (1750)**

The **High Synagogue** and the **Pinkas Synagogue** retain strong elements of the style: the former in its 1586 exterior, the latter in the reworking of an original Gothic building.

The Church of St Roch in the **Strahov Monastery** is probably the best example of Late-Renaissance "Mannerism".

Renaissance-influenced vaulting, Pinkas Synagogue (1535)

BAROQUE

THE COUNTER-REFORMATION *(see pp30–31)* inspired the building of new churches and the revamping of existing ones for a period of 150 years. Prague's first Baroque church

was **Our Lady Victorious**, built in 1611–13. **St Nicholas** in the Little Quarter took almost 60 years to build. Its lush interior and frescoed vault make it Prague's most important Baroque building, followed by **The Loreto** (1626–1750), adjoining the **Capuchin Monastery**. The father-and-son team, Christoph and Kilian Ignaz Dientzenhofer designed both buildings, and **St John on the Rock** and **St Nicholas** in the Old Town.

A special place in Prague's history was occupied by the Jesuit **Clementinum**. This influential university's church was the **Holy Saviour**. The Baroque style is closely linked with Jesuit teachings: Kilian Ignaz Dientzenhofer was educated here.

Klausen Synagogue (now the Jewish Museum) was built in 1689 with Baroque stuccoed barrel vaults.

Many early buildings were given Baroque facelifts. The Gothic nave of **St Thomas** has Baroque vaulting, and the once-Gothic **St James** went Baroque after a fire in 1689.

19th-century Neo-Gothic portal, Church of St Peter and St Paul

NEO-GOTHIC

DURING THE HEIGHT of the 19th-century Gothic Revival *(see pp32–3)*, **St Vitus's Cathedral** was completed, in accordance with the original Gothic plan. Work by Josef Mocker, the movement's leader, aroused controversy but his **St Peter and St Paul** at Vyšehrad is a well-loved landmark. The triple-naved basilica of **St Ludmila** in Náměstí Míru was also designed by Mocker.

Nave ceiling of the Church of St Nicholas in the Little Quarter

Loreto (1725)

Baroque — *Neo-Gothic*

St Peter and St Paul (1903)

Modernist

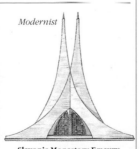

Slavonic Monastery Emauzy (1967)

Prague's Best: Palaces and Gardens

P RAGUE'S PALACES and gardens are among the most important historical and architectural monuments in the city. Many palaces house museums or galleries *(see pp38–41)*, and some are concert venues.

The gardens range from formal, walled oases with fountains and grand statuary, to open spaces beyond the city centre. This map features some of the best palaces and gardens, with a detailed overview on pages 48–9.

Prague Castle and Hradčany

Belvedere

The Singing Fountain (1568) stan in front of the exquisite Renaissan summer palace.

Royal Garden

Though redesigned in the 19th century, the Renaissance garden preserves much of its original character. Historic statues still in place include a pair of Baroque lions (1730) guarding the entrance.

Little Quarter

| 0 metres | 500 |
| 0 yards | 500 |

South Gardens

Starting life as the Castle's defensive bastions, these gardens afford a wonderful view of Prague. First laid out as a park in 1891, their present design was landscaped by Josip Plečnik 40 years later.

Wallenstein Palace

Built in 1624–30 for Duke Albrecht of Wallenstein, this vast Baroque palace was intended to outshine Prague Castle. Over 20 houses and a town gate were demolished to make room for the palace and garden. This Fountain of Venus (1599), stands in front of the arches of the sala terrena.

Wallenstein Garden

The garden statues are copies of 17th-century bronzes. The originals were plundered by the Swedes in 1648.

Kolowrat-Černín Garden

In the Baroque period, several palace gardens with spectacular terraces were laid out on the hillside below Prague Castle.

Kinský Palace

The Kinský coat of arms adorns the pink and white stuccoed façade designed by Kilian Ignaz Dientzenhofer. The Rococo palace is now part of the National Gallery.

Jewish Quarter

Old Town

Clam-Gallas Palace

Four giant statues of Hercules (c1715) by Matthias Bernard Braun show the hero straining to support the weight of the massive Baroque front portals of the palace.

New Town

Michna Summer Palace

This charming villa was designed by Kilian Ignaz Dientzenhofer in 1712. It now houses the Dvořák Museum. The garden's sculptural decorations are from the workshop of Antonín Braun.

Kampa Island

A tranquil waterside park was created on the island after the destruction of its original gardens in World War II.

Exploring the Palaces and Gardens

PRAGUE BOASTS an amazing number of palaces and gardens, spanning centuries. Comparatively few palaces were lost to the ravages of war. Instead, they tended to evolve in style during restoration or enlargement. Palace gardens became fashionable in the 17th century, but could only be laid out where there was space, such as below Prague Castle. More vulnerable to change, most have been relandscaped several times. In the 19th century, and again after 1989, many of the larger parks and private gardens were opened up to the public.

Statue
on Kampa
Island

MEDIEVAL PALACES

THE OLDEST PALACE in Prague is the **Royal Palace** at Prague Castle. In the basement is the Romanesque ground floor, started in about 1135. It has been rebuilt many times, particularly between the 14th and 16th centuries. The heart of the Palace, Vladislav Hall, dates from the 1490s and is late Gothic in structure. Less well known is the **Palace of the Lords of Kunštát**. Here, the vaulted ground floor of the 13th-century building survives as the basement of a later Gothic structure.

RENAISSANCE PALACES

ONE OF THE most beautiful Renaissance buildings in Prague is the 16th-century **Schwarzenberg Palace**. The work of Italian architects, its façade is entirely covered with geometric, two-tone *sgraffito* designs. Italians also

Bronze Singing Fountain in the Royal Garden by the Belvedere

worked on the **Belvedere**. Its graceful arcades and columns, all covered with rich reliefs, make this one of the finest Renaissance buildings north of the Alps. The **Martinic Palace**, built in 1563, was the first example of late-Renaissance building in Prague. Soon after came the **Lobkowicz Palace**. Its terracotta relief-decorated windows and plaster *sgraffito* have survived later Baroque modifications. The huge **Archbishop's Palace** was given a later Rococo façade over its Renaissance structure.

BAROQUE PALACES

MANY PALACES were built in the Baroque style, and examples of all its phases still exist in Prague. A handsome, if ostentatious, early Baroque

Southern façade of Troja Palace and its formal gardens

DECORATIVE PORTALS AND GATES

The elaborate gates and portals of Prague's palaces are among the most beautiful and impressive architectural features in the city. Gothic and Renaissance portals have often survived, even where the buildings themselves have been destroyed or modified by renovations in a later architectural style. The period of most prolific building was the Baroque, and distinctive portals from this time can be seen framing many a grand entrance around the city. Statues of giants, heroes and mythological figures are often depicted holding up the doorways. These were not merely decorative but acted as an integral element of support.

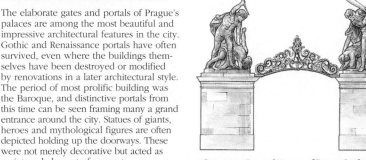

Gateway to Court of Honour of Prague Castle (1768)

example is the **Wallenstein Palace**. Similar ostentation is evident in the **Černín Palace**, one of Prague's most monumental buildings. The mid-Baroque had two strands, one opulent and Italianate, the other formal and French or Viennese in influence. **Troja Palace** and **Michna Summer Palace** are in Italian villa style while the **Sternberg Palace** on Hradčanské náměstí is more Viennese in style. Troja was designed in 1679 by Jean-Baptiste Mathey, who, like the Dientzenhofers (see p129), was a master of the Baroque. The pairs of giants on the portals of the **Clam-Gallas Palace**, and the **Morzin Palace** in Nerudova Street, are a popular Baroque motif. The **Kinský Palace** is a superb Rococo design by Kilian Ignaz Dientzenhofer.

GARDENS

THE FINEST of Prague's palace gardens, such as the **Wallenstein Garden**, are in the Little Quarter. Though the style of Wallenstein Palace is Early Baroque, the garden still displays the geometric formality of the Renaissance, also preserved in the **Royal Garden** behind Prague Castle. The **South Gardens** on the Castle's old ramparts were redesigned in the 1920s.

Many more gardens were laid out in the 17th and 18th centuries, when noble families vied with each other to have fine winter residences in the Little Quarter below the Castle. Many are now the grounds of embassies, but others have been opened to the public. The **Ledebour Garden** has been combined with two neighbouring gardens. Laid out on a steep hillside, the **Kolowrat-Černín Garden**, in particular, makes ingenious use of pavilions, stairs and terraces from which there are wonderful views of the city. The **Vrtba Garden**, landscaped on the site of former vineyards, is a similar Baroque creation with statues and splendid views. Former palace gardens were also used to create a park on **Kampa Island**.

The many old gardens and orchards on Petřín Hill have

The Royal Garden of Prague Castle, planted with spring flowers

Ancient trees in Stromovka

been transformed into the large public area of **Petřín Park**. Another former orchard is **Vojan Park**, laid out by archbishops in the 13th century. The **Botanical Gardens** are one of the few areas of green open to the public in the New Town.

Generally, the larger parks are situated further out of the city. **Stromovka** was a royal deer park, while **Letná Park** was developed in 1858 on the open space of Letná Plain.

WHERE TO FIND THE PALACES AND GARDENS

Troja Palace (c1703)

Clam-Gallas Palace (c1714)

PRAGUE THROUGH THE YEAR

SPRINGTIME in Prague sees the city burst into colour as its gardens start to bloom. Celebrations begin with the Prague Spring Music Festival. In summer, visitors are entertained by street performers and the city's glorious gardens come into their own. When the weather begins to turn cooler, Prague hosts the International Jazz Festival.

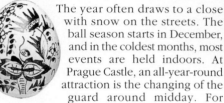
Painted Easter egg

The year often draws to a close with snow on the streets. The ball season starts in December, and in the coldest months, most events are held indoors. At Prague Castle, an all-year-round attraction is the changing of the guard around midday. For details of activities, check the listings magazines *(see p219)* or the Prague Information Service *(see p218)*.

Concert at Wallenstein Palace during the Prague Spring Music Festival

SPRING

AS PRAGUE SEES its first rays of spring sunshine, the city comes alive. A mass of colours, blooms and cultural events makes this one of the most exciting times of the year to visit. The city's blossoming parks and gardens open their gates again, after the colder months of winter. During April the temperatures rise and an entertainment programme begins – dominated by the Prague Spring Music Festival.

EASTER

Easter Monday *(dates vary)* is a public holiday. Easter is observed as a religious holiday but it is also associated with a bizarre pagan ritual in which Czech men beat their women with willow sticks in order to keep them fertile during the coming year. The women retaliate by throwing water over their male tormentors. Peace is finally restored when the women present the men with a painted egg. Church services are held during the entire Easter period *(see p227)*.

MARCH

The Prague-Prčice March *(third Saturday of March)*. Thousands of people walk to the small town of Prčice in celebration of spring.

APRIL

Boat trips *(1 April)*. A number of boats begin trips up and down the Vltava.
Witch-burning *(30 April)*, at the Exhibition Ground *(see p176)*. Concerts accompany

this 500-year-old tradition where old brooms are burnt on bonfires, in a symbolic act to rid nature of evil spirits.

MAY

Labour Day *(1 May)*. Public holiday celebrated with numerous cultural events.
Opening day of Prague's gardens *(1 May)*. Regular summer concerts are held in many parks and gardens.
Anniversary of Prague Uprising *(5 May)*. At noon sirens are sounded for one minute. Flowers are laid at the commemorative plaques of those who died *(see p34)*.
Day of Liberation from Fascism *(8 May)*. Public holiday for VE day. Wreaths are laid on the graves of soldiers at Olšany cemeteries.
Prague International Book Fair *(second week in May)*, Palace of Culture *(see p176)*. The best of Czech and international authors.
Prague International Marathon *(third week in May)*.

THE PRAGUE SPRING MUSIC FESTIVAL

This international festival presents a busy programme of concerts, ballet and opera from 12 May to 3 June. Music lovers can hear a huge selection of music played by some of the best musicians in the world. The main venue is the Rudolfinum *(see p84)* but others include churches and palaces – some of which are only open to the public on these occasions. The festival begins on the anniversary of Bedřich Smetana's death *(see p79)*. A service is held at his grave in Vyšehrad *(see p178)*, and in the evening there is a concert at the Municipal House *(see p64)* where musicians perform his most famous work, *Má Vlast* (My Country). The festival also ends here, with Beethoven's Ninth Symphony.

Bedřich Smetana

AVERAGE DAILY HOURS OF SUNSHINE

Hours

Czechs and tourists enjoying the beauty of Vyšehrad Park on a sunny afternoon

SUMMER

SUMMER arrives with high temperatures, frequent, sometimes heavy, showers and thousands of visitors. This is a beautiful, if busy, time to visit. Every weekend, Czechs set out for the country to go hiking in the surrounding hills or stay in country cottages. Those remaining in Prague visit the reservoirs and lakes *(see p213),* just outside the city to try and escape the heat. There is a wealth of entertainment on offer as culture moves into the open air taking over the squares, streets and gardens. Street performers, buskers and classical orchestras all help to keep visitors entertained. Many cafés have tables outside allowing you to quench your thirst while watching the fun.

JUNE

Mayoral Boat Race *(first weekend in June).* Rowing races are held on the river Vltava, just below Vyšehrad.

Summer Concerts *(throughout the summer).* Prague's gardens *(see pp46–9)* are the attractive and popular setting for a large number of free classical and brass-band concerts. One of the most famous, and spectacular, outdoor classical concerts is held by Křižík Fountain at the Exhibition Ground *(see p162).* Full orchestras play to the stunning backdrop of coloured lights and water, synchronized to the music by computer.

Anniversary of the Murder of Reinhard Heydrich's Assassins *(18 June).* A mass is held in remembrance in the Church of St Cyril and St Methodius *(see p152)* for those who died there.

Golden Prague *(first week of June),* Kaiserstein Palace. International TV festival of prize-winning programmes.

Battle Re-enactments *(throughout summer),* held in Prague's palaces and gardens.

Mozart's Prague *(mid-June to first week in July).* Celebration of Mozart. International orchestras perform his works at Bertramka *(see p160)* and Lichtenstein Palace.

Dance Prague *(last week in June).* An international festival of contemporary dance at the National Theatre *(see p156).*

JULY

Remembrance of the Slavonic Missionaries *(5 July).* Public holiday in honour of St Cyril and St Methodius *(see p152).*

Anniversary of Jan Hus's Death *(6 July).* A public holiday when flowers are laid on his memorial *(see pp26–7).*

AUGUST

Theatre Island *(all of August),* Střelecký Island. Czech theatre and puppet festival.

Changing of the Guard at Prague Castle

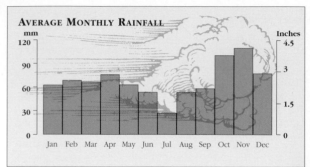

AVERAGE MONTHLY RAINFALL

Rainfall Chart
*Prague has plenty
of rain throughout
the year. The wettest
months are October
and November, but
there are frequent
light showers in the
summer months as
well. Winter snow-
falls can be quite
heavy, but they are
rarely severe.*

AUTUMN

WHEN THE GARDENS below Prague Castle take on the shades of red and gold, and visitors start to leave, the city gets ready for the cold winter months. This is also the traditional mushroom-gathering season when you encounter people with baskets full of freshly-picked mushrooms. Market places are flooded with fruit and vegetables. The tree-lined slopes above the Vltava take on the beautiful colours of autumn. September and October still have a fair number of warm and sunny days, although November often sees the first snowfalls. Football fans fill the stadiums and the popular steeplechase course at Pardubice reverberates to the cheers of fans.

SEPTEMBER

Prague Autumn *(early September)*, at the Rudolfinum *(see p84)*. An international classical music festival.
The Autumn Fair *(dates vary)*, at the Exhibition Ground *(see p176)*. Fairground, food stalls, puppet shows and theatrical and musical performances.
Kite competitions *(third Sunday in September)*, on Letná Plain in front of Sparta Stadium. Very popular competition for children but open to anyone with a kite.
St Wenceslas *(28 September)*. A sacred music festival is held for the feast of the patron saint.
Bohemia Championship *(last Sunday in September)*. This 10-km (6-mile) road race has been run since 1887. Starts from Běchovice, a suburb of Prague, and ends in Žižkov.

Jazz musicians playing at the International Jazz Festival

OCTOBER

The Great Pardubice Steeplechase *(second Sunday in October)*, held at Pardubice, east of Prague. This horse race has been run since 1874 and is considered to be the most difficult in Europe.
Velká Kunratická *(second Sunday in October)*. Popular, but gruelling, cross-country race in Kunratice forest. Anyone can enter.
The Locking of the Vltava *(early October)*. Symbolic conclusion of the water sports season, during which the Vltava is locked with a key until the arrival of spring.
International Jazz Festival *(date varies)*, Lucerna Palace. A famous jazz festival, held since 1964, attracts musicians from around the world.
The Day of the Republic *(28 October)*. Despite the splitting up of Czechoslovakia into two separate republics, the founding of the country in 1918 is still a public holiday.

NOVEMBER

Celebration of the Velvet Revolution *(17 November)*. Peaceful demonstrations take place around Wenceslas Square *(see pp144–5)*.

A view of St Vitus's Cathedral through autumn trees

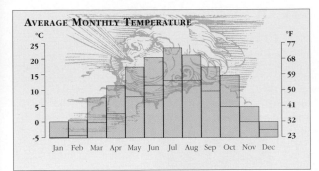

AVERAGE MONTHLY TEMPERATURE

Temperature Chart
The chart shows the average minimum and maximum temperatures for each month in Prague. The summer usually remains comfortably warm, while the winter months can get bitterly cold and temperatures often drop below freezing.

WINTER

IF YOU ARE lucky enough to catch Prague the morning after a snowfall with the sun shining, the effect is magical. The view over the Little Quarter rooftops with their pristine white covering is a memorable sight. Unfortunately Prague is rarely at its best during the winter months. The weather is changeable. Foggy days with temperatures just above freezing can quickly go down to -5° C (23° F). Pollution and Prague's geographical position in the Vltava basin, lead to smog being trapped just above the city.

As if to try and make up for the winter weather's short-comings, the theatre season reaches its climax and there are a number of premieres. Balls and dances are held in these cold months. Just before Christmas Eve large barrels containing live carp – which is the traditional Czech Christmas delicacy – appear on the streets. Christmas trees adorn the city, and carol singers can be heard on street

Barrels of the traditional Christmas delicacy, carp, on sale in Prague

View of the Little Quarter rooftops covered in snow

corners. Christmas mass is held in most churches and New Year's Eve is celebrated, in time-honoured style, throughout the entire city.

DECEMBER

Christmas markets *(throughout December)*, Můstek metro station, 28. října, Na příkopě, Old Town Square. Stalls sell Christmas decorations, gifts, hot wine, punch and the traditional Czech carp *(see p207)*.
Christmas Eve, Christmas Day and Boxing Day *(24, 25 and 26 December)*. Public holidays. Mass is held in churches throughout the city.
Swimming competitions in the Vltava *(26 December)*. Hundreds of hardened and determined swimmers gather together at the Vltava to swim in temperatures of around 3° C (37° F).
New Year celebrations *(31 December)*. Thousands of people congregate around Wenceslas Square.

JANUARY

New Year's Day *(1 January)*. Public holiday.

FEBRUARY

Dances and Balls *(early February)*.
Matthew Fair *(end of February to beginning of April)*, the Exhibition Ground *(see p176)*. Fairground, stalls and various entertainments.

PUBLIC HOLIDAYS

New Year's Day (1 Jan); **Easter Monday**; **Labour Day** (1 May); **Day of Liberation from Fascism** (8 May); **Remembrance of the Slavonic Missionaries** (5 July); **Anniversary of Jan Hus's death** (6 July); **St Wenceslas** (28 Sep); **Foundation of Czechoslovakia** (28 Oct); **Fall of Communism** (17 Nov); **Christmas Eve, Christmas Day, Boxing Day** (24–26 Dec).

A River View
of Prague

THE VLTAVA RIVER has played a vital part in the city's history *(see pp20–21)* and has provided inspiration for artists, poets and musicians throughout the centuries.

Up until the 19th century, parts of the city were exposed to the danger of heavy flooding. To try and alleviate the problem, the river's embankments have been strengthened and raised many times, in order to try to prevent the water penetrating too far (the foundations of today's embankments are made of stone or concrete). During the Middle Ages, year after year of disastrous flooding led to the decision to bury the areas affected under 2 m (6 ft) of earth to try to minimize the damage. Although this strategy was only partially effective, it meant that the ground floors of many Romanesque and Gothic buildings were preserved and can still be seen today *(see pp78–9)*. In 2002

Statues on the wrought-iron Čechův Bridge

however, a state of emergency was declared as flooding devastated large parts of the city. Despite its destructive side, the Vltava has provided a vital method of transport for the city, as well as a source of income. As technology improved, the river became increasingly important; water mills, weirs and water towers were built. In 1912 a large hydroelectric power plant was built on Štvanice Island, supplying almost a third of Prague's electricity. To make the river navigable, eight dams, a large canal and weirs were constructed along the Slapy-Prague-Mělník stretch, where the Vltava flows into the river Elbe. For the visitor, an excursion on one of the many boats and paddle steamers that travel up and down the river, is well worth it. There are trips to Troja *(see pp166–7)* and as far as Slapy Lake. Catching a boat from one of the piers on the river is one of the best ways of seeing the city.

A view of the steamboat landing stage (přístaviště parníků) on Rašínovo nábřeží

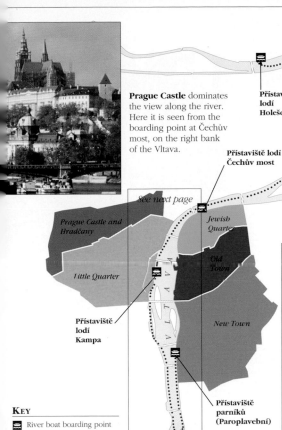

Prague Castle dominates the view along the river. Here it is seen from the boarding point at Čechův most, on the right bank of the Vltava.

Přístaviště lodí Holešovice

Přístaviště lodí Čechův most

See next page

Prague Castle and Hradčany

Jewish Quarter

Little Quarter

Old Town

New Town

V L T A V A

Přístaviště lodí Kampa

Přístaviště parníků (Paroplavební)

0 kilometres   1

0 miles   0.5

KEY

TOURS

There are frequent trips on the Vltava throughout the summer (April to the end of September). Tours range from trips to Troja Palace in the north of Prague and as far away as Slapy Lake in the south. Dining on board while slowly floating through the city centre is another popular option. These trips can be booked in advance at one of the tour companies. Alternatively, you can go directly to one of the river boat boarding points (see left) and buy tickets for one of the many private ships that land here. (Paroplavební pier is where most trips start.) The cost of each trip varies, depending on the vessel and the length of the excursion, but there are trips to suit almost every budget.

Akasi
Jungmannovo náměstí 9.
Map 3 C5.
📞 *22 22 43 067.*
FAX *22 42 37 235.*

Travelex
Národní 28.
Map 3 B5.
📞 *22 11 05 371.*
FAX *22 49 49 002.*
W *www.travelex.cz*

Paroplavební (pier)
Rašínovo nábřeží přistaviště.
Map 5 A2.
📞 *22 49 31 013, 22 49 17 640.*
FAX *22 49 13 862.*

Přístaviště lodí Kampa, a jetty in the Little Quarter, is the starting point for some of the organized boat trips along the Vltava.

Prague River Trip

TAKING A TRIP on the Vltava gives you a unique view of many of the city's historic monuments. Although the left bank was the site of the first Slavonic settlement in the 9th century, it was the right bank, heavily populated by merchants and traders, that developed into a thriving and bustling commercial centre, and the tradition continues today. The left bank was never developed as intensively and much of it is still an oasis of parks and gardens. The river's beauty is enhanced by the numbers of swans which have made it their home.

Hanavský Pavilion
This flamboyant cast-iron staircase is part of a pavilion built for the Jubilee Exhibition of 1891.

Little Quarter Bridge Towers
The smaller tower was built in 1158 to guard the entrance to the original Judith Bridge, while the larger one was built on the site of an old Romanesque tower in 1464 (see p136).

Vltava Weir
The thickly-wooded slopes of Petřín Hill tower above one of several weirs on the Vltava. During the 19th century this weir, along with others on this stretch, were built to make the river navigable to ships.

The Vltava Statue on the northern tip of Children's Island is where, every year, wreaths are placed in memory of the drowned.

Apartment buildings of Art Nouveau design

Little Quarter Water Tower
Built in 1560, the tower supplied river water to 57 fountains throughout the Little Quarter.

0 metres	500
0 yards	500

KEY

🚋 Tram

⛴ River boat boarding point

•• Boat trip

Karlův most

Kampa

Přístaviště lodí Kampa

Grand Priory Mill

most Legií

Střelecký ostrov

Plavební kanál

Jiráskův most

Palackého most

Železniční most

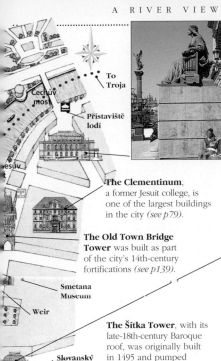

Rudolfinum
This allegorical statue of music by Antonín Wagner is one of two which decorate the imposing entrance to the Neo-Renaissance concert hall (see p84).

To Troja

Čechův most

Přístaviště lodí

The Clementinum, a former Jesuit college, is one of the largest buildings in the city *(see p79)*.

The Old Town Bridge Tower was built as part of the city's 14th-century fortifications *(see p139)*.

National Theatre
This symbol of the Czech revival, with its spectacularly-decorated roof, has dominated the skyline of the right bank since the 1860s (see pp156–7).

Smetana Museum

Weir

The Šítka Tower, with its late-18th-century Baroque roof, was originally built in 1495 and pumped water to the New Town.

Slovanský ostrov

"Ginger and Fred" Building
This charming, quirky office building is home to the stylish Perle de Prague restaurant (see p203).

The Memorial to František Palacký commemorates the life of this eminent 19th-century Czech historian and was built in 1905.

Přístaviště parníků

Výtoň Excise House
The coat of arms on this 16th-century house – built to collect duty on timber transported along the river – is of the New Town from 1671.

The Na Slovanech Monastery was built in 1347 by Charles IV. Its two modern steeples are easily recognizable from the river.

Church of St Peter and St Paul
The Neo-Gothic steeples on this much-rebuilt church were designed by František Mikeš and erected in 1903. They are the dominant feature of Vyšehrad rock (see pp178–9).

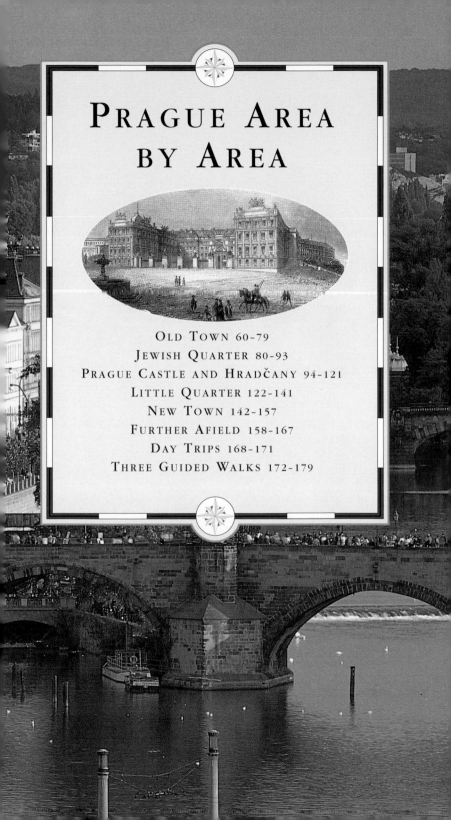

PRAGUE AREA BY AREA

OLD TOWN
STARÉ MĚSTO

THE HEART OF the city is the Old Town and its central square. In the 11th century the settlements around the Castle spread to the right bank of the Vltava. A market-place in what is now Old Town Square (Staroměstské náměstí) was mentioned for the first time in 1091. Houses and churches

Physician, Jan Marek (1595–1667)

sprang up around the square, determining the random network of streets, many of which survive. The area gained the privileges of a town in the 13th century, and, in 1338, a Town Hall. This and other great buildings, such as Clam-Gallas Palace and the Municipal House, reflect the importance of the Old Town.

SIGHTS AT A GLANCE

Churches
Church of St James ④
Church of Our Lady
  before Týn ⑧
Church of St Nicholas ⑪
Church of St Gall ⑭
Church of St Martin
  in the Wall ⑮
Church of St Giles ⑰
Bethlehem Chapel ⑱

Museums and Galleries
Náprstek Museum ⑯
Smetana Museum ㉔

Historic Streets and Squares
Celetná Street ③
*Old Town Square
  pp66–9* ⑦
Mariánské Square ⑳
Charles Street ㉑
Knights of the Cross Square ㉕

Historic Monuments and Buildings
Powder Gate ①
Municipal House ②
Carolinum ⑥
Jan Hus Monument ⑩
Old Town Hall pp72–4 ⑫
House at the Two Golden
  Bears ⑬
Clementinum ㉓

Theatres
Estates Theatre ⑤

Palaces
Clam-Gallas Palace ⑲
Kinský Palace ⑨
Palace of the Lords
  of Kunštát ㉒

GETTING THERE
Můstek on metro lines A and B and Staroměstska on line A are both handy for the area. Trams do not cross the Old Town, but from Charles Bridge or Náměstí Republiky it is only a short walk to Old Town Square and the other sights.

KEY

▮	Street-by-Street map *See pp62–3*
▮	Street-by-Street map *See pp76–7*
🚊	Tram stop
P	Parking

◁ **Café tables and strolling pedestrians in Old Town Square**

Street-by-Street: Old Town (East)

FREE OF TRAFFIC (except for a few horse-drawn carriages) and ringed with historic buildings, Prague's Old Town Square (Staroměstské náměstí) ranks among the finest public spaces in any city. Streets like Celetná and Ovocný trh are also pedestrianized. In summer, café tables spill out onto the cobbles, and though the area draws tourists by the thousands, the unique atmosphere has not yet been destroyed.

Kinský Palace
This stunning Rococo palace now serves as an art gallery **9**

Church of St Nicholas
The imposing façade of this Baroque church dominates one corner of Old Town Square **11**

★ Old Town Square
This late-19th-century watercolour by Václav Jansa shows how little the Square has changed in 100 years **7**

S T A R O M Ě S T S K É
N Á M Ě S T Í

M A L É
N Á M Ě S T Í

Ž
E
L
E
Z
N
Á

Jan Hus Monument
Religious reformer Hus is a symbol of integrity, and the monument brings together the highest and lowest points in Czech history **10**

U Rotta, now Hotel Rott, is a former ironmonger's shop, decorated with colourful paintings by the 19th-century artist Mikuláš Aleš.

House at the Two Golden Bears
The carved Renaissance portal is the finest of its kind in Prague **13**

★ Old Town Hall
The famous astronomical clock draws a crowd of visitors every hour **12**

The Štorch house has painted decoration based on designs by Mikuláš Aleš showing St Wenceslas on horseback.

0 metres	100
0 yards	100

KEY

– – – Suggested route

Church of Our Lady before Týn
The church's Gothic steeples are the Old Town's most distinctive landmark 8

LOCATOR MAP
See Street Finder, maps 3–4

JEWISH QUARTER

OLD TOWN

NEW TOWN

Týn courtyard

JAKUBSKÁ

ŠTUPARTSKÁ

CELETNÁ

OVOCNÝ TRH

U PRAŠNÉ BRÁNY

Church of St James
This wooden Pietà, on the main altar, was made in the 15th century 4

★ Municipal House
This Art Nouveau building is a popular concert venue 2

Powder Gate
This much-restored Gothic gate is a relic of when there was a royal palace here at the entrance to the Old Town 1

House at the Black Madonna

Estates Theatre
The theatre featured in director Miloš Forman's film Amadeus 5

Ovocný trh was Prague's fruit market.

Celetná Street
This ornamental Baroque plaque is the sign of the House at the Black Sun 3

Carolinum
A magnificently carved Oriel window projects from the oldest surviving part of the Carolinum university – founded by Charles IV in the 14th century 6

STAR SIGHTS

★ Old Town Square

★ Old Town Hall

★ Municipal House

Powder Gate ❶
PRAŠNÁ BRÁNA

Náměstí Republiky. **Map** 4 D3.
Náměstí Republiky. 5, 8, 14.
Open Apr–Oct: 10am–6pm daily.

THERE HAS BEEN a gate here since the 11th century, when it formed one of the 13 entrances to the Old Town. In 1475, King Vladislav II laid the foundation stone of the New Tower, as it was to be known. A coronation gift from the city council, the gate was modelled on Peter Parler's Old Town bridge tower built a century earlier. The gate had little defensive value; its rich sculptural decoration was intended to add prestige to the adjacent palace of the Royal Court. Building was halted eight years later when the king had to flee because of riots. On his return in 1485 he opted for the safety of the Castle. Kings never again occupied the Royal Court.

The gate acquired its present name when it was used to store gunpowder in the 17th century. The sculptural decoration, badly damaged during the Prussian occupation in 1757 and mostly removed soon afterwards, was replaced in 1876.

The Powder Gate viewed from outside the Old Town

Karel Špillar's mosaic *Homage to Prague* on Municipal House's façade

Municipal House ❷
OBECNÍ DŮM

Náměstí Republiky 5. **Map** 4 D3.
22 20 02 111. Náměstí Republiky. 5, 8, 14. **Gallery open** for exhibitions only, 10am–6pm daily. by arrangement.

PRAGUE'S MOST prominent Art Nouveau building stands on the site of the former Royal Court palace, the King's residence between 1383 and 1485. Abandoned for centuries, what remained was used as a seminary and later as a military college. It was demolished in the early 1900s to be replaced by the present cultural centre (1905–11) with its exhibition halls and auditorium, designed by Antonín Balšánek assisted by Osvald Polívka.

The exterior is embellished with stucco and allegorical statuary. Above the main entrance there is a huge semi-circular mosaic entitled *Homage to Prague* by Karel Špillar. Inside, topped by an impressive glass dome, is Prague's principal concert venue and the core of the entire building, the Smetana Hall, sometimes also used as a ballroom. The interior of the building is decorated with works by leading Czech artists of the first decade of the century, including Alfons Mucha (*see p149*).

There are numerous smaller halls, conference rooms and offices, as well as cafés and restaurants where visitors can relax and enjoy the centre's flamboyant Art Nouveau decoration at their leisure. On 28 October, 1918, Prague's Municipal House was the scene of the momentous proclamation of the new independent state of Czechoslovakia.

Decorative detail by Alfons Mucha

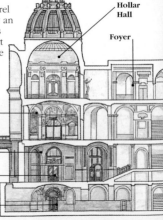

Hollar Hall

Foyer

Mayor's Salon with paintings by Alfons Mucha

Entrance hall

Entrance to Art Nouveau café

Restaurants

Celetná Street ❸
CELETNÁ ULICE

Map 3 C3. 🚇 *Náměstí Republiky, Můstek.* **House of the Black Madonna** 【 *22 42 11 732.* **Open** *10am–6pm Tue–Fri.* ♿

O NE OF THE oldest streets in Prague, Celetná follows an old trading route from eastern Bohemia. Its name comes from the plaited bread rolls that were first baked here in the Middle Ages. It gained prestige in the 14th century as a section of the Royal Route *(see p172)* used for coronation processions. Foundations of Romanesque and Gothic buildings can be seen in some of the cellars, but most of the houses with their picturesque house signs are Baroque remodellings.

At No. 34, the House of the Black Madonna is home to a small but interesting collection of Czech Cubism, including paintings, sculpture, furniture, architectural plans and applied arts.

Church of St James ❹
KOSTEL SV. JAKUBA

Malá Štupartská. **Map** 3 C3. 🚇 *Můstek, Náměstí Republiky.* **Open** *in the season, daily.* 📷 📷

T HIS ATTRACTIVE Baroque church was originally the Gothic presbytery of a Minorite monastery. The order (a branch of the Franciscans) was invited to Prague by King Wenceslas I in 1232. It was

Baroque organ loft in the Church of St James

rebuilt in the Baroque style after a fire in 1689, allegedly started by agents of Louis XIV. Over 20 side altars were added, decorated with works by painters such as Jan Jiří Heinsch, Petr Brandl and Václav Vavřinec Reiner. The tomb of Count Vratislav of Mitrovice (1714–16), designed by Johann Bernhard Fischer von Erlach and executed by sculptor Ferdinand Brokof, is the most beautiful Baroque tomb in Bohemia. The count is said to have been accidentally buried alive – his corpse was later found sitting up in the tomb. Hanging on the right of the entrance is a mummified forearm. It has been there for over 400 years, ever since a thief tried to steal the jewels from the Madonna on the high altar. But the Virgin grabbed his arm and held on so tightly it had to be cut off.

Because of its long nave, the church's acoustics are excellent and many concerts and recitals are given here. There is also a magnificent organ built in 1702.

Estates Theatre ❺
STAVOVSKÉ DIVADLO

Ovocný trh 1. **Map** 3 C4. 【 *22 42 28 503.* 🚇 *Můstek.* **Foyer open** *for performances only.*

B UILT BY COUNT NOSTITZ in 1783, the theatre is one of the finest examples of Neo-Classical elegance in Prague. It is a mecca for Mozart fans *(see p212).* On 29 October 1787, Mozart's opera, *Don Giovanni* had its debut here with Mozart at the piano conducting the orchestra. In 1834 a musical comedy called *Fidlovačka* had its premiere here. One of the songs, *Kde domov můj?* (Where is my Home?), became the Czech national anthem.

Carolinum ❻
KAROLINUM

Ovocný trh 3. **Map** 3 C4. 【 *22 44 91 111.* 🚇 *Můstek.* **Closed** *to the public.* **Open** *for special exhibitions.*

A T THE CORE of the university founded by Charles IV in 1348 is the Carolinum. The chapel, arcade and walls still survive, together with a fine oriel window, but in 1945 the courtyard was reconstructed in Gothic style. In the 15th and 16th centuries the university played a leading role in the movement to reform the church. After the Battle of the White Mountain *(see pp30–31),* the university was taken over by the Jesuits.

Old Town Square ❼
STAROMĚSTSKÉ NÁMĚSTÍ

See pp66–9.

Smetana Hall

Old Town Square: East and North Sides ❼

STAROMĚSTSKÉ NÁMĚSTÍ

Some of Prague's colourful history is preserved around
the Old Town Square in the form of its buildings. On
the north side of the Square, the Pauline Monastery is
the only surviving piece of original architecture. The
east side boasts two superb examples of the architecture
of their times: the House at the Stone Bell, restored to
its former appearance as a Gothic town palace, and the
Rococo Kinský Palace. An
array of pastel-coloured
buildings completes the
Square.

★ House at the Stone Bell
*At the corner of the building,
the bell is the sign of this
medieval town palace.*

Statues by
Ignaz Platzer
from 1760–65

Kinský Palace
*C G Bossi created the
elaborate stucco decoration
on the façade of this Rococo
palace (see p70).*

East side

Rococo
stucco work

North side

**★ Church of
St Nicholas**
*Besides its original
purpose as a parish
church and, later,
a Benedictine
monastery church,
this has served as a
garrison church
and a concert
hall (see p70).*

Star Sights

★ **Church of Our Lady
before Týn**

★ **House at
the Stone Bell**

★ **Church of
St Nicholas**

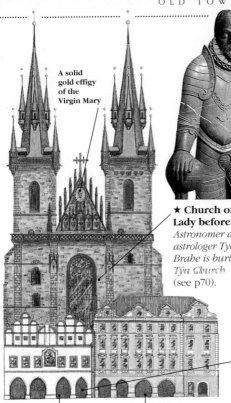

A solid gold effigy of the Virgin Mary

East and north side

Jan Hus Monument

★ Church of Our Lady before Týn
Astronomer and astrologer Tycho Brahe is buried in Týn Church (see p70).

Týn School
Gothic rib vaulting is a primary feature of this building, which was a school from the 14th to the mid-19th century.

Entrance to Týn Church

Romanesque arcaded house with 18th-century façade

Restaurant U Sv. Salvatora façade dates from 1696

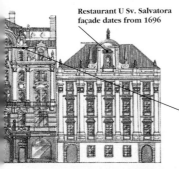

Ministerstvo pro místní rozvoj
Architect Osvald Polívka designed this Art Nouveau building in 1898, with figures of firefighters on the upper façade. It houses the Ministry of Local Development.

Staroměstské náměstí, 1793
The engraving by Filip and František Heger shows the Old Town Square teeming with people and carriages. The Old Town Hall is on the left.

Old Town Square: South Side ⓐ

STAROMĚSTSKÉ NÁMĚSTÍ

A COLOURFUL ARRAY of houses of Romanesque or Gothic origin, with fascinating house signs, graces the south side of the Old Town Square. The block between Celetná Street and Železná Street is especially attractive. The Square has always been a busy focal point, and today offers visitors a tourist information centre, as well as a number of restaurants, cafés, shops, and galleries.

FRANZ KAFKA (1883–1924)

The author of two of the most influential novels of the 20th century, *The Trial* and *The Castle*, Kafka spent most of his short life in the Old Town. From 1893 to 1901 he studied in the Golz-Kinský Palace *(see p70)*, where his father later had a shop. He worked as an insurance clerk, but frequented Berta Fanta's literary salon at the Stone Ram, Old Town Square, along with others who wrote in German. Hardly any of his work was published in his lifetime.

U Lazara (At Lazarus's)
Romanesque barrel vaulting testifies to the house's early origins, though it was rebuilt during the Renaissance. The ground floor houses the Staroměstská restaurace.

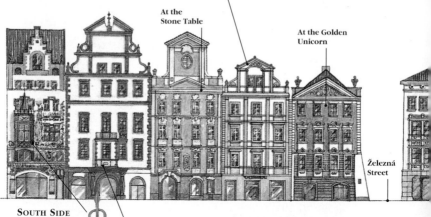

At the Stone Table

At the Golden Unicorn

Železná Street

SOUTH SIDE

★ At the Stone Ram
The early-16th-century house sign shows a young maiden with a ram. The house has been referred to as At the Unicorn due to the similarity between the one-horned ram and a unicorn.

★ Štorch House
The late-19th-century painting of St Wenceslas on horseback by Mikuláš Aleš appears on this ornate Neo-Renaissance building, also known as At the Stone Madonna.

STAR SIGHTS

★ Štorch House

★ At the Stone Ram

Melantrichova Passage
*Václav Jansa's painting (1898)
shows the narrow passageway
leading to the Old Town Square.*

☐ South side

◉ Jan Hus Monument

At the Red Fox
*A golden Madonna and Child
look down from the Baroque
façade of an originally
Romanesque building.*

At The Ox
*Named after its
15th-century owner,
the burgher Ochs,
this house features an
early-18th-century
stone statue of
St Anthony of Padua.*

**At the
Blue Star**

At the Storks

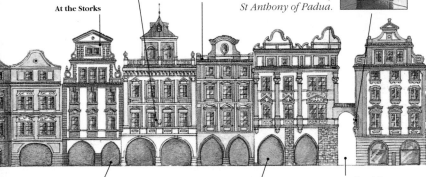

The arcade houses the
Franz Kafka Gallery.

**U Orloje
restaurant**

**Melantrichova
Passage**

TIMELINE

1338 Old Town becomes municipality	*Leopold II's Royal Procession through the Old Town Square in 1791*		**1735** Church of St Nicholas completed	**1948** Klement Gottwald proclaims Communist state from balcony of Golz-Kinský Palace	
	1300	**1450**	**1600**	**1750**	**1900**
1200 Square is meeting point of trade routes and important market	**1365** Building of present Týn Church	**1621** Execution of 27 anti-Habsburg leaders in square *(see p31)*	**1784** Unification of Prague towns		
		1689 Fire destroys large part of Old Town	**1915** Unveiling of Jan Hus Monument		

Hus Monument (detail)

Statue of the Madonna on Our Lady before Týn

Church of Our Lady before Týn ⑧

KOSTEL MATKY BOŽÍ PŘED TÝNEM

Týnská, Štupartská. **Map** 3 C3. **C** 22 23 18 186. **M** Staroměstská, Můstek. **Open** only for services. ✝ 4:30pm Mon–Fri, 1pm Sat, 11:30am & 9pm Sun. ✉

DOMINATING THE Old Town Square are the magnificent multiple steeples of this historic church. The present Gothic church was started in 1365 and soon became associated with the reform movement in Bohemia. From the early 15th century until 1620 Týn was the main Hussite church in Prague. The Hussite king, George of Poděbrady, took Utraquist communion (see Church of St Martin in the Wall p73) here and had a gold chalice – the Utraquist symbol – mounted on the façade. After 1621 the chalice was melted down to become part of the statue of the Madonna that replaced it.

On the northern side of the church is a beautiful entrance portal (1390) decorated with scenes of Christ's passion. The dark interior has some notable features, including Gothic sculptures of *Calvary*, a pewter font (1414) and a 15th-century Gothic pulpit. Behind the church is the Týn Courtyard, with its numerous architectural styles.

Kinský Palace ⑨

PALÁC KINSKÝCH

Staroměstské náměstí 12. **Map** 3 C3. **C** 22 48 10 758. **M** Staroměstská. **Open** 10am–6pm Tue–Sun. 🖼 ✉ 🍴

THIS LOVELY Rococo palace, designed by Kilian Ignaz Dientzenhofer, has a pretty pink and white stucco façade crowned with statues of the four elements by Ignaz Franz Platzer. It was bought from the Golz family in 1768 by Štěpán Kinský, an Imperial diplomat. In 1948 Communist leader, Klement Gottwald, used the balcony to address a huge crowd of party members – a key event in the crisis that led up to his *coup d'état*. The National Gallery now uses the Kinský Palace for temporary art exhibitions.

Kinský arms on Golz-Kinský Palace

Jan Hus Monument ⑩

POMNÍK JANA HUSA

Staroměstské náměstí. **Map** 3 B3. **M** Staroměstská.

AT ONE END of the Old Town Square stands the massive monument to the religious reformer and Czech hero, Jan Hus (see pp26–7). Hus was burnt at the stake after being pronounced a heretic by the Council of Constance in 1415. The monument by Ladislav Šaloun was unveiled in 1915 on the 500th anniversary of his death. It shows two groups of people, one of victorious Hussite warriors, the other of Protestants forced into exile 200 years later, and a young mother symbolizing national rebirth. The dominant figure of Hus emphasizes the moral authority of the man who gave up life rather than his beliefs.

Church of St Nicholas ⑪

KOSTEL SV. MIKULÁŠE

Staroměstské náměstí. **Map** 3 B3. **C** 22 42 15 402. **M** Staroměstská. **Open** 10am–4pm Tue–Sun (to 5pm Wed) and for evening concerts Apr–Nov. ✝ 10:30am Sun. 📷

THERE HAS BEEN a church here since the 12th century. It was the Old Town's parish church and meeting place until Týn Church was completed in the 14th century. After the Battle of the White Mountain in 1620 (see pp30–31) the church became part of a Benedictine monastery. The present church by Kilian Ignaz Dientzenhofer, was completed in 1735. Its dramatic white façade is studded with statues by Antonín Braun.

Defiant Hussites on the Jan Hus Monument in Old Town Square

Church of St Nicholas in the Old Town

When in 1781 Emperor Joseph II closed all monasteries not engaged in socially useful activities, the church was stripped bare. In World War I the church was used by the troops of Prague's garrison. The colonel in charge took the opportunity to restore the church with the help of artists who might otherwise have been sent to the front. The dome has frescoes of the lives of St Nicholas and St Benedict by Kosmas Damian Asam. In the nave is a huge crown-shaped chandelier. At the end of the war, the church of St Nicholas was given to the Czechoslovak Hussite Church. Concerts are given now in the church during the summer.

Old Town Hall ⑫
STAROMĚSTSKÁ RADNICE

See pp72–3.

House at the Two Golden Bears ⑬
DŮM U DVOU ZLATÝCH MEDVĚDŮ

Kožná 1. **Map** 3 B4. Ⓜ *Můstek.* **Closed** to the public.

IF YOU LEAVE the Old Town Square by the narrow Melantrichova Street, make a point of turning into the first alleyway on the left to see the portal of the house called "At the Two Golden Bears". The present Renaissance building was constructed from two earlier houses in 1567. The portal was added in 1590, when a wealthy merchant, Lorenc Štork, secured the services of court architect Bonifaz Wohlmut, who had designed the spire on the tower of St Vitus's Cathedral *(see pp100–3)*. His ornate portal with reliefs of two bears is one of the most beautiful Renaissance portals in Prague. Magnificent arcades, also dating from the 16th century, have been preserved in the inner courtyard. In 1885 Egon Erwin Kisch, known as the "Furious Reporter", was born here. He was a German-speaking Jewish writer and journalist, feared for the force of his left-wing rhetoric.

Church of St Gall ⑭
KOSTEL SV. HAVLA

Havelská. **Map** 3 C4. Ⓜ *Můstek.* 📞 *22 23 18 186.* **Open** only for services. ✝ *12:15pm Mon–Fri, 7:30am Sun.* 🚫

DATING FROM around 1280, this church was built to serve an autonomous German community in the area known as Gall's Town (Havelské Město). In the 14th century this was merged with the Old Town. In the 18th century the church was given a Baroque facelift by Giovanni Santini-Aichel, who created a bold façade decorated with statues of saints by Ferdinand Brokof. Rich interior furnishings include paintings by the leading Baroque artist Karel Škréta, who is buried here. Prague's best-known market has been held in Havelská Street since the middle ages, selling flowers, vegetables, toys, and clothes.

One of nine statues on façade of St Gall's

Carved Renaissance portal of the House at the Two Golden Bears

Old Town Hall ⑫

STAROMĚSTSKÁ RADNICE

ONE OF THE most striking buildings in Prague is the Old Town Hall, established in 1338 after King John of Luxemburg agreed to set up a town council. Over the centuries a number of old houses were knocked together as the Old Town Hall expanded, and it now consists of a row of colourful Gothic and Renaissance buildings, most of which have been carefully restored after heavy damage inflicted by the Nazis in the 1945 Prague Uprising. The tower is 69.5 m (228 ft) high and offers a spectacular view of the city.

Old Council Hall
This 19th-century engraving features the well-preserved 15th-century ceiling.

Old Town Coat of Arms
Above the inscription, "Prague, Head of the Kingdom", is the coat of arms of the Old Town, which was adopted in 1784 for the whole city.

Tourist information and entrance to Tower

Temporary art exhibitions

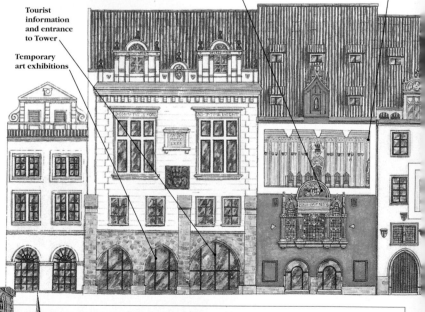

EXECUTIONS IN THE OLD TOWN SQUARE

A bronze tablet below the Old Town Hall chapel records the names of the 27 Protestant leaders executed here by order of the Catholic Emperor Ferdinand on 21 June 1621. This was the humiliating aftermath of the Battle of the White Mountain *(see pp30–31)*. This defeat led to the emigration of Protestants unwilling to give up their faith, a Counter-Reformation drive and Germanization.

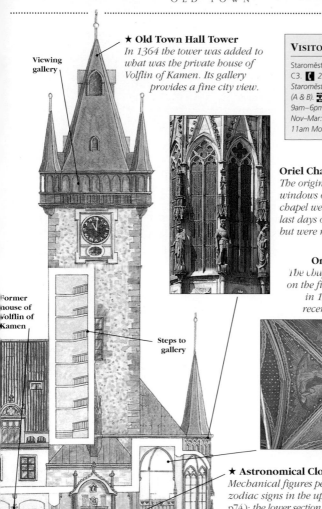

★ Old Town Hall Tower
In 1364 the tower was added to what was the private house of Volflin of Kamen. Its gallery provides a fine city view.

Viewing gallery

Former house of Volflin of Kamen

Steps to gallery

Calendar *(see pp32–3)*

Entrance hall decorated with mosaics

VISITORS' CHECKLIST

Staroměstské náměstí 1. **Map** 3
C3. 22 42 28 456.
Staroměstská (line A), Můstek
(A & B). 17, 18. **Open** Apr–Oct:
9am–6pm daily (from 11am Mon);
Nov–Mar: 9am–5pm daily (from
11am Mon).

Oriel Chapel
The original stained-glass windows on the five-sided chapel were destroyed in the last days of World War II, but were replaced in 1987.

Oriel Chapel Ceiling
The chapel, which was built on the first floor of the tower in 1381, has an ornate, recently restored ceiling.

★ Astronomical Clock
Mechanical figures perform above the zodiac signs in the upper section (see p74); the lower section is a calendar.

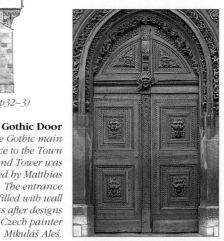

Gothic Door
This late Gothic main entrance to the Town Hall and Tower was carved by Matthias Rejsek. The entrance hall is filled with wall mosaics after designs by the Czech painter Mikuláš Aleš.

STAR FEATURES

★ **Astronomical Clock**

★ **Old Town Hall Tower**

Town Hall Clock

ORLOJ

Jan Táborský

The TOWN HALL acquired its first clock at the beginning of the 15th century. According to legend, in 1490, when it was rebuilt by a master clockmaker called Hanuš (real name Jan Z Růže), the councillors were so anxious to prevent him from re-creating his masterpiece elsewhere, that they blinded the poor man. Though the clock has been repaired many times since, the mechanism was perfected by Jan Táborský between 1552 and 1572.

The Apostles

Vanity and Greed

Arabic numerals 1–24

Astronomical Clock with the sun in Aries

Death

APOSTLES

THE CENTREPIECE of the show that draws a crowd of spectators every time the clock strikes the hour is the procession of

Vojtěch Sucharda's Apostles, sculpted after the last set was burnt in 1945

Blue, representing the daylight hours

Calendar by Josef Mánes *(see pp32–3)*

The Turk, a symbol of lust

the 12 Apostles. First the figure of Death, the skeleton on the right of the clock, gives a pull on the rope that he holds in his right hand. In his left hand is an hourglass, which he raises and inverts. Two windows then open and the clockwork Apostles (or to be precise 11 of the Apostles plus St Paul) move slowly round, led by St Peter.

At the end of this part of the display, a cock crows and the clock chimes the hour. The other moving figures are a Turk, who shakes his head from side to side, Vanity, who looks at himself in a mirror and Greed, adapted from the original medieval stereotype of a Jewish moneylender.

ASTRONOMICAL CLOCK

THE CLOCKMAKER's view of the universe had the Earth fixed firmly at the centre. The purpose of the clock was not to tell you the exact time but to imitate the supposed orbits of the sun and moon about the Earth. The hand with the sun, which points to the hour, in fact records three different kinds of time. The outer ring of medieval Arabic numerals measures Old Bohemian time, in which a day of 24 hours was reckoned from the setting of the sun. The ring of Roman numerals indicates time as we know it. The blue part of the dial represents the

visible part of the sky. This is divided into 12 parts. In so-called Babylonian time, the period of daylight was divided into 12 hours, which would vary in length from summer to winter.

The clock also shows the movement of the sun and moon through the 12 signs of the zodiac, which were of great importance in 16th-century Prague.

The figures of Death and the Turk

Church of St Martin in the Wall ⑮

KOSTEL SV. MARTINA VE ZDI

Martinská. **Map** 3 B5. ⚇ *Národní třída, Můstek.* 🚊 *6, 9, 17, 18, 22.* **Open** *for concerts.*

T HIS 12TH-CENTURY church became part of the newly erected town wall during the fortification of the Old Town in the 13th century, hence its name. It was the first church where blessed wine, usually reserved for the clergy, was offered to the congregation as well as bread. This was a basic tenet of belief of the moderate Hussites *(see pp26–7)*, the Utraquists, who took their name from the Latin *sub utraque specie*, "in both kinds". In 1787 the church was converted into workshops, but rebuilt in its original form in the early years of this century.

Náprstek Museum ⑯

NÁPRSTKOVO MUZEUM

Betlémské náměstí 1. **Map** 3 B4. 🛈 *22 22 21 418.* ⚇ *Národní třída, Staroměstská.* 🚊 *6, 9, 17, 18, 22.* **Open** *9am–5:30pm Tue–Sun.* 🅦 www.aconet.cz/npm

V OJTA NÁPRSTEK, art patron and philanthropist, created this museum as a tribute to modern industry following a decade of exile in America after the 1848 revolution *(see pp32–3)*. On his return in 1862, inspired by London's Victorian museums, he began his collection. He created the Czech Industrial Museum by joining five older buildings together, and in the process virtually destroyed the family brewery and home – an 18th-century house called At the Haláneks (U Halánků). He later turned to ethnography and the collection now consists of artefacts from Asian, African and Native American cultures, including weapons and ritual objects from the Aztecs, Toltecs and Mayas. The museum is part of the National Museum.

Nearby, on Smetanovo nábřeží is Neo-Gothic Kranners Fountain erected in 1850.

Ceiling fresco by Václav Vavřinec Reiner in Church of St Giles

Church of St Giles ⑰

KOSTEL SV. JILJÍ

Husova. **Map** 3 B4. 🛈 *22 42 20 235.* ⚇ *Národní třída.* 🚊 *6, 9, 17, 18, 22.* **Open** *for services only.* 🕐 *7am & 6:30pm Mon–Fri, 6:30pm Sat, 8:30am, 10:30am, noon, 6:30pm Sun.* 📷

D ESPITE A beautiful Gothic portal on the southern side, the inside of this church is essentially Baroque. Founded in 1371 on the site of an old Romanesque church, it became a Hussite parish church in 1420. Following the Protestant defeat in 1620 *(see pp30–31)*, Ferdinand II presented the church to the Dominicans, who built a huge friary on its southern side. It has now been returned to the Dominicans, religious orders having been abolished under the Communists.

The vaults of the church are decorated with frescoes by the painter Václav Vavřinec Reiner, who is buried in the nave before the altar of St Vincent. The main fresco, a glorification of the Dominicans, shows St Dominic and his friars helping the pope defend the Catholic Church from non-believers.

Bethlehem Chapel ⑱

BETLÉMSKÁ KAPLE

Betlémské náměstí. **Map** 3 B4. ⚇ *Národní třída, Staroměstská.* 🚊 *6, 9, 17, 18, 22.* **Open** *Apr–Oct: 9am–6pm daily; Nov–Mar: 9am–5pm daily.* 📷 ♿ 🎫 *organized by the Prague Information Service (see p219).*

T HE PRESENT "chapel" is a reconstruction of a hall built by the followers of the radical preacher Jan Milíč z Kroměříže in 1391–4. The hall was used for preaching in Czech. Between 1402 and 1413 Jan Hus *(see pp26–7)* preached in the Chapel. Influenced by the teachings of the English religious reformer John Wycliffe, Hus condemned the corrupt practices of the Church, arguing that the Scriptures should be the sole source of doctrine. After the Battle of the White Mountain in 1620 *(see pp30–31)*, when Protestant worship was outlawed, the building was handed over to the Jesuits, who completely rebuilt it with six naves. In 1786 it was almost demolished. After World War II the chapel was reconstructed following old illustrations.

16th-century illustration showing Jan Hus preaching in Bethlehem Chapel

Street-by-Street: Old Town (West)

T HE NARROW STREETS near Charles Bridge follow
Prague's medieval street plan. For centuries Charles
Street (Karlova) was the main route across the Old
Town. The picturesque, twisting street is lined with
shops and houses displaying Renaissance and Baroque
façades. In the 17th century the Jesuits bought up a
vast area of land to the north of the street to house
the complex of the Clementinum university.

★ Clementinum
*This plaque records the
founding in 1783 of a state-
supervised seminary in place
of the old Jesuit university* ㉓

**Knights of the
Cross Square**
*From the façade of
the Church of the
Holy Saviour, black-
ened statues overlook
the small square* ㉕

**Church of
St Francis**

★ Smetana Museum
*A museum devoted to the life
and work of composer Bedřich
Smetana is housed in this Neo-
Renaissance building set on the
riverfront, which was once
an old waterworks* ㉔

A N E N S K Á

St Anne's Convent
was abolished in 1782.
Some of its buildings
are now used by the
National Theatre
(see pp156–7).

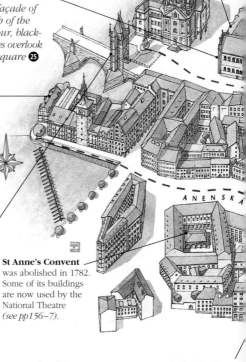

The Old Town Bridge Tower
dates from 1380. The Gothic sculptural
decoration on the eastern façade was
from Peter Parler's workshop. The
kingfisher was the favourite personal
symbol of Wenceslas IV (son of
Charles IV) in whose reign the tower
was completed *(see p139).*

Charles Street
*Among the many decorated houses
along the ancient street, be sure to
look out for this Art Nouveau
statue of the legendary Princess
Libuše (see p21) surrounded by
roses at No. 22/24* ㉑

Mariánské Square
The square used to be flooded so often, it was called "the puddle". The Art Nouveau sculptures on the balcony of the New Town Hall, built here in 1911, are by Stanislav Sucharda **20**

Observatory tower

LOCATOR MAP
See Street Finder, map 3

Clam-Gallas Palace
One of Prague's grandest Baroque palaces and full of wonderful statuary, the Clam-Gallas has been restored and is open for concerts **19**

MARIÁNSKÉ
NÁMĚSTÍ

KARLOVA

LILIOVÁ

HUSOVA

ŘETĚZOVÁ

To Old Town Square

Church of St Giles
Much of the Baroque sculpture, like this angel on the altar (1738), is by František Weiss **17**

Palace of the Lords of Kunštát
George of Poděbrady lived here before he became King in 1458 **22**

Bethlehem Chapel
In this spacious chapel, rebuilt in the 1950s, Hus and other reformers preached to huge congregations **18**

| 0 metres | 100 |
| 0 yards | 100 |

KEY

– – – Suggested route

STAR SIGHTS

★ **Clementinum**

★ **Smetana Museum**

Clam-Gallas Palace ⑲

CLAM-GALLASŮV PALÁC

Husova 20. **Map** 3 B4. 🔲 *22 42 22 496*. Ⓜ *Staroměstská.* **Open** *for concerts and temporary exhibitions only.*

T HE INTERIOR of this magnificent Baroque palace had suffered during its use as a store for the city archives, but has now been lovingly restored. The palace, designed by Viennese court architect Johann Bernhard Fischer von Erlach, was built in 1713–30 for the Supreme Marshal of Bohemia, Jan Gallas de Campo. Its grand portals, each flanked by two pairs of Hercules sculpted by Matthias Braun, give a taste of what lies within. The main staircase is also decorated with Braun statues, set off by a ceiling fresco, *The Triumph of Apollo* by Carlo Carlone. The palace has a theatre, where Beethoven performed some of his works.

Mariánské Square ⑳

MARIÁNSKÉ NÁMĚSTÍ

Map 3 B3. Ⓜ *Staroměstská, Můstek.*

T WO STATUES dominate the square from the corners of the forbidding Town Hall, built in 1912. One illustrates the story of the long-lived Rabbi Löw *(see p88)* finally being caught by the Angel of Death. The other is the Iron Man, a local ghost condemned to roam the Old Town after murdering his mistress. A niche in the garden wall of the Clam-Gallas Palace houses a statue of the River Vltava, depicted as a nymph pouring water from a jug. There is a story that an old soldier once made the nymph sole beneficiary of his will.

Charles Street ㉑

KARLOVA ULICE

Map 3 A4. Ⓜ *Staroměstská.*

A 19th-century sign on the House at the Golden Snake

D ATING BACK to the 12th century, this narrow, winding street was part of the Royal Route *(see pp174–5)*, along which coronation processions passed on the way to Prague Castle. Many original Gothic and Renaissance houses remain, most converted into shops to attract tourists.

A café at the House at the Golden Snake (No. 18) was established in 1714 by an Armenian, Deodatus Damajan, who handed out slanderous pamphlets from here. It is now a restaurant. Look out for At the Golden Well (No. 3), which has a magnificent Baroque façade and stucco reliefs of saints including St Roch and St Sebastian, who are believed to offer protection against plagues.

Palace of the Lords of Kunštát ㉒

DŮM PÁNŮ Z KUNŠTÁTU

Řetězová 3. **Map** 3 B4. 🔲 *22 22 21 240.* Ⓜ *Národní třída, Staroměstská.* 🚊 *6, 9, 17, 18, 22.* **Open** *May–Sep: 10am–6pm Tue–Sun.* 🚫 📷

T HE BASEMENT of the palace, dating from around 1200, contains three of the best-preserved Romanesque rooms in Prague. It was originally the ground floor, but over the years the surrounding ground level was raised by 3m (10 ft) to prevent flooding. In the 15th century the house was enlarged in Gothic style by its owners, the Lords of Kunštát and Poděbrady. The palace

Matthias Braun's statues on a portal of the Clam-Gallas Palace (c.1714)

houses a historical exhibition devoted to Bohemia's only Hussite king, George of Poděbrady *(see pp26–7)*, who lived here for a time.

Clementinum ㉓
KLEMENTINUM

Křižovnické náměstí 4, Mariánské náměstí 5, Seminářská 1. **Map** 3 A4.
📞 *22 16 63 111.* Ⓜ *Staroměstská.*
🚋 *17, 18.* **Library open** *9am–10pm Mon–Fri, 8am–2pm Sat.* **Church open** *only for services.* 🕇 *7pm Tue, 8pm Thu, 2pm & 8pm Sun.* 🚫 ♿ 🅿 *Mar–Oct: 2–9pm daily (from 10am Sat & Sun).* 📞 *6 03 23 12 41.*

Former Jesuit Church of the Holy Saviour in the Clementinum

Iᴎ 1556 ᴇᴍᴘᴇʀᴏʀ Ferdinand I invited the Jesuits to Prague to help bring the Czechs back into the Catholic fold. They established their headquarters in the former Dominican monastery of St Clement, hence the name Clementinum. This soon became an effective rival to the Carolinum *(see p65)*, the Utraquist university. Prague's first Jesuit church, the Church of the Holy Saviour (Kostel sv. Salvátora) was built here in 1601. Its façade, with seven large statues of saints by Jan Bendl (1659), is dramatically lit up at night.

Expelled in 1618, the Jesuits were back two years later more determined than ever to stamp out heresy. In 1622 the two universities were merged, resulting in the Jesuits gaining a virtual monopoly on higher education in Prague. They believed two-thirds of the population were secret heretics,

searched for books in Czech and then burnt them by the thousand. Between 1653 and 1723 the Clementinum expanded eastwards. Over 30 houses and three churches were pulled down to make way for the new complex.

When in 1773 the pope dissolved their order, the Jesuits had to leave Prague and education was secularized. The Clementinum became the Prague University library, today the National Library. Look out for any classical concerts performed in the beautiful Chapel of Mirrors (Zrcadlová kaple).

Smetana Museum ㉔
MUZEUM BEDŘICHA SMETANY

Novotného lávka 1. **Map** 3 A4.
📞 & ꜰᴀx *22 22 20 082.*
Ⓜ *Staroměstská.* 🚋 *17, 18.*
Open *10am–5pm Wed–Mon.* 🎞 🚫

Oᴎ ᴀ ꜱᴘɪᴛ ᴏꜰ ʟᴀɴᴅ beside the Vltava, a former Neo-Renaissance waterworks has been turned into a memorial to Bedřich Smetana, the father of Czech music. The museum contains documents, letters, scores and musical instruments detailing the composer's life and work. Smetana was a fervent patriot and his music helped inspire the Czech national revival. Deaf towards the end of his life, he never heard his cycle of symphonic poems *Má Vlast* (My Country), being performed.

Statue of Charles IV (1848) in Knights of the Cross Square

Knights of the Cross Square ㉕
KŘIŽOVNICKE NÁMĚSTÍ

Map 3 A4. 📞 *22 11 08 227.* Ⓜ *Staroměstská.* 🚋 *17, 18.* 🚌 *135, 207.* **Church of St Francis open** *only for services.* 🕇 *7am Mon–Fri, 9am Sun.* 🚫 ♿ **Gallery Křižovníků open** *10am–1pm, 2–6pm Tue–Sun.*

Tʜɪꜱ ꜱᴍᴀʟʟ ꜱQᴜᴀʀᴇ in front of the Old Town Bridge Tower offers fine views across the Vltava. On the north side is the Church of St Francis (kostel sv. Františka), once part of the monastery of the crusading Knights of the Cross with the Red Star. To the east is the Church of the Holy Saviour, part of the huge Clementinum complex. On the western side is the Gallery Křižovníků, holding the art collection and Treasury of the Knights of the Cross. In the square stands a large bronze Neo-Gothic statue of Charles IV.

Sgraffitoed façade of the Smetana Museum

JEWISH QUARTER

JOSEFOV

I N THE MIDDLE AGES there were two distinct Jewish communities in Prague's Old Town: Jews from the west had settled around the Old-New Synagogue, Jews from the Byzantine Empire around the Old Shul (on the site of today's Spanish Synagogue). The two settlements gradually merged and were confined in an enclosed ghetto. For centuries Prague's Jews suffered from oppressive laws – in the 16th century they had to wear a yellow circle as a mark of shame. Christians

Art Nouveau detail on house in Kaprova

often accused them of starting fires and poisoning wells – any pretext for a pogrom. Discrimination was partially relaxed in 1784 by Joseph II, and the Jewish Quarter was named Josefov after him. In 1850 the area was officially incorporated as part of Prague. In the 1890s the city authorities decided to raze the ghetto slums because the area's complete lack of sanitation made it a health hazard. However, the Town Hall, a number of synagogues and the Old Jewish Cemetery were saved.

SIGHTS AT A GLANCE

Synagogues and Churches
Pinkas Synagogue ❹
Klausen Synagogue ❺
Old-New Synagogue
pp88–9 ❻
High Synagogue ❼
Maisel Synagogue ❾
Church of the Holy Ghost ❿
Spanish Synagogue ⓫
Church of St Simon
and St Jude ⓭
Church of St Castullus ⓮

Concert Hall
Rudolfinum ❶

Museums and Galleries
Museum of Decorative Arts ❷
St Agnes of Bohemia Convent
pp92–3 ⓯

Historic Buildings
Jewish Town Hall ❽
Cubist Houses ⓬

Cemeteries
Old Jewish Cemetery
pp86–7 ❸

GETTING THERE
Staroměstská station on metro line A is close to all the major sights in the Jewish Quarter. The alternative is to take tram 17 or 18 to Náměstí Jana Palacha. For St Agnes of Bohemia Convent, bus 207 is convenient.

```
0 metres        250
0 yards         250
```

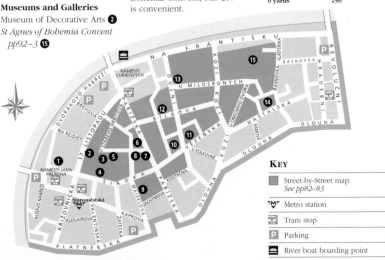

KEY

▦	Street-by-Street map *See pp82–83*
Ⓜ	Metro station
🚋	Tram stop
P	Parking
🚢	River boat boarding point

◁ **Densely-packed gravestones in the Old Jewish Cemetery**

Street-by-Street: Jewish Quarter

Though the old ghetto has disappeared, much of the area's fascinating history is preserved in the synagogues around the Old Jewish Cemetery, while the newer streets are lined with many delightful Art Nouveau buildings. The old lanes to the east of the former ghetto lead to the quiet haven of St Agnes's Convent, beautifully restored as a branch of the National Gallery.

Cubist Houses
One of the new architectural styles used in the rebuilding of the old Jewish Quarter was based on the ideas of Cubism ⓬

★ **Old Jewish Cemetery**
Thousands of gravestones are crammed into the ancient cemetery ❸

★ **Old-New Synagogue**
The Gothic hall with its distinctive crenellated gable has been a house of prayer for over 700 years ❻

High Synagogue
The interior has splendid Renaissance vaulting ❼

Klausen Synagogue
The exhibits of the Jewish Museum include this alms box, dating from about 1800 ❺

★ **Museum of Decorative Arts**
Stained glass panels on the staircase depict the crafts represented in the museum's wide-ranging collection ❷

Pinkas Synagogue
The walls are now a moving memorial to the Czech Jews killed in the Holocaust ❹

To Metro Staroměstská

Jewish Town Hall
The 16th-century building still serves the Czech Jewish community ❽

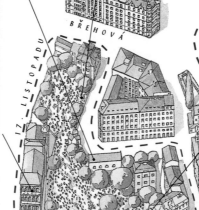

Maisel Synagogue
The original synagogue was built for Mayor Mordechai Maisel in 1591 ❾

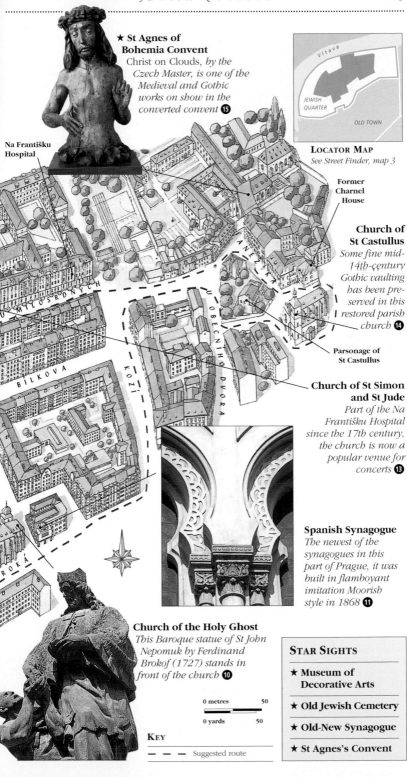

★ **St Agnes of Bohemia Convent**
Christ on Clouds, *by the Czech Master, is one of the Medieval and Gothic works on show in the converted convent* **15**

Na Františku Hospital

LOCATOR MAP
See Street Finder, map 3

Former Charnel House

Church of St Castullus
Some fine mid-14th-century Gothic vaulting has been preserved in this restored parish church **14**

Parsonage of St Castullus

Church of St Simon and St Jude
Part of the Na Františku Hospital since the 17th century, the church is now a popular venue for concerts **13**

Spanish Synagogue
The newest of the synagogues in this part of Prague, it was built in flamboyant imitation Moorish style in 1868 **11**

Church of the Holy Ghost
This Baroque statue of St John Nepomuk by Ferdinand Brokof (1727) stands in front of the church **10**

0 metres 50

0 yards 50

KEY

– – – Suggested route

STAR SIGHTS
★ **Museum of Decorative Arts**
★ **Old Jewish Cemetery**
★ **Old-New Synagogue**
★ **St Agnes's Convent**

Stage of the Dvořák Hall in the Rudolfinum

Rudolfinum ❶

Alšovo nábřeží 12. **Map** 3 A3. 🚇
Staroměstská. 🚋 *17, 18.* 🚌 *135,
207.* **Philharmonic** 📞 *22 70 59 352.*
Galerie Rudolphinum 📞 *22 70 59
204.* **Open** *10am–6pm Tue–Sun.*
♿ 🚫 📷 🖵 Ⓦ www.rudolfinum.cz

NOW THE HOME of the Czech
Philharmonic Orchestra,
the Rudolfinum is one of the
most impressive landmarks
on the Old Town bank of the
Vltava. Many of the major
concerts of the Prague Spring
music festival *(see p50)* are
held here. There are several
concert halls, the sumptuous
Dvořák Hall ranking among
the finest creations of 19th-
century Czech architecture.

The Rudolfinum was built
between 1876 and 1884 to a
design by Josef Zítek and Josef
Schulz and named in honour
of Crown Prince Rudolph of
Habsburg. Like the National
Theatre *(see pp156–7)*, it is an
outstanding example of Czech
Neo-Renaissance style. The
curving balustrade is decorated
with statues of distinguished
Czech, Austrian and German
composers and artists.

Also known as the House of
Artists (Dům umělců), the
building houses the Gallerie

Rudolphinum, a collection of
modern art. Between 1918
and 1939, and for a brief
period after World War II, the
Rudolfinum was the seat of
the Czechoslovak parliament.

Museum of Decorative Arts ❷

**UMĚLECKOPRŮMYSLOVÉ
MUZEUM**

17. listopadu 2. **Map** 3 B3. 📞 *25 10
93 111.* 🚇 *Staroměstská.* 🚋 *17,
18.* 🚌 *135, 207.* **Open** *10am–6pm
Tue–Sun.* 📷 🚫 🖵

FOR SOME YEARS after its
foundation in 1885, the
museum's collections were
housed in the Rudolfinum.
The present building, designed
by Josef Schulz in French
Neo-Renaissance style, was
completed in 1901.

The museum's glass collection
is one of the largest in the
world, but only a fraction
of it is ever on display.
Pride of place goes to the
Bohemian glass, of which
there are many fine Baroque
and 19th- and 20th-century
pieces. Medieval and Venetian
Renaissance glass are also
well represented.

Among the permanent
exhibitions of other crafts are
Meissen porcelain, the Gobelin
tapestries and displays
covering fashion, textiles,
photography and printing.
The furniture collection has
exquisitely carved escritoires
and bureaux from the Renaissance. On the mezzanine
floor are halls for temporary
exhibitions and an extensive
art library housing more than
100,000 publications.

Old Jewish Cemetery ❸

STARÝ ŽIDOVSKÝ HŘBITOV

See pp86–7.

Pinkas Synagogue ❹

PINKASOVA SYNAGÓGA

Široká 3. **Map** 3 B3. 🚇 *Staroměstská.*
🚋 *17, 18.* 🚌 *135, 207.* **Open**
*Apr–Oct: 9am–6pm Sun–Fri;
Nov–Mar: 9am–4:30pm.* 🖼
📷 🚫 Ⓦ www.jewishmuseum.cz

THE SYNAGOGUE was founded
in 1479 by Rabbi Pinkas
and enlarged in 1535 by his
great-nephew Aaron Meshulam
Horowitz. It has been rebuilt
many times over the centuries.
Excavations have turned up
fascinating relics of life in the
medieval ghetto, including a
mikva or ritual bath. The core
of the present building is a
hall with

Names of Holocaust victims on Pinkas Synagogue wall

Gothic vaulting. The gallery for women was added in the early 17th century.

The synagogue now serves as a memorial to all the Jewish Czechoslovak citizens who were imprisoned in Terezín concentration camp and later deported to various Nazi extermination camps. The names of the 77,297 who did not return are inscribed on the synagogue walls. The building now houses an exhibition of children's drawings from the Terezín concentration camp.

Klausen Synagogue ➎
KLAUSOVÁ SYNAGÓGA

U starého hřbitova 3a. **Map** 3 B3. 🚇 Staroměstská. 🚊 17, 18. 🚌 135, 207. **Open** Apr–Oct: 9am–6pm daily; Nov–Mar: 9am–4:30pm. 📷 🚫 🌐 www.jewishmuseum.cz

BEFORE THE FIRE of 1689, this site was occupied by a number of small Jewish schools and prayer houses known as *klausen*. The name was preserved in the Klausen Synagogue, built on the ruins and completed in 1694. The High Baroque structure has a fine barrel-vaulted interior with rich stucco decorations. It now houses Hebrew prints and manuscripts and an exhibition of Jewish traditions and customs, tracing the history of the Jews in Central Europe back to the early Middle Ages. Many exhibits relate to famous figures in the city's Jewish community including the 16th-century Rabbi Löw *(see p88)*, who, according to legend, created an artificial man or *golem* out of clay.

Adjoining the synagogue is a building that looks like a tiny medieval castle. It was built in 1906 as the ceremonial hall of the Jewish Burial Society. In 1944 an exhibition was put on here detailing the history of the Prague ghetto.

18th-century silver-gilt Torah shield in the High Synagogue

Old-New Synagogue ➏
STARONOVÁ SYNAGÓGA

See pp88–9.

High Synagogue ➐
VYSOKÁ SYNAGÓGA

Červená 4. **Map** 3 B3. 🚇 Staroměstská. 🚊 17, 18. 🚌 135, 207. **Open** Apr–Oct: 9am–6pm daily; Nov–Mar: 9am–4:30pm. 📷 🚫

LIKE THE Jewish Town Hall, the building of the High Synagogue was financed by Mordechai Maisel, mayor of the Jewish Town, in the 1570s. Originally the two buildings formed a single complex and to facilitate communication with the Town Hall, the main hall of the synagogue was on the first floor. It was not until the 19th century that the two buildings were separated and the synagogue was given a staircase and street entrance. You can still see the original Renaissance vaulting and stucco decoration.

The exhibition in the synagogue includes richly embroidered Torah mantles, curtains and other religious textiles. There are also silver ornaments,

19th-century Torah pointer in Klausen Synagogue

such as shields and finials, used to decorate the Ark, where the Torah scrolls are kept. These date from the 16th to the 19th centuries.

Jewish Town Hall ➑
ŽIDOVSKÁ RADNICE

Maislova 18. **Map** 3 B3. 📞 & 📠 22 23 19 002. 🚇 Staroměstská. 🚊 17, 18. 🚌 135, 207. **Closed** to the public.

THE CORE of this attractive pink and white building is the original Jewish Town Hall, built in 1570–77 by the immensely rich mayor, Mordechai Maisel. In 1763 it acquired a new appearance in the flowery style of the Late Baroque. The last alterations date from 1908, when the southern wing was enlarged.

On the roof stands a small wooden clock tower with a distinctive green steeple. The right to build the tower was originally granted to the Jewish community after their part in the defence of Charles Bridge against the Swedes in 1648 *(see pp30–31)*. On one of the gables there is another clock. This one has Hebrew figures and, because Hebrew reads from right to left, hands that turn in an anti-clockwise direction. The Town Hall is now the seat of the Council of Jewish Religious Communities in the Czech Republic.

Façade and clock tower of the Jewish Town Hall

Old Jewish Cemetery ❸

STARÝ ŽIDOVSKÝ HŘBITOV

Tᴴⁱˢ ʀᴇᴍᴀʀᴋᴀʙʟᴇ ˢⁱᵗᴇ was, for over 300 years, the only burial ground permitted to Jews. Founded in 1478, it was slightly enlarged over the years but still basically corresponds to its medieval size. Because of the lack of space people had to be buried on top of each other, up to 12 layers deep. Today you can see over 12,000 gravestones crammed into the tiny space, but an estimated 100,000 people are thought to have been buried here. The last burial was of Moses Beck in 1787.

View across the cemetery towards the western wall of the Klausen Synagogue

Jewish printers, Mordechai Zemach (d 1592) and his son Bezalel (d 1589), are buried under this square gravestone.

The Pinkas Synagogue is the second-oldest in Prague (see p84).

David Gans' Tombstone
The tomb of the writer and astronomer (1541–1613) is decorated with the symbols of his name – a star of David and a goose (Gans in German).

The oldest tomb is that of the writer Rabbi Avigdor Kara (1439).

Rabbi David Oppenheim (1664–1736)
The chief rabbi of Prague owned the largest collection of old Hebrew manuscripts and prints in the city.

Klausen Synagogue (see p85)

The gravestone of Moses Beck

Main entrance

The Nephele Mound was where infants who died under a year old were buried.

★ **14th-Century Tombstones**
Embedded in the wall are fragments of Gothic tombstones brought here from an older Jewish cemetery discovered in 1866 in Vladislavova Street in the New Town.

VISITORS' CHECKLIST

Široká 3 (main entrance). **Map** 3
B3. 22 23 17 191 (bookings),
22 48 10 099, 22 48 19 456 (Jewish Museum). Staroměstská.
17, 18 to Staroměstská. **Open**
Apr–Oct: 9am–6pm Sun–Fri; Nov–
Mar: 9–4:30pm Sun–Fri (last admission 30 mins before closing).
W www.jewishmuseum.cz

Prague Burial Society
Founded in 1564, the group carried out ritual burials and performed charitable work in the community. Members of the society wash their hands after leaving the cemetery.

The Museum of
Decorative Arts
(see p84)

★ **Tombstone of
Rabbi Löw**
The most visited grave in the cemetery is that of Rabbi Löw (1520– 1609). Visitors place hundreds of pebbles and wishes on his grave as a mark of respect.

**The Neo-
Romanesque
Ceremonial
Hall**

Mordechai Maisel
(1528–1601) was
Mayor of Prague's
Jewish Town and
a philanthropist.

★ **Tombstone of Hendela Bassevi**
The highly-decorated tomb (1628) was built for the beautiful wife of Prague's first Jewish nobleman.

UNDERSTANDING THE GRAVESTONES

From the late 16th century onwards, tombstones in the Jewish cemetery were decorated with symbols denoting the background, family name or profession of the deceased person.

**Blessing
hands:
Cohen family**

**A pair of
scissors:
tailor**

**A stag:
Hirsch or
Zvi family**

**Grapes:
blessing or
abundance**

Old-New Synagogue ❻

STARONOVÁ SYNAGOGA

Star of David in Červená Street

BUILT AROUND 1270, this is the oldest synagogue in Europe and one of the earliest Gothic buildings in Prague. The synagogue has survived fires, the slum clearances of the 19th century and many Jewish pogroms. Residents of the Jewish Quarter have often had to seek refuge within its walls and today it is still the religious centre for Prague's Jews. It was originally called the New Synagogue until another synagogue was built nearby – this was later destroyed.

The synagogue's eastern side

The 14th-century stepped brick gable

★ **Jewish Standard**
The historic banner of Prague's Jews is decorated with a Star of David and within it the hat that had to be worn by Jews in the 14th century.

These windows formed part of the 18th-century extensions built to allow women a view of the service.

Candlestick holder

RABBI LÖW AND THE GOLEM

The scholar and philosophical writer Rabbi Löw, director of the Talmudic school (which studied the Torah) in the late 16th century,

Rabbi Löw and the Golem

was also thought to possess magical powers. He was supposed to have created a figure, the Golem, from clay and then brought it to life by placing a magic stone tablet in its mouth. The Golem went berserk and the Rabbi had to remove the tablet. He hid the creature among the Old-New Synagogue's rafters.

★ **Five-rib Vaulting**
Two massive octagonal pillars inside the hall support the five-rib vaults.

Right-hand Nave
The glow from the bronze chandeliers provides light for worshippers using the seats lining the walls.

VISITORS' CHECKLIST

Pařížská and Červená. **Map** 3 B2.
22 23 17 191. ᴹ Staroměstská. 17, 18 to Staroměstská,
17 to Law Faculty (Právnická
fakulta). **Open** 9am–6pm Sun–
Fri (to 5pm Fri). **Closed** Jewish
holidays. 8am Mon–
Fri. www.jewishmuseum.cz

The tympanum
above the Ark is decorated with 13th-century leaf carvings

★ Rabbi Löw's Chair
A star of David marks the chair of the Chief Rabbi, placed where the distinguished 16th-century scholar used to sit.

The cantor's platform and its lectern is surrounded by a wrought-iron Gothic grille.

Entrance to the Synagogue in Červená Street

The Ark
This shrine is the holiest place in the synagogue and holds the sacred scrolls of the Torah.

Entrance Portal
The tympanum above the door in the south vestibule is decorated with clusters of grapes and vine leaves growing on twisted branches.

STAR FEATURES

★ Rabbi Löw's Chair

★ Five-rib Vaulting

★ Jewish Standard

18th-century silver Torah crown in the Maisel Synagogue

Maisel Synagogue ⑨
MAISELOVA SYNAGÓGA

Maiselova 10. **Map** 3 B3.
Ⓜ *Staroměstská.* 🚊 *17, 18.*
🚌 *135, 207.* **Open** *9am–6pm Sun–Fri; Nov–Mar: 9am–4.30pm Sun–Fri.*
♿ Ⓦ *www.jewishmuseum.cz*

WHEN IT WAS FIRST built, at the end of the 16th century, this was a private house of prayer for the use of mayor Mordechai Maisel and his family. Maisel had made a fortune lending money to Emperor Rudolph II to finance wars against the Turks, and his synagogue was the most richly decorated in the city. The original building was a victim of the fire that devastated the Jewish Town in 1689 and a new synagogue was built in its place. Its present crenellated, Gothic appearance dates from the start of the 20th century. Since the 1960s the Maisel Synagogue has housed a fascinating collection of Jewish silver and other metalwork dating from Renaissance times to the 20th century. It includes many Torah crowns, shields and finials. Crowns and finials were used to decorate the rollers on which the text of the Torah (the five books of Moses) was kept. The shields were hung over the mantle that was draped over the

Torah and the pointers were used to follow the text so that it was not touched by readers' hands. There are also objects such as wedding plates, lamps and candlesticks. By a tragic irony, nearly all these Jewish treasures were brought to Prague by the Nazis from synagogues throughout Bohemia and Moravia with the intention of founding a museum of a vanished people.

Church of the Holy Ghost ⑩
KOSTEL SV. DUCHA

Dušní, Široká. **Map** 3 B3.
Ⓜ *Staroměstská.* 🚊 *17.*
🚌 *135, 207.* **Open** *only for services.*
✝ *5pm Sun.* ♿ ⚡

THIS CHURCH stands on the narrow strip of Christian soil which once separated the two Jewish communities of the Middle Ages – the Jews of the eastern and western rites. Built in the mid-14th century, the single-naved Gothic church was originally part of a convent of Benedictine nuns. The convent was destroyed in 1420 during the Hussite Wars *(see pp26–7)* and not rebuilt.

The church was badly damaged in the Old Town fire of 1689. The exterior preserves the original Gothic buttresses and high windows, but the vault of the nave was rebuilt in Baroque style after the fire. The furnishings too

are mainly Baroque. The high altar dates from 1760, and there is an altar painting of *St Joseph* by Jan Jiří Heintsch (c1647–1712). In front of the church stands a stone statue of St John Nepomuk *(see p83)* distributing alms (1727) by the prolific sculptor of the Czech Baroque Ferdinand Maximilian Brokof. Inside the church there are a few earlier statues, including a 14th-century *Pietà* (the heads of the figures are later, dating from 1628), a Late Gothic statue of St Ann and busts of St Wenceslas and St Adalbert from the early 16th century.

Church of the Holy Ghost

Spanish Synagogue ⑪
ŠPANĚLSKÁ SYNAGÓGA

Vězeňská 1. **Map** 3 B2.
Ⓜ *Staroměstská.* 🚊 *17.*
Open *Apr–Oct: 9am–6pm Sun–Fri; Nov–Mar: 9am–4.30pm Sun–Fri.*
♿ Ⓦ *www.jewishmuseum.cz*

PRAGUE'S first synagogue, known as the Old School (Stará škola), once stood on this site. In the 11th century the Old School was the centre of the community of Jews of the eastern rite, who lived strictly apart from the Jews of the western rite, who were concentrated round the Old-New Synagogue. The present building dates from the second half of the 19th century. The exterior and interior are both pseudo-Moorish in

Motif of the Ten Commandments on the Spanish Synagogue's façade

appearance. The rich stucco decorations on the walls and vaults are reminiscent of the Alhambra in Spain, hence the name. Once closed to the public, the Spanish Synagogue now houses a permanent exhibition dedicated to the history of the Jews of Bohemia.

Cubist Houses ⑫

KUBISTICKÉ DOMY

Eliška Krásnohorské, 10–14. **Map** 3 B2. ⓂStaroměstská. 🚋 17, 18. **Closed** to the public.

THE REBUILDING of the old Jewish Quarter at the turn of the 20th century gave Prague's architects scope to experiment with many new styles. Most of the blocks in this area are covered with flowing Art Nouveau decoration, but on the corner of Bílkova and Eliška Krásnohorské there is a plain façade with a few simple repeated geometrical shapes. This is an example of Cubist architecture, a fashion that did not really catch on in the rest of Europe, but was very popular with the avant-garde in Bohemia and Austria before and after World War I. This block was built for a cooperative of teachers in 1919–21.

At No. 7 Eliška Krásnohorské you can see the influence of Cubism in the curiously flattened atlantes supporting the windows. Another interesting Cubist building is the House of the Black Mother of God in Celetná *(see pp174–5)*.

Church of St Simon and St Jude ⑬

KOSTEL SV. ŠIMONA A JUDY

U milosrdných. **Map** 3 B2. ⓂStaroměstská. 🚋 17, 18. 🚌 135, 207. **Open** for concerts. W www.festival.cz

MEMBERS OF the Bohemian Brethren built this church with high Late Gothic windows in 1615–20. The Brethren, founded in the mid-15th century, agreed with the Utraquists *(see p75)* in directing the congregation to receive both bread and wine

Cubist-style atlantes framing a window in Eliška Krásnohorské Street

at Holy Communion. In other respects they were more conservative than other Protestant sects, continuing to practise celibacy and Catholic sacraments such as confession. After the Battle of the White Mountain *(see pp30–31)*, the Brethren were expelled from the Empire.

The church was then given to a Catholic order, the Brothers of Mercy, becoming part of a monastery and hospital. Tradition has it that the monastery's wooden steps were built from the scaffold on which 27 Czechs were executed in 1621 *(see p72)*. In the 18th century the city's first anatomy lecture hall was established here and the complex continues to serve as a hospital – the Na Františku. The church is now used as a venue for concerts.

Detail of Baroque façade of Church of St Simon and St Jude

Church of St Castullus ⑭

KOSTEL SV. HAŠTALA

Haštalské náměstí. **Map** 3 C2. 🚋 5, 8, 14. 🚌 135, 125, 207. **Open** irregularly. ✝ 5pm Sun. 🚫 ♿

THIS PEACEFUL little corner of Prague takes its name – Haštal – from the parish church of St Castullus. One of the finest Gothic buildings in Prague, the church was erected on the site of an older Romanesque structure in the second quarter of the 14th century. Much of the church had to be rebuilt after the fire of 1689, but fortunately the double nave on the north side survived. It has beautiful slender pillars supporting a delicate ribbed vault.

The interior furnishings are mainly Baroque, though there are remains of wall paintings of about 1375 in the sacristy and a metal font decorated with figures dating from about 1550. Standing in the Gothic nave is an impressive sculptural group depicting *Calvary* (1716) from the workshop of Ferdinand Maximilian Brokof.

St Agnes of Bohemia Convent ⑮

KLÁŠTER SV. ANEŽKY ČESKÉ

See pp92–3.

St Agnes of Bohemia Convent ⓯
KLÁŠTER SV. ANEŽKY ČESKÉ

IN 1234 A CONVENT of the Poor Clares was founded here by Agnes, sister of King Wenceslas I. She was not canonized until 1989. The convent, one of the very first Gothic buildings in Bohemia, was abolished in 1782 and fell into disrepair.

Head of statue of St Agnes by Josef Myslbek

Following painstaking restoration in the 1960s, it has recovered much of its original appearance and is now used by the National Gallery to display a collection of medieval art from Bohemia and Central Europe. The recent enlargement of the exhibition space, has enabled these to be shown in a much broader Central European context.

First floor

★ **Votive panel of Archbishop Jan Očko of Vlašim**
This detailed panel, painted around 1370 by an anonymous artist, shows Charles IV kneeling before the Virgin in Heaven.

Ground floor

Steps to first-floor gallery

★ **The Annunciation of Our Lady**
Painted around 1350 by the renowned Master of the Vyšší Brod Altar, this panel is one of the oldest and finest works in the museum.

STAR EXHIBITS

★ **The Annunciation by the Master of the Vyšší Brod Altarpiece**

★ **Strakonice Madonna**

★ **Votive panel of Archbishop Jan Očko of Vlašim**

Terrace café

Cloister
The Gothic vaulting around the cloister of the convent dates from the 14th century.

GALLERY GUIDE

The permanent exhibition is housed on the first floor of the old convent in a long gallery and smaller rooms around the cloister. The works are arranged chronologically.

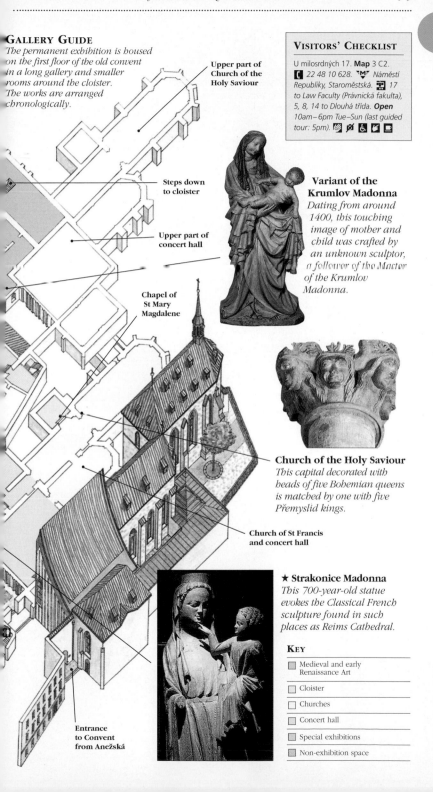

Upper part of Church of the Holy Saviour

Steps down to cloister

Upper part of concert hall

Chapel of St Mary Magdalene

Variant of the Krumlov Madonna

Dating from around 1400, this touching image of mother and child was crafted by an unknown sculptor, a follower of the Master of the Krumlov Madonna.

Church of the Holy Saviour

This capital decorated with heads of five Bohemian queens is matched by one with five Přemyslid kings.

Church of St Francis and concert hall

★ Strakonice Madonna

This 700-year-old statue evokes the Classical French sculpture found in such places as Reims Cathedral.

Entrance to Convent from Anežská

KEY

- Medieval and early Renaissance Art
- Cloister
- Churches
- Concert hall
- Special exhibitions
- Non-exhibition space

PRAGUE CASTLE AND HRADČANY

PRAŽSKÝ HRAD A HRADČANY

THE HISTORY of Prague begins with the Castle, founded in the 9th century by Prince Bořivoj. Its commanding position high above the river Vltava soon made it the centre of the lands ruled by the Přemyslids. The buildings enclosed by the Castle walls included a palace, three churches and a monastery. In about 1320 a town called Hradčany was founded in part of the Castle's

Stained-glass window in St Vitus's Cathedral

outer bailey. The Castle has been rebuilt many times, most notably in the reigns of Charles IV and Vladislav Jagiello. After a fire in 1541, the badly damaged buildings were rebuilt in Renaissance style and the Castle enjoyed its cultural heyday under Rudolph II. Since 1918 it has been the seat of the president of the Republic. The Changing of the Guard takes place every hour. At noon the ceremony includes a fanfare.

SIGHTS AT A GLANCE

Churches and Monasteries
St Vitus's Cathedral
  pp100–3 **2**
St George's Basilica **5**
Capuchin Monastery **19**
The Loreto pp116–17 **20**
Strahov Monastery
  pp120–21 **23**

Palaces
Royal Palace pp104–5 **4**
Lobkowicz Palace **8**
Belvedere **11**
Archbishop's Palace **14**
Martinic Palace **16**
Černín Palace **21**

Historic Buildings
Powder Tower **3**
Dalibor Tower **9**

Museums and Galleries
Picture Gallery
  of Prague Castle **1**
St George's Convent
  pp106–9 **6**
Riding School **13**
Sternberg Palace pp112–15 **15**
Schwarzenberg Palace **17**

Historic Streets
Golden Lane **7**
New World **18**
Pohořelec **22**

Parks and Gardens
South Gardens **10**
Royal Garden **12**

KEY

▨	Street-by-Street map *See pp96–7*
🚊	Tram stop
🅿	Parking
ℹ	Tourist Information
—	Castle wall

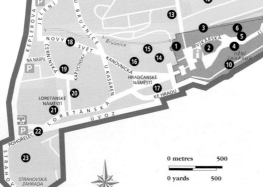

GETTING THERE
Take the 22 or 23 tram to Pražský hrad (Prague Castle) or to Pohořelec. If you feel energetic, take the 12, 18, 20, 22 or 23 tram to Malostranské náměstí in the Little Quarter, then walk up Nerudova or go to Malostranská metro and walk up Staré zámecké schody (Old Castle Steps).

◁ **The main entrance to Prague Castle**

Street-by-Street: Prague Castle

DESPITE PERIODIC FIRES and invasions, Prague Castle has retained churches, chapels, halls and towers from every period of its history, from the the Gothic splendour of St Vitus's Cathedral to the Renaissance additions of Rudolph II, the last Habsburg to use the Castle as his principal residence. The courtyards date from 1753–75 when the whole area was rebuilt in Late Baroque and Neo-Classical styles. The Castle became the seat of the Czechoslovak president in 1918, and the current president of the Czech Republic has an office here.

Powder Tower
Used in the past for storing gunpowder and as a bell foundry, the tower is now a museum ❸

Gothic reliquary of
St George's arm in
St Vitus's Cathedral

★ St Vitus's Cathedral
The decoration on the fence at St Vitus's Golden Portal ❷

Picture Gallery of Prague Castle
Renaissance and Baroque paintings hang in the restored stables of the castle ❶

President's office

To Royal Garden

Second courtyard

Matthias Gate (1614)

First courtyard

To Hradčanské náměstí

Church of the Holy Rood

Steps down to Little Quarter

The Castle gates are crowned by copies of 18th-century statues of Fighting Giants by Ignaz Platzer.

South Gardens
18th-century statues decorate the gardens laid out in the old ramparts ❿

★ **Golden Lane**
The picturesque artisans' cottages along the inside of the castle wall were built in the late 16th century for the Castle's guards and gunners **7**

LOCATOR MAP
See Street Finder, map 2

White Tower

Dalibor Tower
This grim tower takes its name from the first man to be imprisoned in it **9**

Old Castle steps to Malostranská Metro

Lobkowicz Palace
The historical collection of the National Museum is housed here **8**

★ **St George's Basilica**
The vaulted chapel of the royal Bohemian martyr St Ludmilla is decorated with 16th-century paintings **5**

★ **St George's Convent**
The convent houses Renaissance and Baroque art, such as this 16th-century painting, The Resurrection of Christ *by B. Spranger* **6**

KEY

--- Suggested route

| 0 metres | 60 |
| 0 yards | 60 |

★ **Royal Palace**
The uniform exterior of the palace conceals many fine Gothic and Renaissance halls. Coats of arms cover the walls and ceiling of the Room of the New Land Rolls **4**

STAR SIGHTS

★ St Vitus's Cathedral

★ Royal Palace

★ St George's Basilica and Convent

★ Golden Lane

Picture Gallery of Prague Castle **❶**

OBRAZÁRNA PRAŽSKÉHO HRADU

Prague Castle, the second courtyard.
Map 2 D2. ☎ *22 43 73 368.*
ᴹᵧᵣ *Malostranská, Hradčanská.*
🚊 *22, 23* **Open** *10am–6pm daily*
🏛 ♿ [w] www.hrad.cz

T HE GALLERY was created in
1965 to hold works of art
collected since the reign of
Rudolph II *(see pp28–9)*.
Though most of the collection
was looted by the Swedes in
1648, many interesting paintings remain. Paintings from
the 16th–18th centuries form
the bulk of the collection, but
there are also sculptures,
among them a copy of a bust
of Rudolph by Adriaen de
Vries. Highlights include
Titian's *The Toilet of a Young
Lady*, Rubens' *The Assembly of
the Olympic Gods* and Guido
Reni's *The Centaur Nessus
Abducting Deianeira*. Master
Theodoric, Paolo Veronese,
Tintoretto and the Czech
Baroque artists Jan Kupecký
and Petr Brandl are among
other artists represented. The
Picture Gallery houses many
of Rudolph's best paintings.
    You can also see the
remains of the Castle's first
church, the 9th-century Church
of our Lady, thought to have

been built by Prince Bořivoj,
the first Přemyslid prince
to be baptized a Christian
(see pp20 – 21). The historic
site was discovered during
reconstruction.

St Vitus's Cathedral **❷**

CHRÁM SV. VÍTA

See pp100–3.

Powder Tower **❸**

PRAŠNÁ VĚŽ

Prague Castle, Vikářská. **Map** 2 D2.
☎ *22 43 73 368.* ᴹᵧᵣ *Malostranská,
Hradčanská.* 🚊 *22, 23.* **Open** *Apr–
Oct: 9am–5pm; Nov–Mar: 9am–4pm
daily.* 🏛 Ø 🛗 [w] www.hrad.cz

A TOWER WAS BUILT here in
about 1496 by the King
Vladislav II's architect Benedikt
Ried as a cannon bastion overlooking the Stag Moat. The
original was destroyed in the
fire of 1541, but it was rebuilt
as the home and workshop of
gunsmith and bell founder
Tomáš Jaroš. In 1549 he made
Prague's largest bell, the 18-
tonne Sigismund, for the bell
tower of St Vitus's Cathedral.
    During Rudolph II's reign
(1576 –1612), the tower
became a laboratory for
alchemists. It was here that

**View of the Powder Tower from
across the Stag Moat**

adventurers such as Edward
Kelley performed experiments
that convinced the emperor
they could turn lead into gold.
    In 1649, when the Swedish
army was occupying the
Castle, gunpowder exploded
in the tower, causing serious
damage. Nevertheless it was
used as a gunpowder store
until 1754, when it was
converted into flats for the
sacristans of St Vitus's
Cathedral. In the 1960s it
became a museum with
exhibits relating to Jaroš's bell
foundry and alchemy practised
in the reign of Rudolph II.

Royal Palace **❹**

KRÁLOVSKÝ PALÁC

See pp104 – 5.

St George's Basilica **❺**

BAZILIKA SV. JIŘÍ

Jiřské náměstí. **Map** 2 E2. ☎ *22 43 73
368.* ᴹᵧᵣ *Malostranská, Hradčanská.*
🚊 *22, 23.* **Open** *Apr–Oct: 9am–5pm
daily; Nov–Mar: 9am–4pm daily.* 🏛
Ø ♿ [w] www.hrad.cz

F OUNDED by Prince Vratislav
(915–21), the basilica
predates St Vitus's Cathedral

Titian's *The Toilet of a Young Lady* in the Castle Picture Gallery

and is the best-preserved Romanesque church in Prague. It was enlarged in 973 when the adjoining St George's Convent was established here, and rebuilt following a fire in 1142. The massive twin towers and austere interior have been scrupulously restored to give a good idea of the church's original appearance. However, the rusty red façade was a 17th-century Baroque addition.

Buried in the church is St Ludmilla, widow of the 9th-century ruler Prince Bořivoj *(see pp20–21)*. She became Bohemia's first female Christian martyr when she was strangled on the orders of Drahomíra, her daughter-in-law, as she knelt at prayer. Other members of the Přemyslid dynasty buried here include Vratislav. His austere tomb stands on the right-hand side of the nave at the foot of the curving steps that lead up to the choir. The impressive Baroque grille opposite encloses the tomb of Boleslav II (973–99).

St George's Convent ❻
KLÁŠTER SV. JIŘÍ

See pp106–9.

Golden Lane ❼
ZLATÁ ULIČKA

Map 2 E2. 🚇 *Malostranská, Hradčanská.* 🚊 *22, 23.*

N AMED AFTER the goldsmiths who lived here in the 17th century, this short, narrow street is one of the most picturesque in Prague. One side of the lane is lined with

Façade and towers of St George's Basilica

tiny, brightly painted houses which were built right into the arches of the Castle walls. They were constructed in the late 1500s for Rudolph II's 24 Castle guards. A century later the goldsmiths moved in and modified the buildings. But by the 19th century the area had degenerated into a slum and was populated by Prague's poor and the criminal community. In the 1950s all the remaining tenants were moved and the area restored to something like its original state. Most of the houses were converted into shops selling books, Bohemian glass and other souvenirs for tourists, who flock to the narrow lane.

Golden Lane has been home to some well-known writers, including the Nobel prize-winning poet, Jaroslav Seifert, and Franz Kafka *(see p68)* who stayed at No. 22 with his sister for a few months in 1916–17.

Because of its name, legends have spread about the street being filled with alchemists huddled over their bubbling alembics trying to produce gold for Rudolph II. In fact the alchemists had laboratories in Vikářská, the lane between St Vitus's Cathedral and the Powder Tower.

Lobkowicz Palace ❽
LOBKOVICKÝ PALÁC

Jiřská 3. **Map** 2 E2. 📞 *25 75 35 979.* 🚇 *Hradčanská.* 🚊 *22, 23.* **Open** 9am–5pm Tue–Sun. 📷 🚫 ♿ 🔲 **Toy Museum** 📞 *22 43 72 294.* **Open** 9:30am–5:30pm daily. 🔲 *www.nm.cz*

T HIS IS ONE of the palaces that sprang up after the fire of 1541, when Hradčany was almost totally destroyed. It dates from 1570, and some original *sgraffito* on the façade has been preserved, but most of the present palace is Carlo Lurago's 17th-century reconstruction for the Lobkowicz family, who had inherited it in 1627. The most splendid room is the 17th-century banqueting hall with mythological frescoes by Fabian Harovník.

Detail of 16th-century *sgraffito* on façade of Lobkowicz Palace

The palace is part of the National Museum. Its superb permanent exhibition traces Czech history from the first settlements to the revolution of 1848 by means of documents, paintings, jewellery, glass, sculpture and weapons. Copies of the Czech Coronation Jewels, kept in St Vitus's Cathedral, are also on display.

Opposite the palace at No. 6 is a delightful toy museum claiming to be the world's second largest, with toys from ancient Greece to the present.

One of the tiny houses in Golden Lane

St Vitus's Cathedral ❷

KATEDRÁLA SV. VÍTA, VÁCLAVA A VOJTĚCHA

W̶ORK BEGAN ON the city's most distinctive landmark in 1344 on the orders of John of Luxembourg. The first architect was the French Matthew of Arras. After his death, Swabian Peter Parler took over. His masons' lodge continued to work on the building until the Hussite Wars. Finally completed by 19th- and 20th-century architects and artists, the cathedral houses the crown jewels and the tomb of "Good King" Wenceslas *(pp20–21)*.

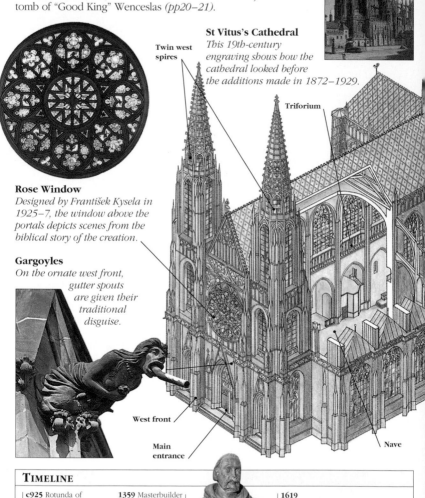

St Vitus's Cathedral
This 19th-century engraving shows how the cathedral looked before the additions made in 1872–1929.

Twin west spires

Triforium

Rose Window
Designed by František Kysela in 1925–7, the window above the portals depicts scenes from the biblical story of the creation.

Gargoyles
On the ornate west front, gutter spouts are given their traditional disguise.

West front

Main entrance

Nave

TIMELINE

Bust of Peter Parler on triforium

Tomb of Přemysl Otakar II

c925 Rotunda of St Vitus built by St Wenceslas	**1359** Masterbuilder Peter Parler summoned to continue work on the cathedral		**1619** Calvinists take over cathedral as house of prayer	**1929** Consecration of completed cathedral, nearly 1,000 years after death of St Wenceslas	

1000	1200	1400	1600	1800

1060 Building of triple-naved basilica begins on orders of Prince Spytihněv		**1421** Hussites occupy St Vitus's	**1589** Royal tomb completed	**1872** Joseph Mocker begins work on west nave
		1344 King John of Luxembourg founds Gothic cathedral. French architect Matthew of Arras begins work		**1770** New steeple added to tower after fire

★ Flying Buttresses
The slender buttresses that sur-round the exterior of the nave and chancel, supporting the vaulted interior, are richly decorated like the rest of the cathedral.

The Renaissance bell tower is capped with a Baroque "helmet".

Chancel

★ Chapel of St Wenceslas
The bronze ring on the chapel's north portal was thought to be the one to which St Wenceslas clung as he was murdered by his brother Boleslav (see pp20–21).

To Royal Palace
(See pp104–5)

The tomb of St Wenceslas is connected to an altar, decorated with semi-precious stones.

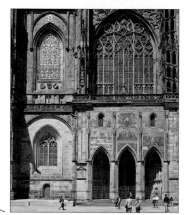

★ Golden Portal
Until the 19th century this was the main cathedral entrance, and it is still used on special occasions. Above it is a mosaic of The Last Judgment *by 14th-century Venetian craftsmen.*

Gothic Vaulting
The skills of architect Peter Parler are never more clearly seen than in the delicate fans of ribbing that support the three Gothic arches of the Golden Portal.

STAR FEATURES

★ Chapel of St Wenceslas

★ Golden Portal

★ Flying Buttresses

A Guided Tour of St Vitus's Cathedral

West door:
St Wenceslas'
murder

A WALK AROUND St Vitus's takes you back through a thousand years of history. Go in through the west portal to see some of the best elements of the modern, Neo-Gothic style and continue past a succession of side chapels to catch glimpses of religious artefacts such as saintly relics, and works of art from Renaissance paintings to modern statuary. Allow plenty of time to gaze at the richly decorated, jewel-encrusted St Wenceslas Chapel before you leave.

② Chancel
The chancel was built by Peter Parler from 1372. It is remarkable for the soaring height of its vault, counterpointed by the intricacy of the webbed Gothic tracery.

Cathedral organ (1757)

New sacristy

① Alfons Mucha Window
The cathedral contains many superb examples of 20th-century Czech stained glass, notably St Cyril and St Methodius.

Main entrance (West Portal)

Thun Chapel

Chapel of St Ludmilla

THE FOUR ERAS OF ST VITUS'S

Excavations have revealed sections of the northern apse of St Wenceslas's original rotunda, and architectural and sculptural remains of the later basilica, beneath the existing cathedral. The western, Neo-Gothic end is a faithful completion of the 14th-century plan.

KEY

- ☐ Rotunda, 10th century
- ☐ Basilica, 11th century
- ☐ Gothic cathedral, 14th century
- ☐ 19th- and 20th-century additions to cathedral

Leopold II
is shown in a contemporary engraving being crowned King of Bohemia at the cathedral in September 1791. Mozart composed an opera, *La Clemenza di Tito*, in honour of the occasion.

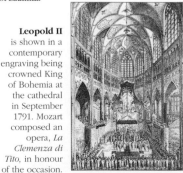

③ **Flight of Frederick of the Palatinate**
In depicting the sad aftermath of the Battle of the White Mountain in 1620 (see p31), this carved wooden panel shows 17th-century Prague in fascinating detail.

Chapel of
St John the
Baptist

Pulpit
(1618)

④ **Tomb of
St John Nepomuk**
Crafted from solid silver in 1736, this elaborate tomb honours the saint who became the focus of a Counter-Reformation cult (see p137).

Chapel of
the Holy Relics

⑤ **Royal Oratory**
The vault of the 15th-century Late-Gothic oratory is carved with branches instead of ribs.

Chapel of the
Holy Rood

Stairs to crypt

⑥ **Crypt**
Steps lead down to the royal tombs, including those of Charles IV and his four wives, as well as vestiges of the early rotunda and basilica.

Golden
Portal

Exit from
crypt

⑧ **St Wenceslas
Chapel**
Gothic frescoes with scenes from the Bible and the life of the saint cover the walls, interspersed with a patchwork of polished gemstones and fine gilding. Every object is a work of art – this golden steeple held the wafers and wine for Holy Communion.

⑦ **Royal Mausoleum**
Ferdinand I died in 1564. His beloved wife and son, Maximilian II, are buried alongside him in the mausoleum.

KEY

– – – Tour route

Royal Palace ④

KRÁLOVSKÝ PALÁC

FROM THE TIME Prague Castle was first fortified in stone in the 11th century (*see pp22–3*), the palace was the seat of Bohemian princes. The building consists of three different architectural layers. A Romanesque palace built by Soběslav I around 1135 forms the cellars of the present building. Přemysl Otakar II and Charles IV then added their own palaces above this, while the top floor, built for Vladislav Jagiello, contains the massive Gothic Vladislav Hall. During the period of Habsburg rule the palace housed government offices, courts and the old Bohemian Diet (parliament). In 1924 it was extensively restored.

Riders'
Staircase
These wide and gently sloping steps, with their Gothic rib vault, were used by knights on horse-back to get to Vladislav Hall for indoor jousting competitions.

The Diet, the medieval parliament, was also the throne room. Destroyed by fire in 1541, it was rebuilt by Bonifaz Wohlmut in 1563.

An overhead passage from the palace leads to the Royal Oratory in St Vitus's Cathedral (*see p103*).

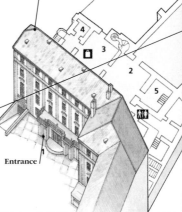

Vladislav Hall
The 17th-century painting by Aegidius Sadeler shows that the Royal Court was very like a public market. The hall's magnificent rib vaulting was designed by Benedikt Ried in the 1490s.

Entrance

TIMELINE

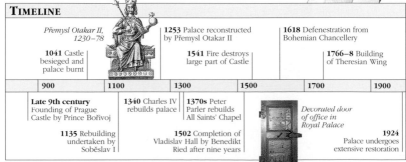

Přemysl Otakar II, 1230–78

1253 Palace reconstructed by Přemysl Otakar II

1618 Defenestration from Bohemian Chancellery

1041 Castle besieged and palace burnt

1541 Fire destroys large part of Castle

1766–8 Building of Theresian Wing

900	1100	1300	1500	1700	1900

Late 9th century Founding of Prague Castle by Prince Bořivoj

1340 Charles IV rebuilds palace

1370s Peter Parler rebuilds All Saints' Chapel

Decorated door of office in Royal Palace

1924 Palace undergoes extensive restoration

1135 Rebuilding undertaken by Soběslav I

1502 Completion of Vladislav Hall by Benedikt Ried after nine years

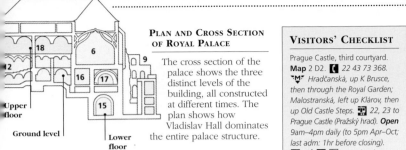

PLAN AND CROSS SECTION OF ROYAL PALACE

The cross section of the palace shows the three distinct levels of the building, all constructed at different times. The plan shows how Vladislav Hall dominates the entire palace structure.

Upper floor

Ground level

Lower floor

All Saints' Chapel was built by Peter Parler for Charles IV. After the 1541 fire, its vault had to be rebuilt and it was redecorated in the Baroque style.

11   **10**

KEY TO ROYAL PALACE

☐	Romanesque and Early Gothic
☐	Late Gothic
☐	Rebuilt after 1541 fire
☐	Baroque and later

1 Eagle Fountain		**10** All Saints' Chapel	
2 Vestibule		**11** Diet Hall	
3 Green Chamber		**12** Riders' Staircase	
4 King's Bedchamber		**13** Court of Appeal	
5 Romanesque tower		**14** Palace courtyard	
6 Vladislav Hall		**15** Hall of the Romanesque palace	
7 Bohemian Chancellery		**16** Old Land Rolls	
8 Imperial Council Room steps		**17** Palace of Charles IV	
9 Terrace		**18** New Land Rolls	

The Theresian Way was built to house the office registers.

Bohemian Chancellery
This 17th-century Dutch-style stove decorates the former royal offices of the Habsburgs. The chancellery is the site of the 1618 defenestration.

DEFENESTRATION OF 1618

Painting by Václav Brožík, 1889

On 23 May, 1618, more than 100 Protestant nobles, led by Count Thurn, marched into the palace to protest against the succession to the throne of the intolerant Habsburg Archduke Ferdinand. The two Catholic Governors appointed by Ferdinand, Jaroslav Martinic and Vilém Slavata, were confronted and, after a row, the Protestants threw both the Governors and their secretary, Philipp Fabricius, out of the eastern window. Falling some 15 m (50 ft), they survived by landing in a dung heap. This event signalled the beginning of the Thirty Years' War. The Catholics attributed the survival of the Governors to the intervention of angels.

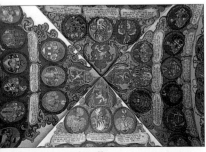

The New Land Rolls
These rooms are decorated with the crests of clerks who worked here from 1561 to 1774.

St George's Convent ❻

KLÁŠTER SV. JIŘÍ

THE FIRST CONVENT in Bohemia was founded here close to the Royal Palace in 973 by Prince Boleslav II. His sister Mlada was its first abbess. Rebuilt over the centuries, the convent was finally abolished in 1782 and converted into barracks. In 1962–74 it was reconstructed and today it houses the National Gallery's collection of Bohemian Baroque art. It shows works by some of the Baroque masters, including the painters Karel Škréta, Petr Brandl and Václav Vavřinec Reiner, and the sculptor Matyáš Bernard Braun.

★ Landscape with Orpheus and Animals
This pre-1720 work by Baroque master Václav Vavřinec Reiner represents a departure from his usual landscape frescoes by including a figure from Greek myth.

Stairs to upper floor

★ Bust of a Talking Apostle
Painted in about 1725 by Petr Brandl, this painting has since been hailed as one of the greatest examples of Czech art. It is noted for its strong sense of movement.

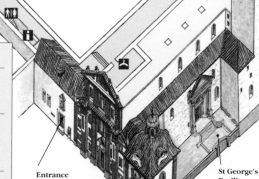

Stairs down to exit

Ground floor

Entrance to Gallery from Jiřské náměstí

St George's Basilica (see pp98–9)

STAR EXHIBITS

- **★ Bust of a Talking Apostle by Petr Brandl**

- **★ Landscape with Orpheus and Animals by V. V. Reiner**

- **★ Self Portrait by Jan Kupecký**

★ Self Portrait
This painting (1711) shows Jan Kupecký working on a portrait of his wife. The artist spent much of his life in exile.

Upper floor

VISITORS' CHECKLIST

Prague Castle, Jiřské náměsti 33.
Map 2 E2. 25 75 31 644.
Hradčanská or Malostranská, then 10 mins up steep steps. 22, 23 to Prague Castle (Pražský hrad).
Open 10am–6pm Tue–Sun.
W www.ngprague.cz

Statue of Moor
This is one of a pair of Moorish warriors (1719) by Ferdinand Brokof, commissioned by the Morzin family (see p130) for their country seat in Kounice.

Bust of Talking Apostle by Petr Brandl

Still Life with Watch
Johann-Adalbert Angermayer (1674–1740) filled his delicate still lifes with symbols of the transience and vanity of human life.

Epitaph of Goldsmith Mikuláš Müller
This work by Bartholomeus Spranger epitomizes the Mannerist style popular in the court of Rudolph II.

KEY

▦	Rudolphian Mannerism (c1600)
☐	Czech art of the Baroque
☐	Chapel of St Anne
☐	St George's Basilica
▦	Special exhibitions
☐	Non-exhibition space

GALLERY GUIDE
The permanent exhibition is located on the first floor of the convent. Beginning with a small collection of Mannerist art, you can follow the development of Czech Baroque painting and sculpture throughout the 17th and 18th centuries.

Exploring the St George's Collection

THIS WONDERFUL COLLECTION gives a fascinating insight into the art and sculpture of one of the periods of Prague's history that is so conspicuous in the city's architecture – the Baroque. The Bohemian school of Baroque art produced dramatic biblical paintings and statues of saints and angels in flamboyant poses. There are also collections of works representing the antecedents of the Baroque: not only the better known late Gothic, but also paintings and sculptures of the Mannerist school that were created under the patronage of Rudolph II.

Wooden statue of St Judas Thaddeus by Matyáš Bernard Braun (1712)

EARLY 16TH-CENTURY CZECH ART

SOME OF THE works in the gallery's collection of late Gothic art show greater similarity with contemporary German and Italian paintings. The finest Bohemian painter of this period is the Master of the Litoměřice Altar, who was active at the beginning of the 16th century. His most impressive works are an altar triptych showing *The Holy Trinity* and *The Visitation of the Virgin Mary*.

Also on display are some fascinating reliefs by a wood-carver who signed his works with the initials I P. His style is that of the so-called Danube school and his figures are clearly influenced by German painter and engraver Albrecht

Dürer. Dating from about 1520, the *Votive Altarpiece of Zlíchov* shows a kneeling knight with the Virgin Mary, St Andrew, Christ and Death.

RUDOLPHIAN MANNERISM (c1600)

BEFORE the Baroque reached Bohemia, there was a short period when Prague was the main centre of Northern Mannerism. This term is used to describe a style that evolved in Italy after the Renaissance. Many 16th-century painters and sculptors strove to outdo the exaggerated poses of Michelangelo's later works just for the sake of creating a startling effect. A typical example of this is *The Last Judgment* by Josef Heintz. A more successful exponent of this style was Bartholomeus

Spranger from Antwerp. He died in Prague in 1611 while in the employment of the Imperial Emperor Rudolph II (*see p28–9*).

With his passion for the unusual and the artificial, Rudolph loved Mannerist artists and invited many to work at his court in Prague. Although the Mannerist style had fallen out of fashion throughout the royal courts of Europe, the paintings made under his patronage represent the last flowering of this dramatic style. They made an impression on the next generation of artists who emerged after the Thirty Years War and who came to define style of the Bohemian school of Baroque art.

Rudolph's great collection was dispersed when Prague Castle was looted in 1648, but the few works on show here give an idea of his tastes. The best are probably the paintings of the German-born Hans von Aachen and the sculptures of the Dutch-born Adriaen de Vries. There are also other sculptures by Hans Mont and Benedict Wurzelbauer.

Not all the works here are typically Mannerist in style. The landscapes of Roelant Savery, for example, show a genuine feeling for the beauty of the Bohemian forests that he gained during an eight-year stay in Prague (1604–12).

Altarpiece of *The Holy Trinity* by Master of the Litoměřice Altar (c1515)

Stag Hunt (c1610) by Roelant Savery, artist at the court of Rudolph II

CZECH ART OF THE BAROQUE

THERE ARE many agreeable surprises in this extensive collection of Baroque art.

The founding personality of Czech Baroque painting is Karel Škréta. The five years he spent in Italy early in his career were profoundly influential on his work. He is the prime representative of the realistic trend in Czech Baroque art. Of his religious paintings, *St Charles Borromeo Visiting the Sick* shows realistic types and detail, and this also applies in full measure to the lunette scene of the *Nativity of St Wenceslas*. His large group portrait of Dionysius Miseroni, the Italian cutter of precious stones, and his family, reveals an interesting glimpse into a workshop, and the rare work, a crystal chalice, made there. Much of his later work, both in portraits and altarpieces, reflects a Dutch and Flemish influence.

Of the paintings of religious subjects, the finest are surely those by Petr Brandl. The old men who feature in many of his works are beautifully painted. Particularly moving is the painting known as *Simeon and the Infant Jesus*. The gallery gives a good idea of his work as a portraitist, but unfortunately his work on Prague and country churches is not represented here.

A contemporary of Brandl, Jan Kupecký was Czech by birth but lived abroad for most of his life. He had a large middle-class and aristocratic clientele throughout Central Europe, and his portraits are among the highlights of the exhibition. The large portrait of Karl Bruni, a painter of miniatures, clearly illustrates the form and content of Baroque portraiture at the beginning of the 18th century.

Václav Vavřinec Reiner's most important contribution to the development of Bohemian Baroque paintings were his strikingly coloured frescoes and vivid landscape paintings. The several pictures housed here give an idea of his art, in particular two of his sketches, one for the ceiling painting in the Prague Church of St Giles, and the other for the Loretto Church of the Nativity. The *Landscape with Orpheus and Animals* and *Landscape with Birds* are highly decorative.

On a smaller scale, look out for the still lifes of flowers and game by the Swiss painter Johann Rudolf Bys and his pupil Johann-Adalbert Angermayer. There are also notable works by Jan Jiří Heinsch, Jan Kryštof Liška and Michal Václav Halbax. The transition to the later Rococo styles is demonstrated in works by Bohemian artists such as Antonín Kern, Norbert Grund and František Xaver Palko.

The sculptures are chiefly by the 18th-century artists whose works decorate so many of the city's Baroque churches: Ferdinand Brokof, Matthias Braun and Ignaz Platzer. Several of the more flamboyant saints and angels are in painted wood, an unexpected link with the early polychrome wood carvings of the Gothic period.

Hedvika Francesca Wussin by Jan Kupecký (1710)

Old prison in the Dalibor Tower

Dalibor Tower ❾
DALIBORKA

Prague Castle, Zlatá ulička. **Map** 2 E2.
〰 *Malostranská.* 🚋 *18, 20, 22,
23.* **Open** *on request.* 🏛 🚫

THIS 15TH-CENTURY tower
with a conical roof was
part of the fortifications built
by King Vladislav Jagiello *(see
p26–7)*. His coat of arms can
be seen on the outer wall.
The tower also served as a
prison and is named after its
first inmate, Dalibor of
Kozojedy, a young knight
sentenced to death for
harbouring some outlawed
serfs. While awaiting execution, he was kept in an
underground dungeon, into
which he had to be lowered
through a hole in the floor.
   According to legend, while
in prison he learnt to play the
violin. People sympathetic to
his plight came to listen to his
playing and provided him
with food and drink, which

they lowered on a rope from a
window – prisoners were often
left to starve to death. The
story was used by Bedřich
Smetana in his opera *Dalibor.*
The tower ceased to serve as
a prison in 1781. Visitors can
see part of the old prison.

South Gardens ❿
JIŽNÍ ZAHRADY

Prague Castle (access from
Hradčanské náměstí). **Map** 2 D3. 〰
Malostranská, Hradčanská. 🚋 *18,
20, 22, 23.* **Open** *Apr–Oct: 10am–
6pm daily.* 📷 Ⓦ www.hrad.cz

THE GARDENS occupy the long
narrow band of land below
the Castle overlooking the
Little Quarter. Several small
gardens have been linked to
form what is now known as
the South Gardens. The oldest,
the Paradise Garden (Rajská
zahrada), laid out in 1562,
contains a circular pavilion
built for Emperor Matthias in
1617. Its carved wooden
ceiling shows the coloured
emblems of the 39 countries
of the Habsburg Empire. The
Garden on the Ramparts
(Zahrada Na valech) dates from
the 19th century. It occupies a
former vegetable patch and is
famous as the site of the
defenestration of 1618 *(see
p105)*, when two Imperial
governors were thrown from a
first-floor window. Two
obelisks were subsequently
erected by Ferdinand II to
mark the spots where they

landed. Extensive modifications
were carried out in the 1920s
by Josip Plečnik, who built
the Bull Staircase leading to
the Paradise Garden and the
observation terrace. Below the
terrace, in the former Hartig
Garden, is a Baroque music
pavilion designed by Giovanni
Battista Alliprandi. Beside it
stand four statues of Classical
gods by Antonín Braun.

**Alliprandi's music pavilion in
the South Gardens**

Belvedere ⓫
BELVEDÉR

Prague Castle, Royal Garden. **Map** 2
E1. 〰 *Malostranská, Hradčanská.*
🚋 *18, 20, 22, 23.* **Open** *only for
exhibitions.* 🏛 ♿ Ⓦ www.hrad.cz

BUILT BY FERDINAND I for his
beloved wife Anne, the
Belvedere is one of the finest
Italian Renaissance buildings
north of the Alps. Also known
as the Royal Summer Palace
(Královský letohrádek), it is

The Belvedere, Emperor Ferdinand I's summer palace in the Royal Garden beside Prague Castle

Antonín Braun's statue of *The Allegory of Night* in front of the *sgraffito* decoration of the Ball Game Hall in the Royal Garden

Riding School ⑬
JÍZDÁRNA

Prague Castle. **Map** 2 D2. 📞 *22 43 73 368.* 🚇 *Malostranská, Hradčanská.* 🚋 *22, 23.* **Open** *10am–6pm during exhibitions.*

THE 17TH-CENTURY Riding School forms one side of U Prašného mostu, a road which runs to the northern side of Prague Castle via Deer Moat. In the 1920s it was converted into an exhibition hall, which now holds important exhibitions of painting and sculpture. A garden provides excellent views of St. Vitus's Cathedral and the northern fortifications of the castle.

Archbishop's Palace ⑭
ARCIBISKUPSKÝ PALÁC

Hradčanské náměstí 16. **Map** 2 D3. 📞 *22 03 92 111.* 🚇 *Malostranská, Hradčanská.* 🚋 *22, 23.* **Not open** *to the public.*

FERDINAND I bought this sumptuous palace in 1562 for the first Catholic Archbishop since the Hussite Wars *(see pp26–7)*. It replaced the old Archbishop's Palace in the Little Quarter, which had been destroyed during the wars, and has remained the Archbishop's seat in Prague ever since. In the period after the Battle of the White Mountain *(see p30–31)*, it was a powerful symbol of Catholic domination of the city and the Czech lands. Its spectacular cream-coloured Rococo façade was designed by Johann Joseph Wirch in the 1760s

Příchovský coat of arms

for Archbishop Antonín Příchovský, whose coat of arms sits proudly above the portal.

Royal Garden ⑫
KRÁLOVSKÁ ZAHRADA

Prague Castle, U Prašného mostu. **Map** 2 D2. 🚇 *Malostranská, Hradčanská.* 🚋 *22, 23.* **Open** *May–Oct: 10am–6pm daily.* 🏛 📷 ♿ 🌐 www.hrad.cz

THE GARDEN was created in 1535 for Ferdinand I. Its appearance has been altered over time, but some examples of 16th-century garden architecture have survived, notably the Belvedere and the Ball Game Hall (Míčovna), built by Bonifaz Wohlmut in 1569. The building is covered in beautiful, though much restored, Renaissance *sgraffito*, a form of decoration created by cutting a design through the wet top layer of plaster on to a contrasting undercoat. The garden is a beautiful place for a stroll, especially in spring when thousands of tulips bloom in its immaculate beds. This is where tulips were first acclimatized to Europe.

an arcaded summerhouse with slender Ionic columns topped by a roof shaped like an inverted ship's hull clad in blue-green copper. The main architect was Paolo della Stella, who was also responsible for the ornate reliefs inside the arcade. Work began in 1538, but was interrupted by the great Castle fire of 1541. The Belvedere was eventually completed in 1564.

In the middle of the small geometrical garden in front of the palace stands the Singing Fountain. Dating from 1568, it owes its name to the musical sound the water makes as it hits the bronze bowl, though you have to place your head very close to appreciate the effect. The fountain was cast by Tomáš Jaroš, the famous bell founder, who lived and worked in the Powder Tower *(see p98)*.

Many of the Belvedere's works of art were plundered by the occupying Swedish army in 1648. The statues stolen included Adriaen de Vries's 16th-century bronze of *Mercury and Psyche*, which is now in the Louvre in Paris. The Belvedere is now used as an art gallery.

Sternberg Palace ⑮
ŠTERNBERSKÝ PALÁC

See pp112–15.

Sternberg Palace ⑮
ŠTERNBERSKÝ PALÁC

FRANZ JOSEF STERNBERG founded the Society of Patriotic Friends of the Arts in Bohemia in 1796. Fellow noblemen would lend their finest pictures and sculpture to the society, which had its headquarters in the early-18th-century Sternberg Palace. Since 1949, the fine Baroque building has been used to house the National Gallery's collection of European art, with its superb range of Old Masters.

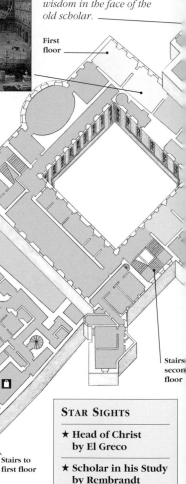

★ Scholar in his Study
In this painting from 1634 Rembrandt used keenly observed detail to convey wisdom in the face of the old scholar.

First floor

Cardinal Cesi's Garden in Rome
Henrick van Cleve's painting (1548) provides a valuable image of a Renaissance collections of antiquities. The garden was later destroyed.

Garden Room

Stairs second floor

Ground floor

Stairs to first floor

Ticket office

Passageway to Hradčanské náměstí

STAR SIGHTS

★ **Head of Christ by El Greco**

★ **Scholar in his Study by Rembrandt**

★ **The Martyrdom of St Thomas by Rubens**

Concerning the Eden *(1618)*
Roelandt Savery studied models of exotic animals, brought to Prague by Persian nobles, at the court of Emperor Rudolf II. He was then able to paint real animals.

★ The Martyrdom of St Thomas
This magnificent work is by Peter Paul Rubens, the foremost Flemish painter of the 17th century.

Chinese Cabinet

Second floor

irs down to er floors d exit

★ Head of Christ
Painted by El Greco in the 1590s, this portrait emphasizes the humanity of Christ. At the same time the curious square halo framing the head gives the painting the qualities of an ancient icon.

GALLERY GUIDE
The gallery is arranged on three floors around the central courtyard of the palace. The ground floor, reached from the courtyard, houses German and Austrian art from the 15th to 19th centuries. The stairs to the collections on the upper floors are opposite the ticket office at the main entrance.

The Lamentation of Christ
The frozen, sculptural figures make this one of the finest paintings by Lorenzo Monaco (1408).

KEY

- ⬛ German and Austrian Art 1400–1800
- ⬜ Flemish and Dutch Art 1400–1600
- ⬛ Italian Art 1400–1500
- ⬛ Roman Art
- ⬛ Flemish and Dutch Art 1600–1800
- ⬜ French Art 1600–1800
- ⬜ Icons, Classical and Ancient Art
- ⬛ Venice 1700–1800 and Goya
- ⬛ Spanish Art 1600–1800
- ⬜ Naples and Venice 1600–1700
- ⬜ Italian Art 1500–1600
- ⬛ Non-exhibition space

Exploring the Sternberg Collections

St John
the Baptist
by Rodin

THE NATIONAL GALLERY'S collection of European art ranks among the best collections of comparable size. Since the transfer of the outstanding 19th- and 20th-century exhibits to Veletržní Palace in 1996 *(see pp164–5)* the Sternberg has been expanding its permanent exhibition, with especially strong representations from Italian medieval art, Neapolitan artists of the 17th and 18th centuries, Dutch and Flemish works, and German art of the 15th to 17th centuries. There is also a fine collection of Renaissance bronzes, and the fascinating Chinese Cabinet is on display again after a restoration lasting several years.

ICONS, CLASSICAL AND ANCIENT ART

TWO SMALL ROOMS contain an odd assortment of paintings that do not quite fit in with the rest of the collection. These include a *Portrait of a Young Woman* dating from the 2nd century AD, discovered during excavations at Fayoum in Egypt in the 19th century.

The majority of the exhibits, however, are icons of the Orthodox church. These come from a variety of Eastern European countries – some are Byzantine, some Italo-Greek and some Russian. The finest examples are two of the later 16th-century works, *The Lamentation of Christ* from Crete and *Christ's Entry Into Jerusalem* from Russia.

Christ's Entry into Jerusalem, a 16th-century Russian icon

GERMAN AND AUSTRIAN ART (1400–1800)

ONE OF THE most celebrated paintings in the Sternberg's collection is Albrecht Dürer's *The Feast of the Rosary*, painted during the artist's stay in Venice in 1506. It has special significance for

Prague since it was bought by Emperor Rudolph II. The two figures seen in front of the Virgin and Child are Maximilian I (Rudolph's great-great-grandfather) and Pope Julius II.

There are works by several other important German painters of the Renaissance, including Hans Holbein the Elder and the Younger and Lucas Cranach the Elder. Cranach is represented by works including a striking *Adam and Eve* whose nudes show the spirit of the Renaissance, tempered by Lutheran Reform.

ITALIAN ART (1300–1800)

WHEN YOU ENTER the Italian galleries, you are greeted by a splendid array of early diptychs, triptychs and other richly gilded panel paintings from the churches of Tuscany and northern Italy. Most came originally from the d'Este collection at Konopiště Castle *(see p169)*. Of particularly high quality are the two triangular panels of saints by the 14th-century Sienese painter Pietro Lorenzetti and a moving *Lamentation of Christ* by Lorenzo Monaco.

A fascinating element of the collection is the display of Renaissance bronze statuettes. Fashionable amongst Italian nobility of the 15th century, these little bronzes were at first cast from famous or newly-discovered works of antiquity. Later, sculptors began to use the medium more freely – Padua, for example, specialized in the depiction of small animals – and producers also adapted items for use as decorative household goods such as oil lamps, ink pots and door knockers. This small collection has representative works from all the major Italian producers except Mantua and, while many variations can be found in other museums throughout the world, there are some pieces here that are both unique and outstanding examples of the craft.

The Feast of the Rosary by Dürer (1506)

Don Miguel de Lardizábal (1815), by Francisco Goya

Among the 16th-century Italian works on display, there are some delightful surprises. These include *St Jerome* by the Venetian painter, Tintoretto, and *The Flagellation of Christ* and *Portrait of an Elderly Man* by another Venetian, Jacopo Bassano. There is also an expressive portrait by the Florentine mannerist, Bronzino, of *Eleanor of Toledo*, the wife of Cosimo de' Medici.

FLEMISH AND DUTCH ART (1400–1800)

THE COLLECTIONS of Flemish and Dutch art are rich and varied, ranging from rural scenes by Pieter Brueghel the Elder to portraits by Rubens and Rembrandt.

Highlights of the former include an altarpiece showing the *Adoration of the Magi* by Geertgen tot Sint Jans. Other early works of great interest include *St Luke Drawing the Virgin* by Jan Gossaert (c1515), one of the first works of art from the Netherlands to show the clear influence of the

Italian Renaissance. The collection from the 17th century includes several major works, notably by Peter Paul Rubens who, in 1639, sent two paintings to the Augustinians of the Church of St Thomas *(see p127)* in the Little Quarter. The originals were lent to the gallery in 1896 and replaced by copies. The violence and drama of *The Martyrdom of St Thomas* is in complete

Eleanor of Toledo (1540s) by the Florentine Mannerist painter Agnolo Bronzino

contrast to the spiritual calm of *St Augustine*. Two other fine portraits are those of Rembrandt's *Scholar in His Study* and Frans Hals' *Portrait of Jasper Schade*.

Also on display is a wide assortment of paintings by other, less-prominent, artists who nonetheless represent the enormous range and quality of this period.

SPANISH, FRENCH AND ENGLISH ART (1400–1800)

FRENCH ART is represented chiefly by the 17th-century painters Simon Vouet (*The Suicide of Lucretia*), Sébastien Bourdon and Charles Le Brun. Spanish painting is even less well represented, but two of the collection's finest works are a haunting *Head of Christ* by El Greco – the only work by the artist on display in the Czech Republic – and a noble half-length portrait of the politician *Don Miguel de Lardizábal* by Goya.

THE CHINESE CABINET

AFTER SEVERAL YEARS of difficult restoration work, this curiosity is once again open to the public. The richly-decorated little chamber was part of the original furnishings of the Sternberg Palace, and was designed as an intimate withdrawing room away from the bustle of the grand state rooms. In its plethora of decorative styles, Baroque mingles with Far Eastern motifs and techniques, which were fashionable at the turn of the 18th century. The vaulted ceiling features the Star of the Sternbergs among its geometric decorations. Black lacquered walls are embellished with cobalt blue and white medallions in golden frames, while gilded shelves once held rare Oriental porcelain.

The Loreto ⑳

LORETA

EVER SINCE ITS CONSTRUCTION in 1626, the Loreto has been an important place of pilgrimage. It was commissioned by Kateřina of Lobkowicz, a Czech aristocrat who was very keen to promote the legend of the Santa Casa of Loreto *(see opposite)*. The heart of the complex is a copy of the house believed to be the Virgin Mary's. The Santa Casa was enclosed by cloisters in 1661, and a Baroque façade 60 years later by Christoph and Kilian Ignaz Dientzenhofer. The grandiose design and miraculous stories about the Loreto were part of Ferdinand II's campaign to re-catholicize the Czechs *(see pp30–31)*.

Kateřina Lobkowicz, founder of the Santa Casa

Bell Tower
Enclosed in this large Baroque tower, is a set of 30 bells cast 1691–94 in Amsterdam by Claudy Fremy.

Chapel of St Joseph

Fountain decorated with a sculpture of the Resurrection

Chapel of St Francis Seraphim

Chapel of St Ann

Entrance from Loretánské náměstí

★ Loreto Treasury
This gold-plated, diamond-encrusted monstrance, for displaying the host, is one of the valuable liturgical items in the Loreto treasury, most of which originated in the 16th–18th centuries.

Baroque Entrance
The balustrade above the Loreto's front entrance is decorated with statues of St Joseph and St John the Baptist by Ondřej Quitainer.

STAR SIGHTS

★ Loreto Treasury

★ Santa Casa

★ Church of the Nativity

★ Santa Casa
Stucco figures of many of the Old Testament prophets and reliefs from the life of the Virgin Mary by Italian artists decorate the chapel.

★ Church of the Nativity
Gruesome relics, including fully-clothed skeletons with death masks made of wax, line the walls of this 18th-century church. The frescoes are by Václav Vavřinec Reiner.

Chapel of the Holy Rood

17th-Century Cloister
Built originally as a shelter for the many pilgrims who visited the shrine, the cloister is covered with frescoes.

Chapel of St Anthony of Padua

Chapel of Our Lady of Sorrows

Fountain Sculpture
This copy of The Ascension of the Virgin Mary *is taken from Jan Brüderle's 1739 sandstone statue, now in the Lapidarium* (see p162).

LEGEND OF THE SANTA CASA

The original house, said to be where the Archangel Gabriel told Mary about the future birth of Jesus, is in the small Italian town of Loreto. It was believed that angels transported the house from Nazareth to Loreto in 1278 following threats by infidels. After the Protestants' defeat in 1620 (see pp30–31), Catholics promoted the legend, and 50 replicas of the Loreto were built in Bohemia and Moravia. This, the grandest, became the most important in Bohemia, and received many visitors.

The stuccoed Santa Casa

Martinic Palace 🔞
MARTINICKÝ PALÁC

Hradčanské náměstí 8. **Map** 1 C2.
📞 *22 43 08 111.* 🚇 *Malostranská, Hradčanská.* 🚋 *22, 23.* **Closed** to the public.

IN THE COURSE of the palace's restoration in the early 1970s, workmen uncovered the original 16th-century façade decorated with ornate cream and brown *sgraffito (see p111).* It depicts Old Testament scenes, including the story of Joseph and Potiphar's wife. More *sgraffito* came to light in the courtyard, showing the story of Samson and the Labours of Hercules.

Martinic Palace was enlarged by Jaroslav Bořita of Martinice, who was one of the imperial governors thrown from a window of the Royal Palace in 1618 *(see p105).*

According to an old legend, between 11pm and midnight the ghost of a fiery black dog appears at the palace and accompanies walkers as far as the Loreto *(see pp116–17),* where it disappears again. Today the palace houses the city architecture department.

Schwarzenberg Palace 🔟
SCHWARZENBERSKÝ PALÁC

Hradčanské náměstí 2. **Map** 2 D3.
📞 *22 02 02 023, 22 02 02 398.* 🚇 *Malostranská, Hradčanská.* 🚋 *22, 23.* **Closed** for renovation.
📷 🚫 🆆 www.militarymuseum.cz

FROM A DISTANCE, the façade of this grand Renaissance palace appears to be clad in projecting pyramid-shaped stonework. On closer inspection, this turns out to be an illusion created by *sgraffito* patterns

incised on a flat wall. Built originally for the Lobkowicz family by the Italian architect Agostino Galli in 1545–76, the gabled palace is Florentine rather than Bohemian in style. It passed through several hands before the Schwarzenbergs, a leading family in the Habsburg Empire, bought it in 1719. Much of the interior decoration has survived, including four painted ceilings on the second floor dating from1580. Since 1945 the palace has housed the Museum of Military History, a collection of arms and uniforms from the wars in Bohemia from the time of the first Slavs up to 1918.

In the square outside is the statue of Tomáš G Masaryk, Czechoslovakia's first president.

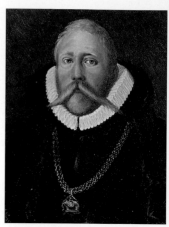
Tycho Brahe, Rudolph II's astronomer

New World 🔞
NOVÝ SVĚT

Map 1 B2. 🚋 *22, 23.*

NOW A CHARMING STREET of small cottages, Nový Svět (New World) used to be the name of this area of Hradčany. Developed in the mid-14th century to provide houses for the castle workers, the area was twice destroyed by fire, the last time being in 1541. Most of the cottages date from the 17th century. They have been spruced up, but are otherwise unspoilt and very different in character from the

rest of Hradčany. In defiance of their poverty, the inhabitants chose golden house signs to identify their modest houses – you will see a Golden Pear, a Grape, a Foot, a Bush and an Acorn. Plaques identify No. 1 as the former home of Rudolph II's brilliant court astronomer, Tycho Brahe, and No. 25 as the 1857 birthplace of the great Czech violinist František Ondříček.

Capuchin Monastery 🔟
KAPUCÍNSKÝ KLÁŠTER

Loretánské náměstí 6. **Map** 1 B3.
🚋 *22, 23.* **Closed** to the public except the church.

BOHEMIA'S FIRST Capuchin monastery was founded here in 1600. It is connected to the neighbouring Loreto *(see pp116–17)* by an overhead roofed passage. Attached to the monastery is the Church of Our Lady Queen of Angels, a single-naved building with plain furnishings, typical of the ascetic Capuchin order.

The church is famous for its miraculous statue of the Madonna and Child. Emperor Rudolph II liked the statue so much he asked the Capuchins to give it to him to place in his private chapel. The monks agreed, but then the statue somehow found its way back to the church. Three times Rudolph had the Madonna brought back but each time

The Carmelite monastery next to the Schwarzenberg Palace

she returned to her original position. The Emperor eventually gave up, left where she was and presented her with a gold crown and a robe. Each year at Christmas the church attracts crowds of visitors to see its delightful Baroque nativity scene of life-sized figures dressed in costumes from the period.

Church of the Capuchin Monastery

The Loreto 🖉

LORETA

See pp116–17.

Černín Palace 🖉

ČERNÍNSKÝ PALÁC

Loretánské náměstí 5. **Map** 1 B3. 📞 22 41 81 111. 🚊 22, 23. **Closed to the public.** 🅦 www.mzv.cz

BUILT IN 1668 for Count Černín of Chudenice, the Imperial Ambassador to Venice, the Černín Palace is 150 m (500 ft) long with a row of 30 massive Corinthian half-columns running the length of its upper storeys. The palace towers over the attractive, small, grassy square that lies between it and the Loreto.

The huge building suffered as a result of its prominent position on one of Prague's highest hills. It was looted by the French in 1742 and badly damaged in the Prussian bombardment of the city in 1757. In 1851 the impoverished Černín family sold the palace to the state and it became a

barracks. After the creation of Czecho-slovakia in 1918 the palace was restored to its original design and became the Ministry of Foreign Affairs. A few days after the Communist Coup in 1948 the Foreign Minister, Jan Masaryk, the popular son of Czechoslovakia's first Presi-dent, Tomáš Masaryk, died as the result of a fall from a top-floor window of the Palace. He was the only non-Communist in the government that had just been formed. No-one really knows whether he was pushed or jumped, but he is still widely mourned.

Capital on Černín Palace

Pohořelec 🖉

Map 1 B3. 🚊 22, 23.

FIRST SETTLED IN 1375, this is one of the oldest parts of Prague. The name is of more recent origin: Pohořelec means "place destroyed by fire", a fate the area has suffered three times in the course of its history – the last time being in 1741. It is now a large open square on a hill high over the city and part of the main access route to Prague Castle. In the centre stands a large monument to St John Nepomuk (1752) *(see p137)*, thought to be by Johann Anton Quitainer. The houses around the square are mainly Baroque and Rococo. In front of the Jan Kepler grammar school stands a monument to Kepler and his predecessor as astronomer at the court of Rudolph II, Tycho Brahe, who died in a house on the school site in 1601.

Strahov Monastery 🖉

STRAHOVSKÝ KLÁŠTER

See pp120–21.

Kučera Palace, a Rococo building in Pohořelec

Strahov Monastery ㉓
STRAHOVSKÝ KLÁŠTER

The bust of Joseph II over entrance gate

W HEN IT WAS FOUNDED in 1140 by an austere religious order, the Premonstratensians, Strahov rivalled the seat of the Czech sovereign in size. Destroyed by fire in 1258, it was rebuilt in the Gothic style, with later Baroque additions. Its famous library, in the theological and philosophical halls, is over 800 years old and despite being ransacked by many invading armies, is one of the finest in Bohemia. Strahov also escaped Joseph II's 1783 dissolution of the monasteries by changing its library into a research institute. It is now a working monastery and museum.

Statue of St John
A Late-Gothic, painted statue of St John the Evangelist situated in the Theological Hall, has the saint's prayer book held in a small pouch.

The Museum of National Literature is devoted to Czech literature.

Refectory

Baroque tower

Entrance to main courtyard of the monastery

Baroque organ on which Mozart played

★ **Church of Our Lady**
The interior of this Baroque church is highly decorated. Above the arcades of the side naves, there are 12 paintings with scenes from the life of St Norbert, founder of the Premonstratensian order, by Jiří Neunhertz.

Entrance to Church of Our Lady

Church Façade
The elaborate statues, by Johann Anton Quitainer, were added to the western façade of the church when it was remodelled by the architect Anselmo Lurago in the 1750s.

VISITORS' CHECKLIST

Královská Kanonie Premonstrátů na Strahově. Strahovské nádvoří 1, Strahovská. **Map** 1 B4. *22 05 16 671.* 22, 23 to Pohořelec. **Open** 9am–noon, 1–5pm Tue–Sun. **Philosophical Hall, Theological Hall, Church of Our Lady, Picture Gallery open** 9am–noon, 12:30–5pm Tue–Sun.

View from Petřín Hill
A gate at the eastern end of the first courtyard leads to Petřín Hill, part of which was once the monastery's orchards.

★ Theological Hall
One of the 17th century astronomical globes by William Blaeu that line the hall. The stucco and wall paintings relate to librarianship.

The façade of the Philosophical Hall is decorated with vases and a gilded medallion of Joseph II by Ignaz Platzer.

Entrance **to libraries**

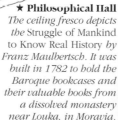

★ Philosophical Hall
The ceiling fresco depicts the Struggle of Mankind to Know Real History *by Franz Maulbertsch. It was built in 1782 to hold the Baroque bookcases and their valuable books from a dissolved monastery near Louka, in Moravia.*

Strahov Gospel Book
A facsimile of this superb and precious 9th-century volume, is now on display in the Theological Hall.

LITTLE QUARTER
MALÁ STRANA

THE LITTLE QUARTER is the part of Prague least affected by recent history. Hardly any new building has taken place here since the late 18th century and the quarter is rich in splendid Baroque palaces and old houses with attractive signs. Founded in 1257, it is built on the slopes below the Castle hill with magnificent views across the river to the Old Town.

Sign from At the Golden Horseshoe in Nerudova

The centre of the Little Quarter has always been Little Quarter Square (Malostranské náměstí), dominated by the Church of St Nicholas. The Grand Prior's millwheel at Kampa Island still turns, pilgrims still kneel before the Holy Infant of Prague in the Church of Our Lady Victorious, and music rings out from churches and palaces as it did when Mozart stayed here.

SIGHTS AT A GLANCE

Churches
Church of St Thomas ❸
Church of St Nicholas pp128–9 ❺
Church of Our Lady Victorious ❾
Church of Our Lady beneath the Chain ⓭
Church of St Lawrence ㉑

Parks and Gardens
Vrtba Garden ❽
Vojan Park ⑰
Ledebour Garden ⑱
Observation Tower ⑲
Mirror Maze ⑳
Observatory ㉒
Petřín Park ㉔
Funicular Railway ㉕

Historic Monuments
Hunger Wall ㉓

Historic Restaurants and Beer Halls
At St Thomas's ❷
At the Three Ostriches ⑮

Historic Streets and Squares
Little Quarter Square ❹
Nerudova Street ❻
Italian Street ❼
Maltese Square ❿
Grand Priory Square ⑫
Bridge Street ⑯

Bridges and Islands
Kampa Island ⓫
Charles Bridge pp136–9 ⑭

Palaces
Wallenstein Palace and Garden ❶
Michna Palace ㉖

KEY

	Street-by-Street map *See pp124–5*
	Street-by-Street map *See pp132–3*
M	Metro station
	Tram stop
	Funicular railway
	River boat boarding point
P	Parking
i	Tourist information
—	City wall

0 metres 250
0 yards 250

GETTING THERE
The area has little public transport, but Malostranská metro on line A is close to most of the sights. Trams 12, 20, 22 and 23 go to Malostranské náměstí and along Újezd to the funicular railway that takes you up Petřín Hill.

◁ **Charles Bridge and the Little Quarter Bridge Towers**

Street-by-Street: Around Little Quarter Square

THE LITTLE QUARTER, most of whose grand Baroque palaces now house embassies, has preserved much of its traditional character. The steep, narrow streets and steps have an air of romantic mystery and you will find fascinating buildings decorated with statues and house signs at every turn. Some smart new restaurants have been established in the old buildings.

At the Three Little Fiddles, now a restaurant, acquired its house sign when it was the home of a family of violin makers around 1700.

Thun-Hohenstein Palace (1721–6) has a doorway crowned with two sculpted eagles by Matthias Braun. The palace is now the seat of the Italian embassy.

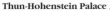

★ **Nerudova Street**
This historic street leading up to Prague Castle is named after the 19th-century writer Jan Neruda ❻

Morzin Palace has a striking Baroque façade with a pair of sculpted moors.

Italian Street
From the 16th to the 18th century, houses in the street, like the House at the Golden Scales, were occupied by Italian craftsmen ❼

STAR SIGHTS

★ **Wallenstein Palace**

★ **Church of St Nicholas**

★ **Nerudova Street**

Vrtba Garden
Laid out in about 1725 by František Maximilián Kaňka, these fine Baroque terraces provide good views over the rooftops of the Little Quarter ❽

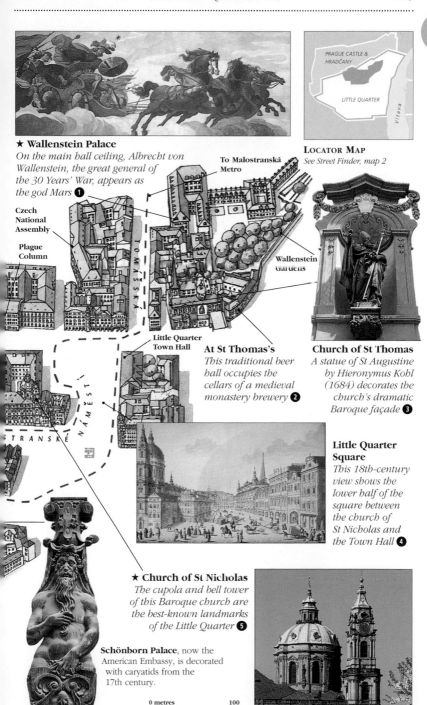

★ **Wallenstein Palace**
On the main hall ceiling, Albrecht von Wallenstein, the great general of the 30 Years' War, appears as the god Mars ❶

Czech National Assembly

Plague Column

To Malostranská Metro

LOCATOR MAP
See Street Finder, map 2

PRAGUE CASTLE & HRADČANY

LITTLE QUARTER

Vltava

Wallenstein Gardens

Little Quarter Town Hall

At St Thomas's
This traditional beer hall occupies the cellars of a medieval monastery brewery ❷

Church of St Thomas
A statue of St Augustine by Hieronymus Kohl (1684) decorates the church's dramatic Baroque façade ❸

Little Quarter Square
This 18th-century view shows the lower half of the square between the church of St Nicholas and the Town Hall ❹

★ **Church of St Nicholas**
The cupola and bell tower of this Baroque church are the best-known landmarks of the Little Quarter ❺

Schönborn Palace, now the American Embassy, is decorated with caryatids from the 17th century.

| 0 metres | 100 |
| 0 yards | 100 |

KEY

– – – Suggested route

Wallenstein Palace and Garden ❶

VALDŠTEJNSKÝ PALÁC

Valdštejnské náměstí 4. **Map** 2 E3.
🚇 *Malostranská.* 🚃 *25 70 71
111.* 🚊 *12, 18, 20, 22, 23.* **Palace
open** *10am–4pm Sat & Sun
(subject to change).* **Riding school
open** *10am–6pm Tue–Sun.* 🚫
♿ *from Valdštejnská.* **Garden
open** *Apr–Oct: 10am–4pm/5pm
daily.* 📷 ♿ *from Valdštejnské
náměstí.* 🖥 W www.senat.cz

THE FIRST LARGE secular
building of the Baroque
era in Prague, the palace
stands as a monument to the
fatal ambition of imperial
military commander Albrecht
von Wallenstein (1581–1634).
His string of victories over the
Protestants in the 30 Years'
War *(see pp30–31)* made him
vital to Emperor Ferdinand II.
Already showered with titles,
Wallenstein soon started to
covet the crown of
Bohemia. Finally
he dared to begin
to negotiate inde-
pendently with the
enemy, and he was
killed on the
emperor's orders
by mercenaries
Wallenstein in 1634.

The main hall of Wallenstein Palace

Wallenstein's intention was to
overshadow even Prague
Castle with his palace, built
between 1624 and 1630. To
obtain a suitable site, he had
to purchase 23 houses, three
gardens and the municipal
brick kiln. The magnificent
main hall rises to a height of
two storeys with a ceiling
fresco of Wallenstein himself
portrayed as Mars, the god of
war, riding in a triumphal
chariot. The architect,
Andrea Spezza, and
nearly all the artists
employed in the
decoration of the
palace were Italians.
   Today the palace
is used as the home
of the Czech Senate,
and will be open to
the public when
restoration work is
complete. The gardens

are laid out as they were when
Wallenstein dined in the huge
sala terrena (garden pavilion)
that looks out over a fountain
and rows of bronze statues.
These are copies of works by
Adriaen de Vries that were
stolen by the Swedes in 1648
(see pp30–31). There is also a
pavilion with fine frescoes
showing scenes from the
legend of the Argonauts and
the Golden Fleece.
   Wallenstein was a holder
of the Order of the
Golden Fleece, the
highest order of
chivalry of the Holy
Roman Empire. At the
far end of the garden
is a large ornamental
pond with a central
statue. Behind this
stands the old Riding
School, now used
to house special
exhibitions by the
National Gallery.
Both gardens and
riding school have
undergone sub-
stantial restoration.

**Copy of a bronze statue of
Eros by Adriaen de Vries**

Palace

**Sala
terrena**

Avenue of sculptures

Riding School

**Valdštejnská
Street
entrance**

The grotesquery is a curious
imitation of the walls of a limestone
cave, covered in stalactites.

**Letenská
Street
entrance**

**Statue of
Hercules**

Klárov entrance

At St Thomas's ❷
U SV. TOMÁŠE

Letenská 12. **Map** 2 E3. 🛎 *25 75 33
466.* Ⓜ *Malostranská.* 🚊 *12, 20,
22, 23.* **Open** *11:30am–11pm daily.* 📷

NO OTHER BEER HALL in
Prague can match the
antiquity of At St Thomas's.
Beer was first brewed here in
1352 by Augustinian monks.
The brewery gained such
renown that it was appointed
sole purveyor of beer to
Prague Castle. It remained in
operation until 1951. Since
then a special dark beer
from the Braník brewery
has been sold here. The
basement of the old brewery
has three beer halls, the
most spectacular being the
so-called "Cave", furnished
in mock medieval style.

Church of
St Thomas ❸
KOSTEL SV. TOMÁŠE

Josefská 8. **Map** 2 E3. 🛎 *25 53 26
75.* Ⓜ *Malostranská.* 🚊 *12, 20,
22, 23.* **Open** *for services.* ✝
*6:45am, 12:15pm Mon–Fri; 12:15pm,
6pm (in English) Sat; 9:30am, 11am
(in English), 5pm Sun.* 🚫 ♿

FOUNDED by Wenceslas II
in 1285 as the monastery
church of the Augustinians,
the original Gothic church
was completed in 1379. In the
Hussite period *(see pp26–7)*
this was one of the few
churches to remain Catholic.
As a result it suffered serious
fire damage. During the reign
of Rudolph II *(see pp28–9)*, St
Thomas's developed strong
links with the Imperial court.
Several prominent members
of Rudolph's entourage were
buried here, including court
architect Ottavio Aostalli and
the sculptor Adriaen de Vries.
In 1723 the church was
struck by lightning and Kilian
Ignaz Dientzenhofer was
called in to rebuild it. The
shape of the original church
was preserved in the Baroque
reconstruction but, apart from
the spire, the church today
betrays little of its Gothic origins. The interior of the dome
and the curving ceiling frescoes
in the nave were painted by

Václav Vavřinec Reiner. Above
the altar are copies of paintings
by Rubens – *The Martyrdom
of St Thomas* and a picture of
St Augustine. The originals
are in the Sternberg Palace
(see pp112–15). The English-
speaking Catholic community
of Prague meets in this church.

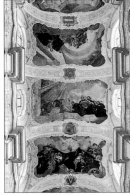

**Baroque ceiling in the nave of
the Church of St Thomas**

Little Quarter
Square ❹
MALOSTRANSKÉ NÁMĚSTÍ

Map 2 E3. Ⓜ *Malostranská.*
🚊 *12, 20, 22, 23.*

THE SQUARE HAS BEEN the
centre of life in the Little
Quarter since its foundation
in 1257. It had started life as
a large marketplace in the
outer bailey of Prague Castle.
Buildings sprang up in the
middle of the square dividing

it in half – a gallows and
pillory stood in its lower part.
Most of the houses around
the square have a medieval
core, but all were rebuilt in
the Renaissance and Baroque
periods. The centre of the
square is dominated by the
splendid Baroque church of
St Nicholas. The large building
beside it was a Jesuit college.
Along the upper side of the
square, facing the church,
runs the vast Neo-Classical
façade of Lichtenstein Palace.
In front of it stands a column
raised in honour of the Holy
Trinity to mark the end of a
plague epidemic in 1713.
Other important buildings
include the Little Quarter
Town Hall with its splendid
Renaissance façade and the
Sternberg Palace, built on the
site of the outbreak of the fire
of 1541, which destroyed most
of the Little Quarter. Beside it
stands the Smiřický Palace. Its
turrets and hexagonal towers
make it an unmistakable
landmark on the northern
side of the lower square. The
Baroque Kaiserstein Palace is
situated at the eastern side.
On the façade is a bust of the
great Czech soprano Emmy
Destinn, who lived there
between 1908 and 1914. She
often sang with the famous
Italian tenor Enrico Caruso.

Church of
St Nicholas ❺
KOSTEL SV. MIKULÁŠE

See pp128–9.

Arcade in front of buildings on the north side of Little Quarter Square

Church of St Nicholas ❺

KOSTEL SV. MIKULÁŠE

THE CHURCH OF ST NICHOLAS divides and dominates the two sections of Little Quarter Square. Building began in 1703, and the last touches were put to the glorious frescoed nave in 1761. It is the acknowledged masterpiece of father-and-son architects Christoph and Kilian Ignaz Dientzenhofer, Prague's greatest exponents of High Baroque *(see opposite)*, although neither lived to see the completion of the church. The statues, frescoes and paintings inside the church are by leading artists of the day, and include a fine *Crucifixion* of 1646 by Karel Škréta. Extensive renovation in the 1950s reversed the damage caused by 200 years of leaky cladding and condensation.

★ Pulpit
Dating from 1765, the ornate pulpit is by Richard and Peter Prachner. It is lavishly adorned with golden cherubs.

Altar Paintings
The side chapels hold many works of art. This painting of St Michael is by Francesco Solimena.

Baroque Organ
A fresco of St Cecilia, patron saint of music, watches over the superb organ. Built in 1746, the instrument was played by Mozart in 1787.

Entrance from west side of Little Quarter Square

Chapel of St Ann

Chapel of St Catherine

STAR FEATURES

★ Dome Fresco

★ Pulpit

★ Statues of the Church Fathers

Façade
St Paul, by John Frederick Kohl, is one of the statues that grace the curving façade. It was completed in 1710 by Christoph Dientzenhofer, who was influenced by Italian architects Borromini and Guarini.

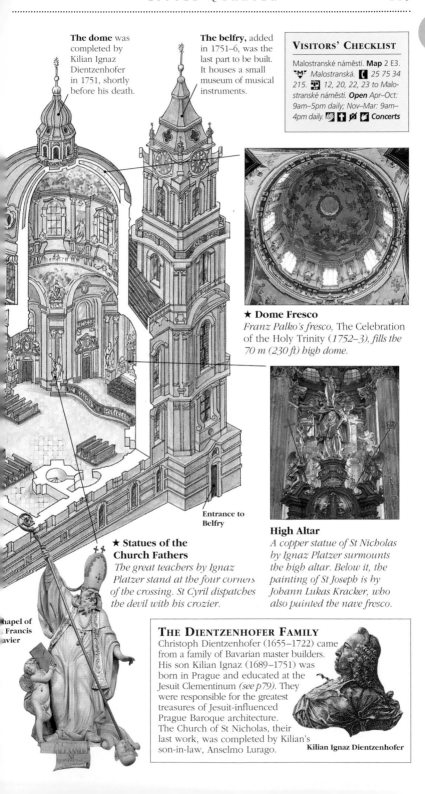

The dome was completed by Kilian Ignaz Dientzenhofer in 1751, shortly before his death.

The belfry, added in 1751–6, was the last part to be built. It houses a small museum of musical instruments.

VISITORS' CHECKLIST

Malostranské náměstí. **Map** 2 E3.
M *Malostranská.* **▮** *25 75 34 215.* **🚋** *12, 20, 22, 23 to Malo-stranské náměstí.* **Open** *Apr–Oct: 9am–5pm daily; Nov–Mar: 9am–4pm daily.* 🖼 ⛪ 🚫 🎵 *Concerts*

★ **Dome Fresco**
Franz Palko's fresco, The Celebration of the Holy Trinity *(1752–3), fills the 70 m (230 ft) high dome.*

Entrance to Belfry

High Altar
A copper statue of St Nicholas by Ignaz Platzer surmounts the high altar. Below it, the painting of St Joseph is by Johann Lukas Kracker, who also painted the nave fresco.

★ **Statues of the Church Fathers**
The great teachers by Ignaz Platzer stand at the four corners of the crossing. St Cyril dispatches the devil with his crozier.

Chapel of
Francis
avier

THE DIENTZENHOFER FAMILY
Christoph Dientzenhofer (1655–1722) came from a family of Bavarian master builders. His son Kilian Ignaz (1689–1751) was born in Prague and educated at the Jesuit Clementinum *(see p79).* They were responsible for the greatest treasures of Jesuit-influenced Prague Baroque architecture. The Church of St Nicholas, their last work, was completed by Kilian's son-in-law, Anselmo Lurago.

Kilian Ignaz Dientzenhofer

Nerudova Street ❻
NERUDOVA ULICE

Map 2 D3. ᵀᴹᶠ *Malostranská.* 🚋 *12, 20, 22, 23.*

A PICTURESQUE narrow street leading up to Prague Castle, Nerudova is named after the poet and journalist Jan Neruda, who wrote many short stories set in this part of Prague. He lived in the house called At the Two Suns (No. 47) between 1845 and 1857.

Up until the introduction of numbers in 1770, Prague's houses were distinguished by signs. Nerudova's houses have a splendid selection of heraldic beasts and emblems. As you make your way up Nerudova's steep slope, look out in particular for the Red Eagle (No. 6), the Three Fiddles (No. 12), the Golden Horseshoe (No. 34), the Green Lobster (No. 43) and the White Swan (No. 49) as well as the Old Pharmacy museum (No. 32).

There are also a number of grand Baroque buildings in the street, including the Thun-Hohenstein Palace (No. 20, now the Italian embassy) and the Morzin Palace (No. 5, the Rumanian embassy). The latter has a façade with two massive statues of moors (a pun on the name Morzin) supporting the semicircular balcony on the first floor. Another impressive façade is that of the Church of Our Lady of Unceasing Succour, the church of the Theatines, an order founded during the Counter-Reformation.

Italian Street, heart of the former colony of Italian craftsmen

Italian Street ❼
VLAŠSKÁ ULICE

Map 1 C4. ᵀᴹᶠ *Malostranská.* 🚋 *12, 20, 22, 23.*

I TALIAN IMMIGRANTS started to settle here in the 16th century. Many were artists or craftsmen employed to rebuild and redecorate the Castle. If you approach the street from Petřín, on the left you will see the former Italian Hospital, a Baroque building with an arcaded courtyard. Today it maintains its traditional allegiance as the cultural section of the Italian embassy.

The grandest building in the street is the former Lobkowicz Palace, now the German embassy. One of the finest Baroque palaces in Prague, it has a large oval hall on the ground floor leading out onto a magnificent garden. Look out too for the pretty stucco sign on the house called At the Three Red Roses, dating from the early 18th century.

Vrtba Garden ❽
VRTBOVSKÁ ZAHRADA

Karmelitská 25. **Map** 2 D4. ᵀᴹᶠ *Malostranská.* 🚋 *12, 20, 22, 23.* **Open** *Apr–Oct: 10am–6pm daily.* 📷 ♿

B EHIND VRTBA PALACE lies a beautiful Baroque garden with steep flights of steps and balustraded terraces. From the highest part of the garden there are magnificent views of Prague Castle and the Little Quarter. The Vrtba Garden was designed by František Maximilián Kaňka in about 1720. The statues of Classical gods and stone vases are the work of Matthias Braun and the paintings in the *sala terrena* (garden pavilion) in the lower part of the garden are by Václav Vavřinec Reiner.

View of the Little Quarter from the terrace of the Vrtba Garden

Church of Our Lady Victorious ❾
KOSTEL PANNY MARIE VÍTĚZNÉ

Karmelitská. **Map** 2 E4. 📞 *25 75 33 646.* 🚋 *12, 20, 22, 23.* **Open** *9am–7pm daily.* ✝ *9am, 6:15pm Mon–Fri, 9am, 6pm, 7:30pm Sat, 10am, noon (English), 8pm (Oct–May: 7pm) Sun.*

T HE FIRST BAROQUE building in Prague was the Church of the Holy Trinity, built for the German Lutherans by Giovanni Maria Filippi. It was finished in 1613 but after the Battle of the White Mountain (*see p31*) the Catholic authorities gave the church to the Carmelites, who rebuilt it and renamed it in honour of the victory.

Sign of Jan Neruda's house, At the Two Suns, 47 Nerudova Street

The fabric has survived including the portal. Enshrined on a marble altar in the right aisle is a glass case containing the Holy Infant of Prague (better-known by its Italian name – *il Bambino di Praga*). This wax effigy has a record of miracle cures and is one of the most revered images in the Catholic world. It was brought from Spain and presented to the Carmelites in 1628 by Polyxena of Lobkowicz. A small museum adjacent to the church traces its history.

Maltese Square ⑩
MALTÉZSKÉ NÁMĚSTÍ

Map 2 E4. 🚋 *12, 20, 22, 23.*

THE SQUARE TAKES its name from the Priory of the Knights of Malta, which used to occupy this part of the Little Quarter. At the northern end stands a group of sculptures featuring St John the Baptist by Ferdinand Brokof – part of a fountain erected in 1715 to mark the end of a plague epidemic.

Most of the buildings were originally Renaissance houses belonging to prosperous townspeople, but in the 17th and 18th centuries the Little Quarter was taken over by the Catholic nobility and many were converted to flamboyant Baroque palaces. The largest, Nostitz Palace, stands on the southern side. Part of the palace now houses the Dutch embassy. It was built in the mid-17th century, then in about 1720 a balustrade was added with Classical vases and statues of emperors. In summer, concerts are given at the Palace. The Japanese embassy is housed in the Turba Palace (1767), an attractive pink Rococo building designed by Joseph Jäger.

Ferdinand Brokof's statue of John the Baptist in Maltese Square

Čertovka (the Devil's Stream) with Kampa Island on the right

Kampa Island ⑪
KAMPA

Map 2 F4. 🚋 *6, 9, 12, 20, 22, 23.*

KAMPA, AN ISLAND formed by a branch of the Vltava known as the Devil's Stream (Čertovka), is a delightfully peaceful corner of the Little Quarter. The stream got its name in the 19th century, allegedly after the diabolical temper of a lady who owned a house nearby in Maltese Square. For centuries the stream was used as a millrace and from Kampa you can see the remains of three old mills. Beyond the Grand Prior's Mill the stream disappears under a small bridge below the piers of Charles Bridge. From here it flows between rows of houses. Predictably, the area has become known as "the Venice of Prague", but instead of gondolas you will see canoes.

For most of the Middle Ages there were only gardens on Kampa, though the island was also used for washing clothes and bleaching linen. In the 17th century the island became well-known for its pottery markets. There are some enchanting houses from this period around Na Kampě Square. Most of the land from here to the southern tip of the island is a park, created from several old palace gardens.

The island all but vanished beneath the Vltava during the floods of 2002, which caused widespread devastation to homes, businesses and historic buildings, many of which are still being rebuilt and restored.

Grand Priory Square ⑫
VELKOPŘEVORSKÉ NÁMĚSTÍ

Map 2 F4. Ⓜ *Malostranská.* 🚋 *12, 20, 22, 23.*

ON THE NORTHERN SIDE of this small leafy square stands the former seat of the Grand Prior of the Knights of Malta. In its present form the palace dates from the 1720s. The doorways, windows and decorative vases were made at the workshop of Matthias Braun. On the opposite side of the square is the Buquoy Palace, now the French embassy, a delightful Baroque building roughly contemporary with the Grand Prior's Palace.

The only incongruous features are a painting of John Lennon and graffiti exhorting the world to "give peace a chance". These have decorated the wall of the Grand Prior's garden since Lennon's death.

Street-by-Street: Little Quarter Riverside

O N EITHER SIDE of Bridge Street lies a delightful half-hidden world of gently decaying squares, picturesque palaces, churches and gardens. When you have run the gauntlet of the trinket-sellers on Charles Bridge, escape to Kampa Island to enjoy a stroll in its informal park, the views across the Vltava weir to the Old Town and the flocks of swans gliding along the river.

The Church of St Joseph dates from the late 17th century. The painting of *The Holy Family* (1702) on the gilded high altar is by the leading Baroque artist Petr Brandl.

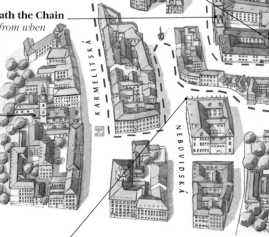

The House at the Golden Unicorn in Lázeňská Street has a plaque commemorating the fact that Beethoven stayed here in 1796.

Bridge Street
A major thoroughfare for 750 years, the narrow street leads to Little Quarter Square

To Little Quarter Square

Grand Priory Square
The Grand Prior's Palace is the former seat of the Knights of Malta and dates from the 1720s. Its street wall features colourful murals and graffitti ⑫

Church of Our Lady beneath the Chain
Two massive towers survive from when this was a fortified priory ⑬

Church of Our Lady Victorious
This Baroque church houses the famous effigy, the Holy Infant of Prague ⑨

Maltese Square
Grand palaces surround the oddly-shaped square. This coat of arms decorates the 17th-century Nostitz Palace, a popular venue for concerts ⑩

| 0 metres | 100 |
| 0 yards | 100 |

KEY

– – – Suggested route

Vojan Park
Quiet shady paths have been laid out under the apple trees of this former monastery garden **17**

At the Three Ostriches
A restaurant and hotel have kept the sign of a seller of ostrich plumes **15**

LOCATOR MAP
See Street Finder, map 2

★ Charles Bridge
The approach to this magnificent 14th-century bridge, with its files of Baroque statues, passes under an arch below a Gothic tower **14**

U LUŽICKÉHO · SEMINÁŘE

Čertovka (the Devil's Stream)

The Grand Priory Mill has had its wheel meticulously restored, though it now turns very slowly in the sluggish water of the Čertovka, the former millrace.

N A KAMPĚ

Lichtenstein Palace

★ Kampa Island
This 19th-century painting by Soběslav Pinkas shows boys playing on Kampa. The island's park is still a popular place for children **11**

STAR SIGHTS

★ Charles Bridge

★ Kampa Island

Church of Our Lady beneath the Chain ⑬

KOSTEL PANNY MARIE POD ŘETĚZEM

Lázeňská. **Map** 2 E4. **℡** *25 75 30 876.* **Ⓜ** *Malostranská.* **🚃** *12, 20, 22, 23.* **Open** *for concerts and services.* **🕐** *4:30pm (4pm in winter) Sat, 10am Sun.*

T HIS CHURCH, the oldest in the Little Quarter, was founded in the 12th century. King Vladislav II presented it to the Knights of St John, the order which later became known as the Knights of Malta. It stood in the centre of the Knights' heavily fortified monastery that guarded the approach to the old Judith Bridge. The church's name refers to the chain used in the Middle Ages to close the monastery gatehouse.

A Gothic presbytery was added in the 13th century, but in the following century the original Romanesque church was demolished. A new portico was built with a pair of massive square towers, but work was then abandoned and the old nave became a courtyard between the towers and the church. This was given a Baroque facelift in 1640 by Carlo Lurago. The painting by Karel Škréta on the high altar shows the Virgin Mary and John the Baptist coming to the aid of the Knights of Malta in the famous naval victory over the Turks at Lepanto in 1571.

Charles Bridge ⑭

KARLŮV MOST

See pp136–9.

Fresco that gave At the Three Ostriches its name

View along Bridge Street through the tower on Charles Bridge

At the Three Ostriches ⑮

U TŘÍ PŠTROSŮ

Dražického náměstí 12. **Map** 2 F3. **℡** *25 75 32 410.* **Ⓜ** *Malostranská.* **🚃** *12, 20, 22, 23.* See **Where to Stay** *pp182–9,* **Restaurants** *pp198–209.* **Ⓦ** *www.upstrosu.cz*

M ANY OF PRAGUE'S colourful house signs indicated the trade carried on in the premises. In 1597 Jan Fux, an ostrich-feather merchant, bought this house by Charles Bridge. At the time ostrich plumes were very fashionable as decoration for hats among courtiers and officers at Prague Castle. Fux even supplied feathers to foreign armies. So successful was his business, that in 1606 he had the house rebuilt and decorated with a large fresco of ostriches. He even employed a respected artist to paint his sign rather than the usual journeymen.

The first floor of the house was added in 1657 and some beamed ceilings painted with vine motifs have been preserved from that time. In 1714 Prague's first coffee house opened here. The building is now an expensive hotel and restaurant.

Bridge Street ⑯

MOSTECKÁ ULICE

Map 2 E3. **Ⓜ** *Malostranská.* **🚃** *12, 20, 22, 23.*

S INCE THE MIDDLE AGES this street has linked Charles Bridge with the Little Quarter Square. Crossing the bridge from the Old Town you can see the doorway of the old customs house built in 1591 in front of the Judith Tower. On the first floor of the tower there is a 12th-century relief of a king and a kneeling man.

Throughout the 13th and 14th centuries the area to the north of the street was the Court of the Bishop of Prague. This was destroyed during the Hussite Wars *(see pp26–7),* but one of its Gothic towers is preserved in the courtyard of the house called At the Three Golden Bells. It can be seen from the higher of the two bridge towers. The street is lined with a mixture of Renaissance and Baroque houses. As you walk up to Little Quarter Square, look out for the house called At the Black Eagle on the left. It has rich sculptural decoration and a splendid Baroque wrought-iron grille. Kaunic Palace, also on the left, was built in the 1770s. Its Rococo façade has striking stucco decoration and sculptures by Ignaz Platzer.

Vojan Park ⑰
VOJANOVY SADY

U lužického semináře. **Map** 2 F3.
🚇 *Malostranská.* 🚃 *12, 18, 20, 22, 23.* **Open** *9am–6pm daily.*

A TRANQUIL SPOT hidden behind high white walls, the park dates back to the 17th century, when it was the garden of the Convent of Barefooted Carmelites. Two chapels erected by the Order have survived among the park's lawns and fruit trees. One is the Chapel of Elijah, who, because of his Old Testament associations with Mount Carmel, is regarded as the founder of the Order. His chapel takes the form of a stalagmite and stalactite cave. The other chapel, dedicated to St Theresa, was built in the 18th century as an expression of gratitude for the convent's preservation during the Prussian siege of Prague in 1757. In a niche to the left of the entrance to the park, there is an 18th-century statue of St John Nepomuk *(see p137)* by Ignaz Platzer. The saint is depicted standing on a fish – a reference to his martyrdom by drowning in the Vltava.

Ledebour Garden ⑱
LEDEBURSKÁ ZAHRADA

Valdštejnská. **Map** 2 F2.
📞 *25 70 10 401.* 🚇 *Malostranská.* 🚃 *12, 18, 20, 22, 23.* **Open** *Apr–Jun, Sep–Oct: 10am–6pm daily; Jul–Aug: 10am–8pm daily.* 📷

THE STEEP SOUTHERN slope below Prague Castle was covered with vineyards and gardens during the Middle Ages. But in the 16th century, when nobles started building

palaces here, they laid out larger formal terraced gardens based on Italian Renaissance models. Most of these gardens were rebuilt during the 18th century and decorated with Baroque garden statuary and fountains. Three of the gardens – those belonging to the former Ledebour, Černín and Pálffy Palaces – have been linked together. They have recently undergone a much-needed programme of restoration work, and they again are delighting visitors with their elegant land-scaping and attractive plants.

The refined and pleasantly atmospheric old-world elegance of the gardens is enhanced by magnificent views of Prague from their terraces. The Ledebour Garden, designed in the early 18th century, has a fine *sala terrena* (garden pavilion) by Giovanni Battista Alliprandi. The Pálffy Garden was laid out in the mid-18th century with terraces (the second still has its original sundial) and loggias. The most beautiful of the three

18th-century statue of Hercules located in the Ledebour Garden

and architecturally the richest is the Kolowrat-Černín Garden, created in 1784 by Ignaz Palliardi. The highest terrace has a *sala terrena* decorated with statues and Classical urns. Below this there is a wonderful assortment of staircases, archways and balustrades, and the remains of Classical statuary and old fountains.

The foot of the Ledebour Garden, prior to restoration work

Charles Bridge (Little Quarter Side) ⓮

KARLŮV MOST

Prague's most familiar monument, connects the Old Town with the Little Quarter. Although it is now pedestrianized, at one time it could take four carriages abreast. Today, due to wear and tear, many of the statues on the bridge are copies; the originals are kept in the Lapidarium of the National Museum *(see p162)* and at Vyšehrad *(see p179)*. The Gothic Old Town Bridge Tower *(see p139)* is one of the finest buildings of its kind in existence.

★ **View from Little Quarter Bridge Tower**
The tall pinnacled wedge tower, gives a superb view of the city of 100 spires. The shorter tower is the remains of Judith Bridge.

St Adalbert, 1709
Adalbert, Bishop of Prague, founded the Church of St Lawrence (see p141) on Petřín Hill in 991. He is known to the Czechs as Vojtěch.

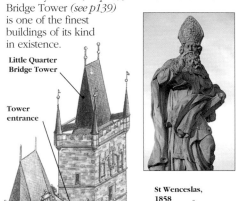

Little Quarter Bridge Tower

Tower entrance

St Wenceslas, 1858

St Philip Benizi,

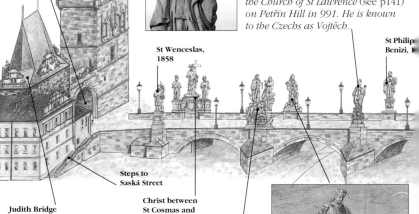

Steps to Saská Street

Judith Bridge Tower, 1158

Christ between St Cosmas and St Damian, 1709

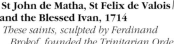

St John de Matha, St Felix de Valois and the Blessed Ivan, 1714
These saints, sculpted by Ferdinand Brokof, founded the Trinitarian Order of mendicants to collect money to buy the freedom of Christians enslaved by the infidels (represented at the foot of the sculpture).

St Vitus, 1714
This engraving of the statue shows the 3rd-century martyr with the lions which were supposed to maul him, but licked him instead. St Vitus is the patron saint of dancers and often invoked against convulsive disorders.

STAR FEATURES

★ **Little Quarter Bridge Tower and View**

★ **St John Nepomuk**

★ **St Luitgard**

★ **St Luitgard, 1710**
This statue, regarded as the most artistically remarkable on the bridge, was sculpted by Matthias Braun when he was only 26. It is based on the blind Cistercian nun's celebrated vision when Christ appeared and she kissed his wounds.

VISITORS' CHECKLIST

Map 2 F4. 🚊 12, 22, 23 to Malostranské náměstí, then walk down Mostecká. **Little Quarter Bridge Tower open** 10am–6pm daily (Jul–Aug: 10am–10pm). 🅰 🅾

★ **St John Nepomuk, 1683**
Reliefs on the bridge depict the martyrdom of St John Nepomuk. Here the saint is polished bright from people touching it for good luck.

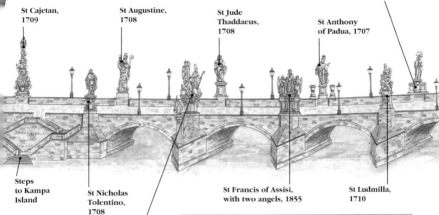

St Cajetan, 1709

St Augustine, 1708

St Jude Thaddaeus, 1708

St Anthony of Padua, 1707

Steps to Kampa Island

St Nicholas Tolentino, 1708

St Francis of Assisi, with two angels, 1855

St Ludmilla, 1710

St Vincent Ferrer and St Procopius, 1712
This detail shows a rabbi saddened by St Vincent's success in converting many Jews to Christianity. St Procopius is one of Bohemia's patron saints.

ST JOHN NEPOMUK

The cult of St John Nepomuk, canonized in 1729, was promoted by the Jesuits to rival the revered Jan Hus *(see p27)*. Jan Nepomucký, vicar-general of the Archdiocese of Prague, was arrested in 1393 by Wenceslas IV along with the archbishop and others who had displeased the king over the election of an abbot. The archbishop escaped, but John died under torture. The body was bound and thrown off Charles Bridge. Statues modelled on the one placed here in 1683 can be seen throughout central Europe, especially on bridges.

Charles Bridge (Old Town Side) ⑭

KARLŮV MOST

U NTIL 1741, CHARLES BRIDGE was the only crossing over the Vltava. It is 520 m (1,706 ft) long and is built of sandstone blocks, rumoured to be strengthened by mixing mortar with eggs. The bridge was commissioned by Charles IV in 1357 to replace the Judith Bridge and built by Peter Parler. The bridge's original decoration was a simple cross. The first statue – of St John Nepomuk – was added in 1683, inspired by Bernini's sculptures on Rome's Ponte Sant'Angelo.

★ 17th-Century Crucifixion

For 200 years, the wooden crucifix stood alone on the bridge. The gilded Christ dates from 1629 and the Hebrew words "Holy, Holy, Holy Lord", were paid for by a Jew as punishment for blasphemy.

St Francis Xavier, 1711
The Jesuit missionary is supported by three Moorish and two Oriental converts. The sculptor Brokof is seated on the saint's left.

St Norbert, St Wenceslas and St Sigismund, 1853

St Francis Borgia, 1710

St John the Baptist, 1857

St Cyril and St Methodius, 1938

St Christopher, 1857

St Ann, 1707

St Joseph, 1854

Thirty Years' War
In the last hours of this war, the Old Town was saved from the Swedish army. The truce was signed in the middle of the bridge in 1648.

STAR FEATURES

★ **Old Town Bridge Tower**

★ **17th-Century Crucifixion**

TIMELINE

1357 Charles IV commissions new bridge

1342 Judith Bridge destroyed by floods

1621 Heads of ten Protestant nobles exhibited on the Old Town Bridge Tower

1648 Swedes damage part of the bridge and Old Town Bridge Tower

1890 flood damage

1100	1300	1500	1700	1900

1158 Europe's second medieval stone bridge, Judith Bridge, is built

1393 St John Nepomuk thrown off Bridge on the orders of Wenceslas IV

Sculptor Matthias Braun (1684–1738)

1890 Three arches destroyed by flood

1713 Bridge decorated with 21 statues by Braun, Brokof and others

1938 Karel Dvořák's sculpture of St Cyril and St Methodius

The Madonna, St Dominic and St Thomas, 1708
The Dominicans, (known in a Latin pun as Domini canes, *the dogs of God), are shown with the Madonna and their emblem, a dog.*

VISITORS' CHECKLIST

Map 3 A4. ⊞ 17, 18 to Křižovnické náměstí. **Old Town Bridge
Tower open** 10am–5pm daily
(Mar: to 6pm; Apr–May & Oct: to
7pm; Jun–Sep: to 10pm). 🖼 📷

Madonna and St Bernard, 1709
Cherubs and symbols of the Passion, including the dice, the cock and the centurion's gauntlet, form part of the statue.

Old Town Bridge Tower

Tower entrance

Pietà, 1859

St Barbara, St Margaret and St Elizabeth, 1707

★ OLD TOWN BRIDGE TOWER

This magnificent Gothic tower, designed by Peter Parler, was built at the end of the 14th century. A fitting ornament to the new Charles Bridge, it was also an integral part of the Old Town's fortifications.

Pinnacled wedge spire

Roof viewing point

The viewing gallery is a rib-vaulted room, on the tower's first floor. It provides a wonderful view of Prague Castle and the Little Quarter.

Bridge Tower sculptures by Peter Parler include St Vitus, the bridge's patron saint, Charles IV (left) and Wenceslas IV.

Observation Tower ⑲
PETŘÍNSKÁ ROZHLEDNA

Petřín. **Map** 1 C4. 🚋 *6, 9, 12, 20, 22, 23, then take funicular railway.* 🚌 *132, 143, 149, 217.* **Open** *Jun–Aug: 10am–7pm daily; Sep–Oct: 10am–6pm daily. Subject to alteration.* 📷 📷

THE MOST conspicuous landmark in Petřín Park is an imitation Eiffel Tower, built for the Jubilee Exhibition of 1891. The octagonal Petřín tower is only 60 m (200 ft), a quarter the height of the Eiffel Tower. The only way to the viewing platform is to climb up the 299 steps of its spiral staircase. On a clear day, you can see as far as Bohemia's highest peak, Sněžka in the Krkonoše (Giant) Mountains, 150 km (100 miles) to the northeast. The tower is currently undergoing major renovation work.

Mirror Maze ⑳
ZRCADLOVÉ BLUDIŠTĚ

Petřín. **Map** 1 C4. ☎ *25 73 15 212.* 🚋 *6, 9, 12, 20, 22, 23, then take funicular railway.* 🚌 *132, 143, 149, 217.* **Open** *Apr–Aug: 10am–7pm daily; Sep & Oct: 10am–6pm daily; Nov–Mar: 10am–5pm Sat & Sun.* 📷 🚫 ♿

LIKE THE Observation Tower, the maze, which has walls lined with distorting mirrors, is a relic of the Exhibition of 1891. It is in a wooden pavilion in the shape of the old Špička Gate, part of the Gothic

The 100-year-old Observation Tower overlooking the city

fortifications of Vyšehrad *(see pp178–9)*. This amusement house moved to Petřín at the end of the exhibition and has stood here ever since.

When you have navigated your way through the maze and laughed at your reflection, your reward is to view the vivid diorama of *The Defence of Prague against the Swedes*, which took place on Charles Bridge *(see p138)* in 1648.

Church of St Lawrence ㉑
KOSTEL SV. VAVŘINCE

Petřín. **Map** 1 C5. 🚋 *6, 9, 12, 20, 22, 23, then take funicular railway.* 🚌 *132, 143, 149, 217.* **Closed** to the public.

ACCORDING TO LEGEND, the church was initially founded in the 10th century by the pious Prince Boleslav II and St Adalbert on the site of a pagan shrine. The ceiling of the sacristy is decorated with a painting illustrating this legend. The painting dates from the 18th century when the Romanesque church was swallowed up by a large new Baroque structure, featuring a cupola flanked by two onion-domed towers.

The small Calvary Chapel, which dates from 1735, is situated just to the left of the entrance to the church. Its façade has been decorated with modern graffito that portrays *The Resurrection of Christ*.

Observatory ㉒
HVĚZDÁRNA

Petřín 205. **Map** 2 D5. ☎ *25 73 20 540.* 🚋 *6, 9, 12, 20, 22, 23, then funicular.* **Open** *Tue–Sun year-round; opening hours vary monthly, so phone ahead.* 📷 🚫 🌐 www.observatory.cz

One of the telescopes in the Observatory on Petřín Hill

SINCE 1930, PRAGUE'S amateur astronomers have been able to enjoy the facilities of this observatory on Petřín Hill. You can use its telescopes to view anything from the craters of the moon to unfamiliar distant galaxies. There is an exhibition of old astronomical instruments and special events for children are held on Saturdays and Sundays.

Hunger Wall ㉓
HLADOVÁ ZEĎ'

Újezd, Petřín, Strahovská. **Map** 2 D5. 🚋 *6, 9, 12, 20, 22, 23, then take funicular railway.* 🚌 *132, 143, 149, 217.*

THE FORTIFICATIONS built around the southern edge of the Little Quarter on the orders of Charles IV in

Diorama of *The Defence of Prague against the Swedes* in the Mirror Maze

1360–62 have been known for centuries as the Hunger Wall. Nearly 1,200 m (1,300 yards) of the wall have survived, complete with crenellated battlements and a platform for marksmen on its inner side. It runs from Újezd across Petřín Park to Strahov. The story behind the name is that Charles commissioned its construction with the aim of giving employment to the poor during a period of famine. It is true that a great famine did break out in Bohemia in the 1360s and the two events, the famine and the building of the wall, became permanently linked in the people's memory.

Petřín Park ㉔
PETŘÍNSKÉ SADY

Map 2 D5. 🚇 6, 9, 12, 20, 22, 23, then take funicular railway. See **Three Guided Walks** pp176–7.

To the west of the Little Quarter, Petřín hill rises above the city to a height of 318 m (960 ft). The name derives either from the Slavonic god Perun, to whom sacrifices were made on the hill or from the Latin name Mons Petrinus, meaning "rocky hill". A forest used to stretch from here as far as the White Mountain *(see p31).* In the 12th century the southern side of the hill was planted with vineyards, but by the 18th century most of these had been transformed into gardens and orchards.

Today a path winds up the slopes of Petřín, offering magnificent views of Prague. The park is especially popular in spring when the fruit trees are in blossom and young lovers lay flowers on the monument to Karel Hynek Mácha, the most famous Czech Romantic poet, who died aged 26 in 1836. Also in the park is the *Monument to the Victims of Communism* (2002) by the sculptor Olbram Zoubek.

Statue of Karel Hynek Mácha in Petřín Park

Nebozízek, the station halfway up Petřín's funicular railway

Funicular Railway ㉕
LANOVÁ DRÁHA

Újezd. **Map** 2 D5. 🚇 6, 9, 12, 20, 22, 23. **In operation** summer: 9am–11:30pm daily; winter: 9:15am–8:45pm daily. 🏭 📷 ♿

Built to carry visitors to the 1891 Jubilee Exhibition up to the Observation Tower at the top of Petřín hill, the funicular was originally powered by water. In this form, it remained in operation until 1914, then between the wars was converted to electricity. In 1965 it had to be shut down because part of the hillside collapsed – coal had been mined here during the 19th century. Shoring up the slope and rebuilding the railway took 20 years, but since its reopening in 1985 it has proved a reliable way of getting up Petřín Hill. At the halfway station, Nebozízek, there is a restaurant *(see p202)* with fine views of the Castle and the city.

Michna Palace ㉖
MICHNŮV PALÁC

Újezd 40. **Map** 2 E4. 🕿 25 73 11 831. 🚇 12, 20, 22, 23. **Open** 9am–5pm Thu, Sat, Sun. 🏭 🚫 ♿

In about 1580 Ottavio Aostalli built a summer palace here for the Kinský family on the site of an old Dominican convent. In 1623 the building was bought by Pavel Michna of Vacínov, a supply officer in the Imperial Army, who had grown rich after the Battle of the White Mountain. He commissioned a new Baroque building that he hoped would rival the palace of his late commander, Wallenstein *(see p126).*

In 1767 the Michna Palace was sold to the army and over the years it became a crumbling ruin. After 1918 it was bought by Sokol (a physical culture association) and converted into a gym and sports centre with a training ground in the old palace garden. The restored palace was renamed Tyrš House in honour of Sokol's founder. The ground floor now houses the Museum of Physical Culture and Sport.

Restored Baroque façade of the Michna Palace (Tyrš House)

NEW TOWN

NOVÉ MĚSTO

Art Nouveau decoration on No. 12 Wenceslas Square

THE NEW TOWN, founded in 1348 by Charles IV, was carefully planned and laid out around three large central market-places: the Hay Market (Senovážné Square), the Cattle Market (Charles Square) and the Horse Market (Wenceslas Square). Twice as large as the Old Town, the area was mainly inhabited by tradesmen and craftsmen such as blacksmiths, wheelwrights and brewers. During the late 19th century, much of the New Town was demolished and completely redeveloped, giving it the appearance it has today.

SIGHTS AT A GLANCE

Churches and Monasteries
Church of Our Lady of the Snows **2**
Church of St Ignatius **8**
Church of St Cyril and St Methodius **11**
Church of St John on the Rock **13**
Slavonic Monastery Emauzy **14**
Church of St Catherine **16**
Church of St Stephen **19**
Church of St Ursula **22**

Historic Buildings
Hotel Europa **4**
Jesuit College **9**
Faust House **12**
New Town Hall **20**

Theatres and Opera Houses
State Opera **6**
National Theatre pp156–7 **23**

Historic Squares
Wenceslas Square **1**
Charles Square **10**

Museums and Galleries
National Museum **5**
Mucha Museum **7**
Dvořák Museum **18**

Historic Restaurants and Beer Halls
Chalice Restaurant **17**
U Fleků **21**

Parks and Gardens
Franciscan Garden **3**
Botanical Gardens **15**

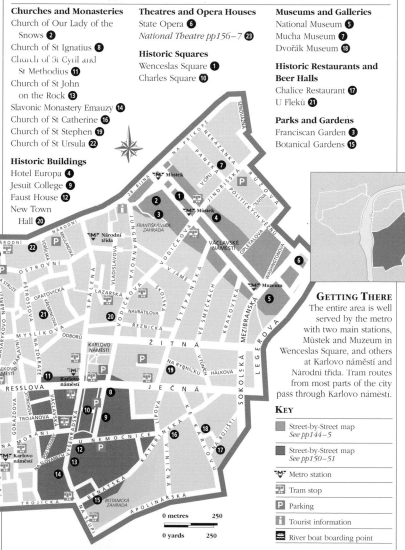

GETTING THERE
The entire area is well served by the metro with two main stations, Můstek and Muzeum in Wenceslas Square, and others at Karlovo náměstí and Národní třída. Tram routes from most parts of the city pass through Karlovo náměstí.

KEY

	Street-by-Street map *See pp144–5*
	Street-by-Street map *See pp150–51*
M	Metro station
	Tram stop
P	Parking
i	Tourist information
	River boat boarding point

◁ **Art Nouveau sculptures on the Hlahol Choir Building (1905) on Masarykovo nábřeží**

Street-by-Street: Wenceslas Square

HOTELS AND RESTAURANTS occupy many of the buildings around Wenceslas Square, though it remains an important commercial centre – the square began life as a medieval horse market. As you walk along, look up at the buildings, most of which date from the turn of this century, when the square was redeveloped. There are fine examples of the decorative styles used by Czech architects of the period. Many blocks have dark covered arcades leading to shops, clubs, theatres and cinemas.

Statue of St Lawrence at U Pinkasů

U Pinkasů became one of Prague's most popular beer halls when it started serving Pilsner Urquell *(see pp196–7)* in 1843.

Koruna Palace (1914) is an ornate block of shops and offices. Its corner turret is topped with a crown (*koruna*).

To Powder Gate

NA PŘÍKOPĚ

Můstek Ⓜ

Church of Our Lady of the Snows
The towering Gothic building is only part of a vast church planned during the 14th century ❷

Můstek Ⓜ

Můs

VODIČKOVA

Jungmann Square is named after Josef Jungmann (1773–1847), an influential scholar of language and lexicographer, and there is a statue of him in the middle. The Adria Palace (1925) used to be the Laterna Magika Theatre *(see p214)*, which was where Václav Havel's Civic Forum worked in the early days of the 1989 Velvet Revolution.

Franciscan Garden
An old monastery garden has been laid out as a small park with this fountain, rosebeds, trellises and a children's playground ❸

Lucerna Palace

Wiehl House, named after its architect Antonín Wiehl, was completed in 1896. The five-storey building is in striking Neo-Renaissance style, with aloggia and colourful *sgraffito*. Mikuláš Aleš designed some of the Art Nouveau figures.

STAR SIGHTS

★ Wenceslas Square

★ Hotel Europa

★ National Museum

★ **Wenceslas Square**
The dominant features of the square are the bronze, equestrian statue of St Wenceslas (1912) and the National Museum behind it. St Wenceslas, a former king who was murdered by his brother Boleslav, is the patron saint of Bohemia ❶

OLD TOWN

NEW TOWN

Vltava

LOCATOR MAP
See Street Finder, maps 3, 4 & 6

The Assicurazioni Generali Building was where Franz Kafka *(see p68)* worked as an insurance clerk for 10 months in 1906–7.

The Monument to the Victims of Communism is on the spot where Jan Palach staged his protest. Since the Velvet Revolution in 1989 an unofficial shrine has been maintained here.

★ **Hotel Europa**
Both the façade and the interior of the hotel (1906) preserve most of their original Art Nouveau features ❹

Café Tramvaj 11

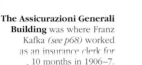

St Wenceslas Monument

State Opera
Meticulously refurbished in the 1980s, the interior retains the luxurious red plush, crystal chandeliers and gilded stucco of the original late-19th-century theatre ❻

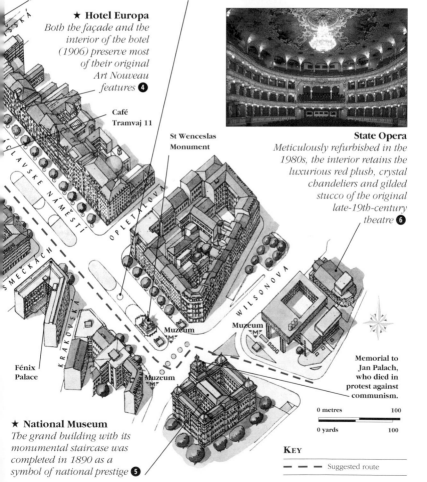

VÁCLAVSKÉ NÁMĚSTÍ

OPLETALOVA

WILSONOVA

VE SMEČKÁCH

KRAKOVSKÁ

Muzeum Ⓜ

Muzeum Ⓜ

Muzeum Ⓜ

Fénix Palace

Memorial to Jan Palach, who died in protest against communism.

0 metres · · · · 100

0 yards · · · · 100

★ **National Museum**
The grand building with its monumental staircase was completed in 1890 as a symbol of national prestige ❺

KEY

— — — Suggested route

Wenceslas Monument in Wenceslas Square

Wenceslas Square ❶
VÁCLAVSKÉ NÁMĚSTÍ

Map 3 C5. Můstek, Muzeum.
3, 9, 14, 24.

THE SQUARE HAS witnessed many key events in recent Czech history. It was here that the student Jan Palach burnt himself to death in 1969, and in November 1989 a protest rally in the square against police brutality led to the Velvet Revolution and the overthrow of Communism.

Wenceslas "Square" is something of a misnomer, for it is some 750 m (825 yd) long and only 60 m (65 yd) wide. Originally a horse market, today it is lined with hotels, restaurants, clubs and shops, reflecting the seamier side of global consumerism. The huge equestrian statue of St Wenceslas that looks the length of the square from in front of the National Museum was erected in 1912. Cast in bronze, it is the work of Josef Myslbek, the leading Czech sculptor of the late 19th century. At the foot of the pedestal there are several other statues of Czech patron saints. A memorial near the statue commemorates the victims of the former regime.

Church of Our Lady of the Snows ❷
KOSTEL PANNY MARIE SNĚŽNÉ

Jungmannovo náměstí 18. **Map** 3 C5.
22 22 46 243. Můstek.
Open 7am–7pm daily. 6:45am,
8am, 6pm Mon–Fri, 9am, 10:15am,
11:30am, 6pm Sun.

CHARLES IV FOUNDED this church to mark his coronation in 1347. The name refers to a 4th-century miracle in Rome, when the Virgin Mary appeared to the pope in a dream telling him to build a church to her on the spot where snow fell in August. Charles's church was to have been over 100 m (330 ft) long, but was never completed. The towering building we see today was just the presbytery of the projected church. Over 33 m (110 ft) high, it was finished in 1397, and was originally part of a Carmelite monastery. On the northern side there is a gateway with a 14th-century pediment that decorated the entrance to the monastery graveyard.

In the early 15th century a steeple was added, but further building was halted by the Hussite Wars (see pp26–7). The Hussite firebrand Jan Želivský preached at the church and was buried here after his execution in 1422. The church suffered considerable damage in the wars and in 1434 the steeple was destroyed. For a long time the church was left

to decay. In 1603 Franciscans restored the building. The intricate net vaulting of the ceiling dates from this period, the original roof having collapsed. Most of the interior decoration, apart from the 1450s pewter font, is Baroque. The monumental three-tiered altar is crowded with statues of saints, and is crowned with a crucifix.

Franciscan Garden ❸
FRANTIŠKÁNSKÁ ZAHRADA

Jungmannovo náměstí 18.
Map 3 C5. Můstek.
Open 6am–7pm daily.

ORIGINALLY the physic garden of a Franciscan monastery, the area was opened to the public in 1950 as a tranquil oasis close to Wenceslas Square. By the entrance is a Gothic portal leading down to a cellar restaurant – U františkánů (At the Franciscans). In the 1980s several of the beds were replanted with herbs, cultivated by the Franciscans in the 17th century.

Hotel Europa ❹
HOTEL EVROPA

Václavské náměstí 29. **Map** 4 D5.
22 42 28 117. Můstek.
3, 9, 14, 24. See **Where
to Stay** pp182–9, **Restaurants,
Pubs and Cafés** pp198–205.

THOUGH A trifle shabby in places, the Europa Hotel is a wonderfully preserved reminder of the golden age

Art Nouveau decoration on façade of the Hotel Europa

Façade of the State Opera, formerly the New German Theatre

of hotels. It was built in highly decorated Art Nouveau style between 1903 and 1906. Not only has its splendid façade crowned with gilded nymphs survived, but many of the interiors on the ground floor have remained virtually intact, including all the original bars, large mirrors, panelling and light fittings.

National Museum ❺
NÁRODNÍ MUZEUM

Václavské náměstí 68. **Map** 6 E1. ☎ 22 44 97 111. Ⓜ *Muzeum.* **Open** Oct–Apr: 9am–5pm daily; May–Sep: 10am–6pm (but closed first Tue of month). 📷 for a fee. ⓦ www.nm.cz

THE VAST Neo-Renaissance building at one end of Wenceslas Square houses the National Museum. Designed by Josef Schulz as a triumphal affirmation of the Czech national revival, the museum was completed in 1890. The entrance is reached by a ramp decorated with allegorical statues. Seated by the door are History and Natural History.

Inside, the rich marbled decoration is impressive, but overwhelms the collections devoted mainly to mineralogy, archaeology, anthropology, numismatics and natural history. The museum also has a Pantheon containing busts and statues of Czech scholars, writers and artists. It is decorated with many paintings by František Ženíšek, Václav Brožík and Vojtěch Hynais.

State Opera ❻
STÁTNÍ OPERA

Wilsonova 4. **Map** 4 E5. ☎ 22 42 27 266 (box office). Ⓜ *Muzeum.* **Open** for performances only. See **Entertainment** pp210–15. ⓦ www.opera.cz

THE FIRST THEATRE built here, the New Town Theatre, was pulled down in 1885 to make way for the present building. This was originally known as the New German Theatre, built to rival the Czechs' National Theatre

(see pp156–7). A Neo-Classical frieze decorates the pediment above the columned loggia at the front of the theatre. The figures include Dionysus and Thalia, the muse of comedy. The interior is stuccoed and original paintings in the auditorium and on the curtain have been preserved. In 1945 the theatre became the city's main opera house.

Mucha Museum ❼
MUCHOVO MUZEUM

Panská 7. **Map** 4 D4. ☎ 22 14 51 333. Ⓜ Můstek, Náměstí Republiky. 🚊 3, 5, 9, 14, 24, 26. **Open** 10am–6pm daily. ⓦ www.mucha.cz

THE 18TH-CENTURY Kaunicky Palace is home to the first museum dedicated to this Czech master of Art Nouveau. A selection of over 80 exhibits include paintings and drawings, sculptures, photographs and personal memorabilia. The central courtyard becomes a terrace for the café in the summer, and there is a museum shop offering exclusive gifts with Mucha motifs.

Main staircase of the National Museum

Art Nouveau in Prague

Façade detail,
10 Masaryk
Embankment

THE DECORATIVE STYLE known as Art Nouveau originated in Paris in the 1890s. It quickly became international as most of the major European cities quickly responded to its graceful, flowing forms. In Prague it was called "Secese" and at its height in the first decade of the 20th century but died out during World War I, when it seemed frivolous and even decadent. There is a wealth of Art Nouveau in Prague, both in the fine and decorative arts and in architecture. In the New Town and the Jewish Quarter (see pp80–93), entire streets were demolished at the turn of the century and built in the new style.

Praha House
This house was built in 1903 for the Prague Insurance Company. Its name is in gilt Art Nouveau letters at the top.

ARCHITECTURE

ART NOUVEAU made its first appearance in Prague at the Jubilee exhibition of 1891. Architecturally, the new style was a deliberate attempt to break with the 19th-century tradition of monumental buildings. In Art Nouveau the important aspect was ornament, either painted or sculpted, often in the form of a female figure, applied to a fairly plain surface. This technique was ideally suited to wrought iron and glass, popular at the turn of the century. These materials were light but strong. The effect of this, together with Art Nouveau decoration, created buildings of lasting beauty.

Hotel Central
Built by Alois Dryák and Bedřich Bendelmayer in 1900, the façade of this hotel has plasterwork shaped like tree branches.

Hlahol Choir Building, 1905
The architect Josef Fanta embellished this building with mosaics and sculptures by Karl Mottl and Josef Pekárek (see also p142).

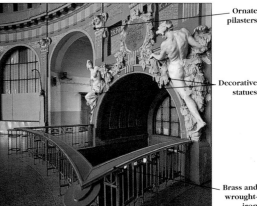

Ornate pilasters

Decorative statues

Brass and wrought-iron balustrade

Hlavní nádraží
Prague's main railway station was completed in 1901. With its huge interior glazed dome and elegant sculptural decoration, it shows many Art Nouveau features.

Hotel Meran
Finished in 1904, this grand Art Nouveau building is notable for its fine detailing inside and out.

DECORATIVE AND FINE ARTS

MANY PAINTERS, sculptors and graphic artists were influenced by Art Nouveau. One of the most successful exponents of the style was the artist Alfons Mucha (1860–1939). He is celebrated chiefly for his posters. Yet he designed stained glass (see p102), furniture, jewellery, even postage stamps. It is perhaps here, in the decorative and applied arts, that Art Nouveau had its fullest expression in Prague. Artists adorned every type of object – doorknobs, curtain ornaments, vases and cutlery – with tentacle- and plant-like forms in imitation of the natural world from which they drew their inspiration.

Postage Stamp, 1918
A bold stamp design by Alfons Mucha marked the founding of the Czechoslovak Republic.

Poster for Sokol Movement
Mucha's colour lithograph for the sixth national meeting of the Sokol gymnastic movement (1912) is in Tyrš's Museum (Physical Culture and Sports).

Záboj and Slavoj
These mythical figures (invented by a forger of old legends) were carved by Josef Myslbek for Palacký Bridge in 1895. They are now in Vyšehrad.

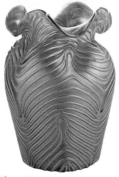

Glass Vase
This iridescent green vase made of Bohemian glass has relief decoration of intertwined threads. It is in the Museum of Decorative Arts.

Curtain Ornament and Candlestick
The silver and silk ornament adorns the Mayor's room of the Municipal House. The candlestick by Emanuel Novák with fine leaf design is in the Museum of Decorative Arts.

WHERE TO SEE ART NOUVEAU IN PRAGUE

Detail of doorway, Široká 9, Jewish Quarter

ARCHITECTURE
Apartment Building, Na příkopě 7
Hanavský Pavilion *p161*
Hlahol Choir Building, Masarykovo nábřeží 10
Hlavní nádraží, Wilsonova
Hotel Central, Hybernská 10 *see also p185*
Hotel Evropa *p146*
Industrial Palace *p162 and Four Guided Walks pp176–7*
Ministerstvo pro místní rozvoj *p67*
Municipal House *p64*
Palacký Bridge (Palackého most)
Praha House, Národní třída 7
Wiehl House *p144*

PAINTING
St Agnes's Convent *pp92–3*

SCULPTURE
Jan Hus Monument *p70*
Vyšehrad Garden and Cemetery *p160 and Three Guided Walks pp178–9*
Zbraslav Monastery *p163*

DECORATIVE ARTS
Mucha Museum *p147*
Museum of Decorative Arts *p84*
Prague Museum *p161*

Street-by-Street: Charles Square

Detail of house in Charles Square

THE SOUTHERN PART of the New Town resounds to the rattle of trams, as many routes converge in this part of Prague. Fortunately, the park in Charles Square (Karlovo náměstí) offers a peaceful and welcome retreat. Some of the buildings around the Square belong to the University and the statues in the centre represent writers and scientists, reflecting the academic environment. There are several Baroque buildings and towards the river stands the historic 14th-century Slavonic Monastery.

The Czech Technical University was founded here in 1867 in a grand Neo-Renaissance building.

Charles Square Centre

Church of St Wenceslas

RESLOVA

To the river

VÁCLAVSKÁ

KARLOVO

NA MORÁNI

★ **Church of St Cyril and St Methodius**
A plaque and a bullet-scarred wall are reminders of the siege of the church in 1942, when German troops mounted an assault on the Czech and Slovak agents who were hiding there **⑪**

To metro Karlovo náměstí

★ **Charles Square**
The centre of the square is a pleasant 19th-century park with lawns, formal flowerbeds, fountains and statues **⑩**

Church of St Cosmas and St Damian

POD SLOVANY

VYŠEHRADSKÁ

Slavonic Monastery Emauzy
In 1965 a pair of modern concrete spires by František Černý were added to the church of the 14th-century monastery **⑭**

TROJICKÁ

STAR SIGHTS

★ **Charles Square**

★ **Church of St Cyril and St Methodius**

Church of St John on the Rock
This view of the organ and ceiling shows the dynamic Baroque design of Kilian Ignaz Dientzenhofer **⑬**

Church of St Ignatius
The sun rays and gilded cherubs on the side altars are typical of the gaudy decoration in this Baroque church built for the Jesuits **8**

Eliška Krásnohorská was a 19th-century poet who wrote the libretti for Smetana's operas. A statue of her was put up here in 1931.

LOCATOR MAP
See Street Finder, map 5

A statue of Jan Purkyně (1787–1869), an eminent physiologist and pioneer of cell theory, was erected in 1961. It is the most recent of the many memorials in the square.

Jesuit College
Founded in the mid-17th century, this imposing building has been a hospital since the suppression of the Jesuits in 1773 (see pp30–31) **9**

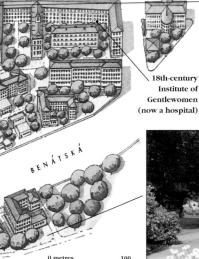

18th-century Institute of Gentlewomen (now a hospital)

Faust House
In the 18th century this house was owned by Count Ferdinand Mladota of Solopysky. The chemical experiments he performed reinforced the associations that gave the building its name **12**

Botanical Gardens
Though part of the Charles University, the gardens are open to the public and are known for their profusion of rare plants. This is an agreeable place to relax **15**

| 0 metres | 100 |
| 0 yards | 100 |

KEY

= = = Suggested route

Sculptures on the façade of the Jesuit College by Tomasso Soldati

Church of St Ignatius ❽

KOSTEL SV. IGNÁCE

Ječná 2. **Map** 5 C2. 〖 22 49 21 254. 〝M〟 Karlovo náměstí. 🚊 3, 4, 6, 10, 14, 18, 22, 23, 24. **Open** 6am– 6:30pm daily. ✝ frequent. 📷

WITH ITS WEALTH of gilding and flamboyant stucco decoration, St Ignatius is typical of the Baroque churches built by the Jesuits to impress people with the power and glamour of their faith. The architects were the same two men responsible for the adjoining Jesuit College, Carlo Lurago, who started work on the church in 1665, and Paul Ignaz Bayer, who added the tower in 1687.

The painting on the high altar of *The Glory of St Ignatius* (St Ignatius Loyola, the founder of the Jesuit order) is by Jan Jiří Heinsch.

The Jesuits continued to embellish the interior right up until the suppression of their order in 1773, adding stuccowork and statues of Jesuit and Czech saints.

Jesuit College ❾

JEZUITSKÁ KOLEJ

Karlovo náměstí 36. **Map** 5 B2. 〝M〟 Karlovo náměstí. 🚊 3, 4, 6, 10, 14, 16, 18, 22, 23, 24. **Closed** to the public.

HALF THE EASTERN side of Charles Square is occupied by the former college of the Jesuit order in the New Town. As in other parts of Prague, the Jesuits were able to demolish huge

swathes of the city to put up another bastion of their formidable education system. The college was built between 1656 and 1702 by Carlo Lurago and Paul Ignaz Bayer. The two sculptured portals are the work of Johann Georg Wirch who extended the building in 1770. After the suppression of the Jesuit order in 1773 the college was converted into a military hospital. It is now a teaching hospital and part of Charles University.

Charles Square ❿

KARLOVO NÁMĚSTÍ

Map 5 B2. 〝M〟 Karlovo náměstí. 🚊 3, 4, 6, 10, 14, 16, 18, 22, 23, 24.

SINCE THE MID-19TH CENTURY the square has been a park. Though surrounded by busy roads, it is a pleasant place to sit and read or watch people exercising their dachshunds.

The square began life as a vast cattle market, when Charles IV founded the New Town in 1348. Other goods sold in the square included firewood, coal and pickled herrings from barrels.

In the centre of the market Charles had a wooden tower built, where the coronation jewels were put on display once a year. In 1382 the tower was replaced by a chapel, from which, in 1437, concessions made to the Hussites by the pope at the Council of Basle were read out to the populace.

Church of St Cyril and St Methodius ⓫

KOSTEL SV. CYRILA A METODĚJE

Resslova 9. **Map** 5 B2. 〖 22 49 20 686. 〝M〟 Karlovo náměstí. 🚊 3, 4, 6, 10, 14, 16, 18, 22, 23, 24. **Open** Oct–Apr: 10am–4pm Tue–Sun; May– Sep: 10am–5pm Tue–Sun. 🚫

THIS BAROQUE CHURCH, with a pilastered façade and a small central tower, was built in the 1730s. It was dedicated to St Charles Borromeo and served as the church of a community of retired priests, but both were closed in 1783. In the 1930s the church was restored and given to the Czechoslovak Orthodox Church, and rededicated to St Cyril and St Methodius, the 9th-century "Apostles to the Slavs" *(see pp20–21)*. In May 1942 parachutists who had assassinated Reinhard Heydrich, the Nazi governor of Czechoslovakia, hid in the crypt along with members of the Czech Resistance. Surrounded by German troops, they took their own lives rather than surrender. Bullet holes made by the German machine guns during the siege can still be seen below the memorial plaque on the outer wall of the crypt, which now houses a museum of these times.

Main altar in the Church of St Cyril and St Methodius

Faust House ⑫
FAUSTŮV DŮM

Karlovo náměstí 40, 41. **Map** 5 B3.
ᵀᴹᵀ *Karlovo náměstí.* 🚊 *3, 4, 14,
16, 18.* **Closed** *to the public.*

P RAGUE THRIVES on legends
of alchemy and pacts with
the devil, and this Baroque
mansion has attracted many.
There has been a house here
since the 14th century when
it belonged to Prince Václav
of Opava, an alchemist and
natural historian. In the 16th
century it was owned by the
alchemist Edward Kelley. The
chemical experiments of
Count Ferdinand Mladota of
Solopysky, who owned the
house in the mid-18th century,
gave rise to its association
with the legend of Faust.

Baroque façade of Faust House

Church of St John
on the Rock ⑬
KOSTEL SV. JANA NA SKALCE

Vyšehradská 49. **Map** 5 B3.
📞 *22 49 15 371.* 🚊 *3, 4, 14, 16,
18, 24.* **Open** *for services only.*
✝ *8am Sun.* 🚫

O NE OF PRAGUE'S smaller
Baroque churches,
St John on the Rock is one of
Kilian Ignaz Dientzenhofer's
most daring designs. Its twin
square towers are set at a
sharp angle to the church's
narrow façade and the
interior is based on an
octagonal floorplan. The
church was completed in

1738, but the double staircase
leading up to the west front
was not added until the
1770s. On the high altar there
is a wooden version of Jan
Brokof's statue of St John
Nepomuk *(see p137)* which
stands on the Charles Bridge.

Slavonic Monastery
Emauzy ⑭
KLÁŠTER NA SLOVANECH-EMAUZY

Vyšehradská 49. **Map** 5 B3.
📞 *221 979 296.* 🚊 *3, 4, 14, 18, 24.*
Monastery church open *7am–7pm
Mon–Fri.* **Cloisters open** *by appoint-
ment.* ✝ *noon Mon, Wed, Fri.*
📷 🚫 ♿

B OTH THE MONASTERY and its
church were almost
destroyed in an American air
raid in 1945. During their
reconstruction, the church
was given a pair of modern
reinforced concrete spires.
The monastery was founded
in 1347 for the Croatian
Benedictines, whose services
were held in the Old Slavonic
language, hence its name
"Na Slovanech". In the course
of Prague's tumultuous
religious history it has since
changed hands many times.
In 1446 a Hussite order was
formed here, then in 1635 the
monastery was acquired by
Spanish Benedictines. In the
18th century the complex was
given a thorough Baroque
treatment, but in 1880 it was
taken over by some German
Benedictines, who rebuilt
almost everything in Neo-
Gothic style. The monastery
has managed to preserve some
historically important 14th-
century wall paintings in the
cloister, though many were
damaged in World War II.

**Remains of 14th-century wall
paintings in the Slavonic Monastery**

Botanical
Gardens ⑮
BOTANICKÁ ZAHRADA

Na slupi 16. **Map** 5 B3. 📞 *22 49 18
970.* 🚊 *18, 24.* 🚌 *148.*
Glasshouses open *10am–4pm daily.*
Gardens open *Jan–Feb: 8am–5pm
daily; Mar–Oct: 8am–6pm daily;
Nov–Dec: 8am–4pm daily.* 📷 🚫 ♿

C HARLES IV founded Prague's
first botanical garden in
the 14th century. This is a
much later institution. The
university garden was founded
in the Smíchov district in 1775,
but in 1897 it was moved to
its present site. The huge
greenhouses date from 1938.
Special botanical exhibitions
and shows of exotic birds and
tropical fish are often held
here. One star attraction of the
gardens is the giant water lily,
Victoria cruziana, whose huge
leaves can support a small
child. During the summer it
produces dozens of flowers
which only survive for a day.

Entrance to the university's Botanical Gardens

Octagonal steeple of St Catherine's

Church of
St Catherine 🟢
KOSTEL SV. KATEŘINY

Kateřinská. **Map** 5 C3. 🚊 *4, 6, 10, 16, 22, 23.* **Closed** to the public.

ST CATHERINE'S stands in the garden of a former convent, founded in 1354 by Charles IV to commemorate his victory at the Battle of San Felice in Italy in 1332. In 1420, during the Hussite revolution *(see pp26–7)*, the convent was demolished, but in the following century it was rebuilt by Kilian Ignáz Dientzenhofer as an Augustinian monastery. The monks remained here until 1787, when the monastery was shut down. Since 1822 it has been used as a hospital. In 1737 a new Baroque church was built, but the slender steeple of the old Gothic church was retained. Its conspicuous octagonal shape has gained it the nickname of "the Prague minaret".

Chalice
Restaurant 🟢
RESTAURACE U KALICHA

Na bojišti 14. **Map** 6 D3. 🏛 *29 61 89 600.* ᴍ *IP Pavlova.* 🚊 *4, 6, 10, 16, 22, 23.* **Open** *11am–11pm daily.* 📷 ♿ *See **Restaurants** pp198–205.*

THIS PILSNER URQUELL beer hall owes its fame to the novel *The Good Soldier Švejk* by Jaroslav Hašek. It was Švejk's favourite drinking

place and the establishment trades on the popularity of the best-loved character in 20th-century Czech literature. The staff dress in period costume from World War I, the era of this novel.

Dvořák Museum 🟢
MUZEUM ANTONÍNA DVOŘÁKA

Ke Karlovu 20. **Map** 6 D2. 🏛 *22 49 23 363.* ᴍ *IP Pavlova.* 🚌 *148.* **Open** *10am–5pm Tue–Sun and for concerts.* 📷 🚫 ♿ 🌐 www.nm.cz

ONE OF THE most enchanting secular buildings of the Prague Baroque, this red and ochre villa now houses the Antonín Dvořák Museum. On display are Dvořák scores and editions of his works, plus photographs and memorabilia of the great 19th-century Czech composer, including his piano, his viola and his desk.

The building is by the great Baroque architect Kilian Ignaz Dientzenhofer *(see p129)*. Just two storeys high with an elegant tiered mansard roof, the house was completed in 1720, for the Michnas of Vacínov and was originally known as the Michna Summer Palace. It later became known as Villa Amerika, after a nearby inn called Amerika. Between the two pavilions flanking the house is a fine iron

gateway, a replica of the Baroque original. In the 19th century villa and garden fell into decay. The garden statues and vases, from the workshop of Matthias Braun, date from about 1735. They are original but heavily restored, as is the interior of the palace. The ceiling and walls of the large room on the first floor, often used for recitals, are decorated with 18th-century frescoes by Jan Ferdinand Schor.

Church of
St Stephen 🟢
KOSTEL SV. ŠTĚPÁNA

Štěpánská. **Map** 5 C2. 🚊 *4, 6, 10, 16, 22, 23.* **Open** *only for services.* 🕆 *5pm Thu, 11am Sun.* 🚫

FOUNDED BY CHARLES IV in 1351 as the parish church of the upper New Town, St Stephen's was finished in 1401 with the completion of the multi-spired steeple. In the late 17th century the Branberg Chapel was built on to the north side of the church. It contains the tomb of the prolific Baroque sculptor Matthias Braun.

Most of the subsequent Baroque additions were removed when the church was scrupulously re-Gothicized in the 1870s by Josef Mocker. There are several fine Baroque paintings,

The Michna Summer Palace, home of the Dvořák Museum

Renaissance painted ceiling in the New Town Hall

however, including *The Baptism of Christ* by Karel Škréta at the end of the left hand aisle and a picture of St John Nepomuk *(see p137)* by Jan Jiří Heinsch to the left of the 15th-century pulpit. The church's greatest treasure is undoubtedly a beautiful Gothic panel painting of the Madonna, known as *Our Lady of St Stephen's*, which dates from 1472.

Gothic pulpit in St Stephen's

New Town Hall ⑳
NOVOMĚSTSKÁ RADNICE

Karlovo náměstí 23. **Map** 5 B1. Karlovo náměstí. 3, 4, 6, 10, 14, 16, 18, 22, 24. 22 49 47 131. **Tower open** May–Sep: 10am–6pm Tue–Sun.

IN 1960 a statue of Hussite preacher Jan Želivský was unveiled at the New Town Hall. It commemorates the first and bloodiest of many defenestrations. On 30 July 1419 Želivský led a crowd of demonstrators to the Town Hall to demand the release of some prisoners. When they were refused, they stormed the building and threw the Catholic councillors

out of the windows. Those who survived the fall were finished off with pikes.

The Town Hall already existed in the 14th century, the Gothic tower was added in the mid-15th century and contains an 18th-century chapel. In the 16th century it acquired an arcaded courtyard. After the joining-up of the four towns of Prague in 1784 the Town Hall ceased to be the seat of the municipal administration and became a courthouse and a prison. It is now used for cultural and social events, and its splendid Gothic hall can be hired for wedding receptions.

U Fleků ㉑

Křemencova 11. **Map** 5 B1. 22 49 34 019. Národní třída, Karlovo náměstí. 6, 9, 17, 18, 22. **Museum open** 10am–5pm Mon–Fri. See **Restaurants** pp198–205. www.ufleku.cz

RECORDS INDICATE that beer was brewed here as early as 1459. This archetypal Prague beer hall has been fortunate in its owners, who have kept up the tradition of brewing as

an art rather than just a means of making money. In 1762 the brewery was purchased by Jakub Flekovský, who named it U Fleků (At the Fleks). The present brewery, the smallest in Prague, makes a special strong, dark beer, sold only here. The restaurant now also features a small museum of Czech brewing history.

Church of St Ursula ㉒
KOSTEL SV. VORŠILY

Ostrovní 18. **Map** 3 A5. 22 49 30 502. Národní třída. 6, 9, 18, 22, 23. **Open** only for services. 5pm daily.

THE DELIGHTFUL Baroque church of St Ursula was built as part of an Ursuline convent founded in 1672. The original sculptures still decorate the façade and in front of the church stands a group of statues featuring St John Nepomuk (1747) by Ignaz Platzer the Elder. The light airy interior has a frescoed, stuccoed ceiling and on the various altars there are lively Baroque paintings. The main altar has one of St Ursula.

The adjoining convent has been returned to the Ursuline order and has now become a Catholic school. One part of the ground floor is still used for secular purposes – the Klášterní Vinárna (Convent Restaurant).

National Theatre ㉓
NÁRODNÍ DIVADLO

See pp156–7.

U Fleků, Prague's best-known beer hall

National Theatre ❷❸

NÁRODNÍ DIVADLO

A bronze sculpture in the foyer

THIS GOLD-CRESTED THEATRE has always been an important symbol of the Czech cultural revival. Work started in 1868, funded largely by voluntary contributions. The original Neo-Renaissance design was by the Czech architect Josef Zítek. After its destruction by fire *(see opposite)*, Josef Schulz was given the job of rebuilding the theatre and all the best Czech artists of the period contributed towards its lavish and spectacular decoration. During the late 1970s and early 80s the theatre was restored and the New Stage was built by architect Karel Prager.

The theatre from Marksmen's Island

A bronze three-horse chariot, designed by Bohuslav Schnirch, carries the Goddess of Victory.

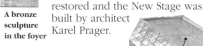

Laterna Magika

The New Stage auditorium

★ Auditorium
The elaborately-painted ceiling is adorned with allegorical figures representing the arts by František Ženíšek.

STAR FEATURES
★ Auditorium
★ Lobby Ceiling
★ Stage Curtain

The five arcades of the loggia are decorated with lunette paintings by Josef Tulka, entitled *Five Songs*.

★ Lobby Ceiling
This ceiling fresco is the final part of a triptych painted by František Ženíšek in 1878 depicting the Golden Age of Czech Art.

★ **Stage Curtain**
This sumptuous gold and red stage curtain, showing the origin of the theatre, is the work of Vojtěch Hynais.

Façade Decoration
This standing figure on the attic of the western façade is one of many figures representing the Arts sculpted by Antonín Wagner in 1883.

The startling sky-blue roof covered with stars, is said to symbolize the summit all artists should aim for.

The President's Box
The former royal box, lined in red velvet, is decorated with famous historical figures from Czech history by Václav Brožík.

NATIONAL THEATRE FIRE

On 12 August, 1881, just days before the official opening, the National Theatre was completely gutted by fire. It was thought to have been started by metalworkers on the roof. But just six weeks later, enough money had been collected to rebuild the theatre. It was finally opened two years late in 1883 with a performance of Czech composer Bedřich Smetana's opera *Libuše (see p79)*.

FURTHER AFIELD

VISITORS TO PRAGUE, finding the old centre packed with sights, tend to ignore the suburbs. It is true that once you start exploring away from the centre, the language can become more of a problem. However, it is well worth the effort, firstly to escape the crowds of tourists milling around the Castle and the Old Town Square, secondly to realize that Prague is a living city as well as a picturesque time capsule. Most of the museums and other sights

Vaulting in Church of St Barbara, Kutná Hora

in the first part of this section are easily reached by Metro, tram or even on foot. If you are prepared to venture a little further, do not miss the grand palace at Troja or the former monastery at Zbraslav, which houses the Asian Art collection of the National Gallery. The Day Trips *(pp168–70)* include visits to castles close to Prague and the historic spa towns of Marienbad and Karlsbad, which attracted the first tourists to Bohemia during the 19th century.

SIGHTS AT A GLANCE

Museums and Galleries
Mozart Museum ❶
Prague Museum ❻
National Technical Museum ❽
Trades Fair Palace pp164–5 ❾
Zbraslav Monastery ⓯

Monasteries
Břevnov Monastery ⓭

Historic Districts
Vyšehrad ❷
Žižkov ❹
Náměstí Míru ❺

Cemeteries
Olšany Cemeteries ❸

Historic Sites
White Mountain and
  Star Hunting Lodge ⓮

Historic Buildings
Troja Palace pp166–7 ⓫

Parks and Gardens
Letná Park ❼
Exhibition Ground and
  Stromovka Park ❿
Zoo ⓬

KEY

Central Prague

Greater Prague

✈ Airport

▬ Major road

= Minor road

15 km = 10 miles

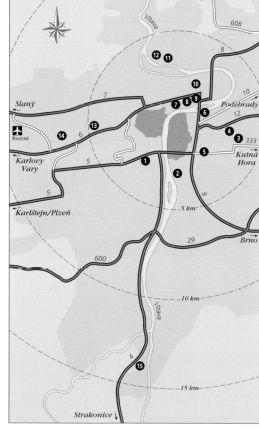

◁ **Part of the garden staircase at the 17th-century Troja Palace**

Bertramka, the villa that houses the Mozart Museum

Mozart Museum ●
BERTRAMKA

Mozartova 169. **(** 25 73 18 461.
M̂ Anděl. 4, 7, 9. **Open** Apr–
Oct: 9:30am–6pm daily; Nov–Mar:
9:30am–4pm daily.
W www.bertramka.cz

T HOUGH SLIGHTLY off the
beaten track, the museum
is well signposted because of
Prague's reverence for Mozart.
Bertramka is a 17th-century
farmhouse, enlarged in the
second half of the 18th century
into a comfortable suburban
villa. Mozart and his wife
Constanze stayed here as the
guests of the composer
František Dušek and his wife
Josefina in 1787, when Mozart
was working on *Don Giovanni*.

**Well-tended grave in the eastern
part of the Olšany Cemeteries**

He composed the overture
to the opera in the garden
pavilion just a few hours
before its premiere at the
Nostitz (now the Estates)
Theatre *(see p65)*. The house,
with a small exhibition on
Mozart, is at its best in the late
afternoon when it is quietest.
During the summer, recitals
take place on the terrace.

Vyšehrad ●

Map 5 B5. M̂ Vyšehrad. 7, 18, 24.

A ROCKY OUTCROP above the
Vltava, Vyšehrad means
"castle on the heights" *(see
pp178–9)*. It was fortified in
the 10th century and, at
times, used as the seat of the
Přemyslid princes. The area
has great historical and
mythological significance for
the Czech people, and in the
1870s it was chosen as the
site for a national cemetery.

Olšany Cemeteries ●
OLŠANSKÉ HŘBITOVY

Vinohradská 153, Jana Želivského. M̂
Želivského. **(** 26 73 10 652. 5,
6, 10, 11, 16, 19, 26. **Open** Mar–
Sep: 8am–7pm; Oct–Feb: 8am–6pm.

A T THE NORTHWEST corner
of the main cemetery
stands the small Church of
St Roch (1682), protector
against the plague – the
first cemetery was founded
here in 1679 specifically for
the burial of plague victims.
In the course of the 19th
century, the old cemetery
was enlarged and new ones

developed, including a
Russian cemetery,
distinguished by its old-
fashioned Orthodox church
(1924–5), and a Jewish one,
where Franz Kafka *(see p68)*
is buried. Tombs include
those of painter Josef Mánes
(1820–71) who worked during
the Czech Revival movement
(see pp32–3), and Josef Jungmann (1773–1847), compiler
of a five-volume Czech-
German dictionary.

Žižkov ●

M̂ Jiřího z Poděbrad, Želivského,
Flóra. **National Monument**, Vítkov,
U památníku. 133, 168, 207.
Closed to the public.

Equestrian statue of Jan Žižka

T HIS QUARTER of Prague was
the scene of a historic
victory for the Hussites *(see
pp26–7)* over Crusaders sent
by the Emperor Sigismund to
destroy them. On 14 July 1420
on Vítkov hill, a tiny force of
Hussites defeated an army of
several thousand well-armed
men. The determined, hymn-
singing Hussites were led by
the one-eyed Jan Žižka.
In 1877 the area around
Vítkov was renamed Žižkov in
honour of Žižka's victory, and
in 1950 a bronze equestrian
statue of Žižka by Bohumil
Kafka was erected on the hill.
About 9m (30 ft) high, this is
the largest equestrian statue
in the world. It stands in front
of the equally massive National
Monument (1927–32), built as
a symbol of the struggle for
independence of the Czechoslovak people. The Monument
later served as a mausoleum
for Klement Gottwald and
other Communist leaders.
Their remains have since
been removed, but the future
of the building is uncertain.

Relief by Josef Myslbek on portal of St Ludmilla in Náměstí Míru

An even more conspicuous landmark is a giant television transmitter, 260 m (850 ft) high. The locals have always been somewhat suspicious of the rays emanating from this great tube of reinforced concrete, built in 1984–8.

Náměstí Míru ❺

Map 6 F2. ᴹ *Náměstí Míru.* 🚊 *4, 6, 10, 16, 22.* 🚌 *135, 148, 272.* **Church of St Ludmila open** *only for services.*

THIS ATTRACTIVE SQUARE, with a well-kept central garden, is the focal point of the Vinohrady quarter. At the top of its sloping lawns stands the attractive, brick Neo-Gothic Church of St Ludmila (1888–93), designed by Josef Mocker, architect of the west end of St Vitus's Cathedral *(see pp100–3)*. Its twin octagonal spires are 60 m (200 ft) high. On the tympanum of the main portal is a relief of Christ with St Wenceslas and St Ludmila by the great 19th-century sculptor Josef Myslbek. Leading artists also contributed designs for the stained-glass windows and the church's colourful blue and gold interior.

The outside of the square is lined with attractive buildings, the most conspicuous being the Vinohrady Theatre, a spirited Art Nouveau building completed in 1907. The façade is crowned by two huge winged figures sculpted by Milan Havlíček, symbolizing Drama and Opera.

Prague Museum ❻

MUZEUM HLAVNÍHO MĚSTA PRAHY

Na Poříčí 52. **Map** 4 F3.
☎ *22 48 16 772/22 48 16 773.*
ᴹ *Florenc.* 🚊 *3, 8, 24, 26.* **Open** *9am–6pm Tue–Sun (9am–8pm first Thu of every month).* 📷 ⬚
W *www.muzeumprahy.cz*

THE COLLECTION records the history of Prague from primeval times. A new museum was built to house the exhibits in the 1890s. Its Neo-Renaissance façade is rich with stucco and sculptures, and the interior walls are painted with historic views of the city. On display are examples of Prague china and furniture, relics of the medieval guilds and paintings of Prague

through the ages. The most remarkable exhibit is the paper and wood model of Prague by Antonín Langweil. Completed in 1834, it covers 20 sq m (25 sq yards). The scale of the extraordinarily accurate model is 1:500.

Letná Park ❼

LETENSKÉ SADY

Map 3 A1. ᴹ *Malostranská, Hradčanská.* 🚊 *1, 8, 12, 18, 20, 22, 23, 25, 26.*

ACROSS THE RIVER from the Jewish Quarter, a large plateau overlooks the city. It was here that armies gathered before attacking Prague Castle. Since the mid-19th century it has been a wooded park.

On the terrace at the top of the granite steps that lead up from the embankment stands a curious monument – a giant metronome built in 1991. It was installed after the Velvet Revolution on the pedestal formerly occupied by the gigantic stone statue of Stalin leading the people, which was blown up in 1962. Nobody likes the metronome any more than they did Stalin and it may soon be replaced. A far more durable monument is the Hanavský Pavilion, a Neo-Baroque cast iron structure, built for the 1891 Exhibition. It was later dismantled and erected on its present site in the park, where it houses a popular restaurant and café.

View of the Vltava and bridges from Letná Park

National Technical Museum ❽
NÁRODNÍ TECHNICKÉ MUZEUM

Kostelní 42. ☎ *22 03 99 111.* 🚊 *1, 8, 25, 26.* **Open** *9am–5pm Tue –Sun.* 📷 🚫 🎞 👶 ♿ Ⓦ www.ntm.cz

Though it tries to keep abreast of all scientific developments, the museum's strength is its collection of machines from the Industrial Revolution to the present day, the largest of its kind in Europe. The section that attracts the most visitors is the History of Transportation in the vast central hall. This is filled with locomotives, railway carriages, bicycles, veteran motorcars and motorcycles, with aeroplanes and a hot-air balloon suspended overhead.

The photography and cinematography section is well worth a visit, as is the collection of astronomical instruments. The section on measuring time is also popular, especially on the hour when everything starts to chime at once. In the basement there is a huge reconstruction of a coal mine, with an assortment of tools tracing the development of mining from the 15th to the 19th century.

Trades Fair Palace ❾
VELETRŽNÍ PALÁC

See pp164–5.

Exhibition Ground and Stromovka Park ❿
VÝSTAVIŠTĚ A STROMOVKA

🚊 *1, 14, 17, 25.* **Exhibition Ground open** *10am–11pm daily.* 🌳 **Stromovka Park open** *24hrs daily.* **Lapidarium** ☎ *23 33 75 636.* **Open** *noon–5pm Tue–Fri, 10am–5pm Sat, Sun.* ♿

Laid out for the Jubilee of 1891, the Exhibition Ground has been used for trade fairs, sports and artistic events ever since. With its lively funfair, it is the obvious destination for a day out from central Prague with the children. All kinds of exhibitions, sporting events,

The Industrial Palace, centrepiece of the 1891 Exhibition Ground

spectacles and concerts are staged throughout the summer. The large park to the west was the former royal hunting enclosure and deer park, first established in the late 16th century. The name Stromovka means "place of trees", a reminder that a large area of the park was once a flourishing tree nursery. Opened to the public in 1804, the park is still a pleasant wooded area and an ideal place for a walk. The Lapidarium holds an exhibition of 11th–19th century sculpture, including some originals from the Charles Bridge (*see pp136-9*).

Troja Palace ⓫
TROJSKÝ ZÁMEK

See pp164–5.

Zoo ⓬
ZOOLOGICKÁ ZAHRADA

U trojského zámku 3. ☎ *26 61 12 111.* 🚇 *Holešovice, then* 🚌 *112.* **Open** *Jun–Aug: 9am–7pm daily; Apr, May, Sep, Oct: 9am–6pm daily; Nov–Feb: 9am–4pm daily; Mar: 9am–5pm daily.* 🌳 📷 ♿ 🍴 Ⓦ www.zoo.cz

Attractively situated on a rocky slope overlooking

the right bank of the Vltava, the zoo was founded in 1924. It now covers an area of 64 hectares (160 acres) and there is a chair lift to take visitors to the upper part. To travel on the lift, you can use an ordinary metro/tram ticket.

The zoo's 2,500 animals represent 500 species, 50 of them extremely rare in the wild. It is best known for its breeding programme of Przewalski's horses, the only species of wild horse in the world. It has also enjoyed success in breeding big cats, gorillas and orang-utans. In addition there are two pavilions, one for lions, tigers and other beasts of prey and one for elephants.

Red panda, relative of the famous giant panda, in Prague Zoo

Břevnov Monastery ⓭
BŘEVNOVSKÝ KLÁŠTER

Markétská 28. 📞 *22 04 06 111.* 🚇 *8, 22.* 🚌 *only, Sat & Sun; tour times vary.* 📷 💳 ⓦ *www.brevnov.cz*

FROM THE surrounding suburban housing, you would never guess that Břevnov is one of the oldest inhabited parts of Prague. A flourishing community grew up here around the Benedictine abbey founded in 993 by Prince Boleslav II *(see p20)* and Bishop Adalbert (Vojtěch) – the first monastery in Bohemia. An ancient well called Vojtěška marks the spot where prince and bishop are supposed to have met and decided to found the monastery.

The gateway, courtyard and most of the present monastery buildings are by the great Baroque architects Christoph and Kilian Ignaz Dientzenhofer *(see p129)*. The monastery Church of St Margaret is the work of Christoph. Completed in 1715, it is based on a floorplan of overlapping ovals, as ingenious as any of Bernini's churches in Rome. In 1964 the crypt of the original 10th-century church was discovered below the choir and is open to the public. Of the other buildings, the most interesting is the abbey's meeting hall, or Theresian Hall, with a painted ceiling dating from 1727.

White Mountain and Star Hunting Lodge ⓮
BÍLÁ HORA A HVĚZDA

🚇 *8, 22 (White Mountain), 18 (Star Hunting Lodge).* **White Mountain enclosure open** *24hrs daily.* **Star Hunting Lodge open** *Apr–Oct: 10am–5pm Tue–Sun.* 📷 💳

THE BATTLE of the White Mountain *(see p30–31)*, fought on 8 November 1620, had a very different impact for the two main communities of Prague. For the Protestants it was a disaster that led to 300 years of Habsburg domination;

Star Hunting Lodge

for the Catholic supporters of the Habsburgs it was a triumph, so they built a memorial chapel on the hill In the early 1700s this was converted into the grander Church of Our Lady Victorious and decorated by leading Baroque artists, including Václav Vavřinec Reiner.

In the 16th century the woodland around the battle site had been a royal game park. The hunting lodge, completed in 1556, survives today. This fascinating building is shaped as a six-pointed star – *hvězda* means star. In 1950 it was converted into a museum and dedicated to the writer of historical novels Alois Jirásek (1851–1930), and the painter Mikoláš Aleš (1852–1913). The museum also houses

exhibits relating to the Battle of the White Mountain and temporary exhibitions about Czech culture.

Zbraslav Monastery ⓯
ZBRASLAVSKÝ KLÁŠTER

Zámek Zbraslav. 📞 *25 79 21 638.* 🚌 *129, 240, 241, 243, 255, 360.* **Open** *10am–6pm Tue –Sun.* 📷 💳 ♿

IN 1279 WENCESLAS II founded a monastery to serve as the burial place for the royal family, though only he and Wenceslas IV were ever buried here. Destroyed during the Hussite Wars *(see pp26 7)*, the monastery was rebuilt in 1709–39, only to be abolished in 1785 and made into a factory. Earlier this century it was restored and in 1941 was given to the National Gallery. It now houses a unique collection of Asian art with exhibits including art and artefacts from China, Japan, India, South East Asia and Tibet. A collection of Japanese sculpture is featured which visually impaired visitors are encouraged to touch. The exhibition also includes a section dedicated to Islamic art. Informative guided tours are available.

Zbraslav Monastery, home to the National Gallery's Asian Art Collection

Trades Fair Palace **❾**

VELETRŽNÍ PALAC

THE NATIONAL GALLERY IN PRAGUE opened its Centre for Modern and Contemporary Art in 1995, housed in a reconstruction of a former Trades Fair building of 1929. Its vast, skylit spaces make an ideal backdrop for the collection, which ranges from French 19th-century art through superb examples of Impressionist and Post-Impressionist painting, to works by Munch, Klimt, Picasso and Miró, and a splendid collection of Czech modern art.

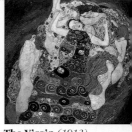

The Virgin *(1913)*
This colourful work epitomizes the distinctive, erotic Art Nouveau style of painter Gustav Klimt.

Screening Room

Third Floor

The Blind *(1926)*
This intriguing work by František Bílek is one of the sculptures on display.

Fourth Floor

★ George of Poděbrady and Matthias Corvinus
Mikuláš Aleš painted many patriotic historical scenes. Here, Corvinus King of Hungary, signs a treaty with King George in 1469.

Cleopatra *(1942-57)*
This painting by Jan Zrzavy clearly made him a major representative of Czech modern art.

Pomona *(1910)*
Aristide Maillol was a pupil of Rodin. This work is part of an exceptional collection of bronzes.

STAR SIGHTS

★ George of Poděbrady and Matthias Corvinus by Aleš

★ Evening in Hradčany by Schikaneder

★ Torso by Pešánek

★ Evening in Hradčany *(1909-13)*
This incredibly atmospheric painting by Jakub Schikaneder, typically captures the magic and nostalgia of the city of Prague at dusk.

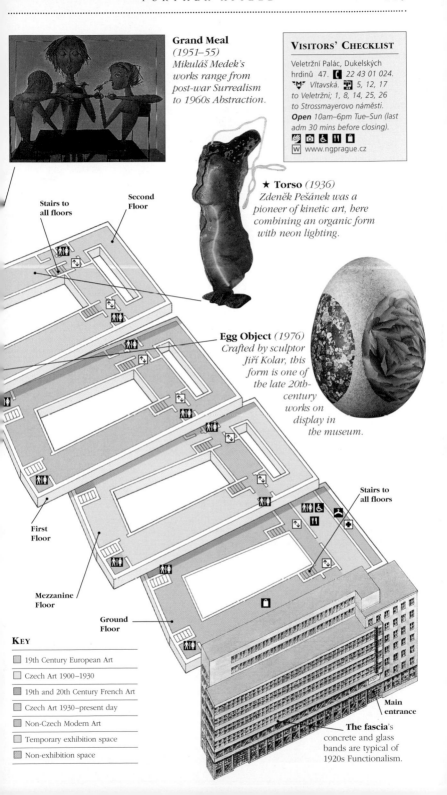

Grand Meal
(1951–55)
*Mikuláš Medek's
works range from
post-war Surrealism
to 1960s Abstraction.*

★ Torso *(1936)*
*Zdeněk Pešánek was a
pioneer of kinetic art, here
combining an organic form
with neon lighting.*

Egg Object *(1976)*
*Crafted by sculptor
Jiří Kolar, this
form is one of
the late 20th-
century
works on
display in
the museum.*

**Stairs to
all floors**

**Second
Floor**

**First
Floor**

**Mezzanine
Floor**

**Ground
Floor**

**Stairs to
all floors**

**Main
entrance**

The fascia's
concrete and glass
bands are typical of
1920s Functionalism.

KEY

- ☐ 19th Century European Art
- ☐ Czech Art 1900–1930
- ☐ 19th and 20th Century French Art
- ☐ Czech Art 1930–present day
- ☐ Non-Czech Modern Art
- ☐ Temporary exhibition space
- ☐ Non-exhibition space

Troja Palace **⓫**

TROJSKÝ ZÁMEK

O NE OF THE MOST STRIKING summer palaces in Prague, Troja was built in the late 17th century by Jean-Baptiste Mathey for Count Sternberg, a member of a leading Bohemian aristocratic family. Situated at the foot of the Vltava Heights, the exterior of the palace was modelled on a Classical Italian villa, while its garden was laid out in formal French style. The magnificent interior took over 20 years to complete and is full of extravagant frescoes expressing the Sternberg family's loyalty to the Habsburg dynasty. Troja houses a good collection of 19th-century art and costumes.

Terracotta urn on the garden balustrade

Defeat of the Turks
This turbaned figure, tumbling from the Grand Hall ceiling, symbolizes Leopold I's triumph over the Turks.

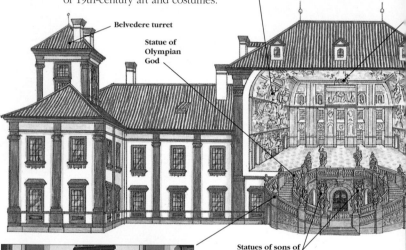

Belvedere turret

Statue of Olympian God

Statues of sons of Mother Earth

Personification of Justice
Abraham Godyn's image of Justice gazes from the lower east wall of the Grand Hall

★ Garden Staircase
The two sons of Mother Earth which adorn the sweeping oval staircase (1685–1703) are part of a group of sculptures by Johann Georg Heermann and his nephew Paul, depicting the struggle of the Olympian Gods with the Titans.

VISITORS' CHECKLIST

U trojského zámku 1, Prague 7. 283 851614. see p55. 112 from Holešovice. **Open** Apr–Oct: 10am–6pm Tue–Sun; Nov–Mar: 10am–5pm Sat & Sun. W www.citygalleryprague.cz

★ **Grand Hall Fresco**
The frescoes in the Grand Hall (1691–7), by Abraham Godyn, depict the story of the first Habsburg Emperor, Rudolph I, and the victories of Leopold I over the archenemy of Christianity, the Sublime Porte (Ottoman Empire).

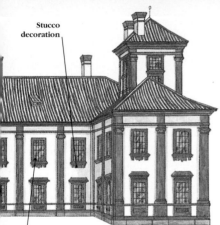

Stucco decoration

★ **LANDSCAPED GARDENS**

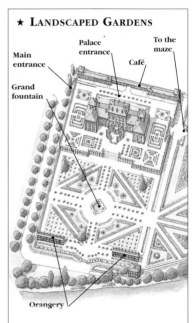

To the maze

Palace entrance

Main entrance

Café

Grand fountain

Orangery

STAR FEATURES

★ **Grand Hall Fresco**

★ **Landscaped Gardens**

★ **Garden Staircase**

Chinese Rooms
Several rooms feature 18th-century murals of Chinese scenes. This room makes a perfect backdrop for a ceramics display.

Sloping vineyards were levelled, hillsides excavated and terraces built to fulfil the elaborate and grandiose plans of French architect, Jean-Baptiste Mathey, for the first Baroque French-style formal gardens in Bohemia. The palace and its geometric network of paths, terracing, fountains, statuary and beautiful terracotta vases, is best viewed from the south of the garden between the two orangeries. The gardens have been carefully restored according to Mathey's original plans.

Day Trips from Prague

THE SIGHTS THAT ATTRACT most visitors away from the city are Bohemia's picturesque medieval castles. Karlstein, for example, stands in splendid isolation above wooded valleys that have changed little since the Emperor Charles IV hunted there in the 14th century. We have chosen four castles, very varied in character. There are regular organized tours *(see p219)* to the major sights around Prague, to the historic mining town of Kutná Hora and, if you have more time to spare, to the famous spa towns of Karlsbad and Marienbad in western Bohemia.

St George and Dragon, Konopiště

SIGHTS AT A GLANCE

Castles	Historic Towns
Veltrusy ❶	Kutná Hora ❺
Karlstein ❷	Karlsbad ❻
Konopiště ❸	Marienbad ❼
Křivoklát ❹	

KEY

▇	Central Prague
▢	Greater Prague
✈	Airport
══	Motorway
══	Major road
══	Minor road

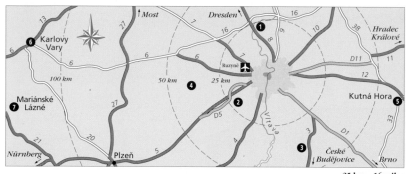

25 km = 16 miles

Veltrusy Château ❶

VELTRUSKÝ ZÁMEK

20 km (12 miles) north of Prague. 🚌 31 57 81 144/146. 🚆 from Smíchov to Kralupy nad Vltavou, then local bus. **Open** May–Sep: 8am–5pm Tue–Sun (Sep: from 9am); Oct, Nov, Apr: 9am–4pm Sat & Sun. 🎟 Ø ♿ (park only). **Nelahozeves Castle** 🚌 31 57 09 111. 🚆 from Masarykovo to Nelahozeves – zastávka. **Open** 9am–4pm Tue–Sun (Jun–Aug: to 5pm). 🎟 🍴 🏠 🛍

VELTRUSY is a small town beside the Vltava, famous for the 18th-century château built by the aristocratic Chotek family. The building is in the shape of a cross, with a central dome and a grand staircase decorated with statues representing the months of the year and the four seasons.

The estate was laid out as an English-style landscaped deer park, covering an area of 300 hectares (750 acres). Near the entrance there is still an enclosure with a herd of deer. The Vltava flows along one side and dotted around the grounds are several summer houses.

The Doric and Maria Theresa pavilions, the orangery and the grotto date from the late 18th century. The park is planted with some 100 different kinds of tree.

Just across the river, and easily accessible from Veltrusy by bus or train, is one of the most important Renaissance buildings in Bohemia, Nelahozeves Castle. The castle houses one of the finest private museums in Europe, the Lobkowicz Collection, which includes works by Veronese, Rubens, Canaletto and Velásquez, as well as rare books and manuscripts. The highlight of the collection, however, is *Haymaking*, a painting by Brueghel the Elder. The birthplace of Czech composer Antonín Dvorak is near the castle.

Karlstein Castle, built by Emperor Charles IV in the 14th century

Karlstein Castle ❷
KARLŠTEJN

25 km (16 miles) southwest of Prague.
📞 31 16 81 617/695. 🚆 from Hlavní
nádraží to Karlštejn (1.5 km/1 mile from
castle. The uphill walk takes around
40 minutes). **Open** Tue–Sun: Apr, Oct:
9am–4pm; May, Jun, Sep: 9am–5pm;
Jul–Aug: 9am–6pm; Nov: 9am–3pm.
📷 🎫 compulsory. 🚫

THE CASTLE WAS founded by
Charles IV as a country
retreat, a treasury for the crown
jewels and a symbol of his
divine right to rule the Holy
Roman Empire. It stands on a
crag above the River Berounka.
The castle is largely a 19th-
century reconstruction by Josef
Mocker. The original building
work (1348–67) was super-
vised by French master mason
Matthew of Arras, and then
by Peter Parler. You can still
see the audience hall and
the bedchamber of Charles
IV in the Royal Palace. On
the third floor, the Emperor's
quarters are below those of
the Empress.

The central tower houses the
Church of Our Lady, decorated
with faded 14th-century wall
paintings. A narrow passage
leads to the tiny Chapel of St
Catherine, the walls of which
are adorned with semiprecious
stones set into the plaster.

Konopiště Castle ❸

40 km (25 miles) southeast of Prague.
📞 31 77 21 366. 🚆 from Hlavní
nádraží to Benešov, then local bus.
Open Apr, Oct: 9am–12:30pm, 1–
3pm Tue–Fri, 9am–12:30pm, 1–4pm
Sat–Sun; May–Aug: 9am–12:30pm,
1–5pm Tue–Sun; Sep: 9am–12:30pm,
1–4pm Tue–Sun; Nov: 9am–3pm Sat
& Sun. 📷 🚫

THOUGH IT DATES back to the
13th century, this moated
castle is essentially a late 19th-
century creation. In between,
Konopiště had been rebuilt
by Baroque architect František
Kaňka and in front of the
bridge across the moat is a
splendid gate (1725) by Kaňka
and sculptor Matthias Braun.

In 1887 Konopiště was
bought by Archduke Franz
Ferdinand, who later became
heir to the Austrian throne. It

View of the castle at Křivoklát, dominated by the Great Tower

was his assassination in 1914
in Sarajevo that triggered off
World War I. To escape the
Habsburg court's harsh
disapproval of his wife,
Ferdinand spent much of his
time at Konopiště. He amassed
arms, armour and Meissen
porcelain, all on display in
the fine furnished interiors.
However, the abiding memory
of the castle is of the hundreds
of stags' heads lining the walls.

Hunting trophies at Konopiště

Křivoklát Castle ❹

45 km (28 miles) west of Prague. 📞
31 35 58 120. 🚆 from Smíchov to
Křivoklát (1 km /0.6 miles) from castle).
🚌 from Anděl. **Open** Mar, Nov, Dec:
9am–noon, 1–3pm Sat, Sun; Apr, Oct:
9am–noon, 1–3pm Tue–Sun; May, Sep:
9am–noon, 1–4pm Tue–Sun; Jun–Aug:
9am–noon, 1–5pm Tue–Sun. 📷 🚫

THIS CASTLE, like Karlstein,
owes its appearance to
the restoration work of Josef
Mocker. It was originally a
hunting lodge belonging to the
early Přemyslid princes and
the seat of the royal master of
hounds. In the 13th century
King Wenceslas I built a stone
castle here, which remained in
the hands of Bohemia's kings
and the Habsburg emperors
until the 17th century.

Charles IV spent some of his
childhood here and returned
from France in 1334 with his
first wife Blanche de Valois.
Their daughter Margaret was
born in the castle. To amuse
his queen and young princess,
Charles ordered the local vil-
lagers to trap nightingales and
set them free in a wooded
area just below the castle.
Today you can still walk
along the "Nightingale Path".

The royal palace is on the
eastern side of the triangular
castle. This corner is dominated
by the Great Tower, 42 m
(130 ft) high. You can still see
some 13th-century stonework,
but most of the palace dates
from the reign of Vladislav
Jagiello. On the first floor
there is a vaulted Gothic hall,
reminiscent of the Vladislav
Hall in the Royal Palace at
Prague Castle (see pp104–5).
It has an oriel window and a
beautiful loggia that was used
by sentries. Also of interest is
the chapel, which has a fine
Gothic altar carving. Below the
chapel lies the Augusta Prison,
so-called because Bishop Jan
Augusta of the Bohemian
Brethren was imprisoned here
for 16 years in the mid-16th
century. The dungeon now
houses a grim assortment of
instruments of torture.

Kutná Hora ❺

70 km (45 miles) east of Prague. ☎
32 75 12 378 (tourist information).
🚇 *from Hlavní nádraží, Masarykovo
nádraží or Holešovice to Kutná Hora,
then bus 1 to Kutná Hora-Město.* 🚌
from Florenc. **Church of St Barbara
open** *Nov–Mar: 9–noon, 2–4pm Tue–
Sun; Apr & Oct: 9–noon, 1–4pm Tue–
Sun; May–Sep: 9am–6pm.* 🏛 **Italian
Court open** *Nov–Feb: 10am–4pm daily;
Mar, Oct: 10am–5pm daily; Apr–Sep:
9am–6pm daily.* 🏛 **Hrádek open** *Apr,
Oct: 9am–5pm Tue–Sun; May, Jun, Sep:
9am–6pm Tue–Sun; Jul, Aug 10am–
6pm Tue–Sun.* 🏛 **Stone House open**
as Hrádek. 🌐 www.kutnahora.cz

T HE TOWN ORIGINATED as a
small mining community
in the second half of the 13th
century. When rich deposits of
silver were found, the king
took over the licensing of the
mines and Kutná Hora became
the second most important
town in Bohemia.

In the 14th century five to
six tonnes of pure silver were
extracted here each year,
making the king the richest
ruler in Central Europe. The
Prague *groschen*, a silver coin
that circulated all over Europe,
was minted here in the Italian
Court (Vlašský dvůr), so-called
because Florentine experts
were employed to set up the
mint. Strongly fortified, it was
also the ruler's seat in the town.

In the late 14th century a
superb palace was con-
structed with reception
halls and the Chapel of St
Wenceslas and St
Ladislav, below which lay
the royal treasury.

When the silver started
to run out in the 16th
century, the town began
to lose its importance;
the mint finally closed in
1727. The Italian Court
later became the town
hall. On the ground floor
you can still see a row
of forges. Since 1947 a
mining museum has
been housed in another
building, the Hrádek,
which was originally a
fort. A visit includes a
tour of a medieval mine.
There is museum in the
Stone House (Kamenný dům),
a restored Gothic building of
the late 15th century.

To the southwest of the
town stands the Church of St
Barbara, begun in 1380 by the
workshop of Peter Parler, also
the architect of St Vitus's
Cathedral *(see pp100–3).* The
presbytery (1499) has a fine
net vault and windows with
intricate tracery. The slightly
later nave vault is by royal
architect Benedikt Ried. Catch
the murals in the nave, many
of which show mining scenes.
The cathedral, with its three

The Italian Court, Kutná Hora's first mint

massive and tent-shaped spires
rising above a forest of flying
buttresses, is a wonderful
example of Bohemian Gothic.

Karlsbad ❻
KARLOVY VARY

140 km (85 miles) west of Prague.
🚇 *from Masarykovo nádraží.*
🚌 *from Florenc.*

L EGEND HAS IT that Charles IV
(see pp24–5) discovered
one of the sources of mineral
water that would make the
town's fortune when one of his
staghounds fell into a hot
spring. In 1522 a medical
description of the springs was
published and by the end of
the 16th century over 200 spa
buildings had been built there.
Today there are 12 hot mineral
springs – *vary* means hot
springs. The best-known is the
Vřídlo (Sprudel), which rises to
a height of 12 m (40 ft). At
72°C, it is also the hottest. The
water is good for digestive
disorders, but you do not have
to drink it; you can take the
minerals in the form of salts.

The town is also known for
its Karlovy Vary china and
Moser glass, and for summer
concerts and other cultural
events. The race course is
popular with the more sporting
invalids taking the waters.

Outstanding among the local
historic monuments is the
Baroque parish church of Mary

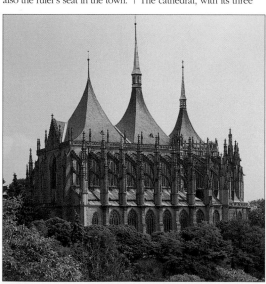

The three steeples of Kutná Hora's great Church of St Barbara

Magdalene by Kilian Ignaz Dientzenhofer (1732–6). More modern churches built for foreign visitors include a Russian church (1896) and an Anglican one (1877). The 19th-century Mill Colonnade (Mlýnská kolonáda) is by Josef Zítek, architect of the National Theatre *(see p156–7)* in Prague. There have been many royal visitors over the centuries – from Peter the Great of Russia in 1711 to England's Edward VII in 1907.

Marienbad ⑦

MARIÁNSKÉ LÁZNĚ

170 km (105 miles) west of Prague.
from [illegible].
from Florenc.

Bronze statue of a chamois at Jeleni skok (Stag's Leap), with a view across the valley to the Imperial Sanatorium, Karlsbad

THE ELEGANCE of Marienbad's hotels, parks and gardens has faded considerably since it was the playground of kings and princes at the turn of the century. The area's health-giving waters – *lázně* means bath (or spa) – have been known since the 16th century, but the spa was not founded until the beginning of the last century. The waters are used to treat all kinds of disorders; mud baths are also popular.

Most of the spa buildings date from the latter half of the 19th century. The great cast-iron colonnade with frescoes by Josef Vyletěl is still an impressive sight. In front of it is a "singing fountain", its jets of water now controlled by computer. Churches were provided for visitors of all denominations, including an Evangelical church (1857), an Anglican church (1879) and the Russian Orthodox church of St Vladimír (1902). Visitors can learn the history of the spa in the house called At the Golden Grape (U zlatého hroznu), where the German poet Johann Wolfgang von Goethe stayed in 1823. Musical visitors during the 19th century included the composers Weber, Wagner and Bruckner, while writers such as Ibsen, Gogol, Mark Twain and Rudyard Kipling also found its treatments beneficial. King Edward VII came here frequently. In 1905 he agreed to open the golf course (Bohemia's first), even though he hated the game.

There are many pleasant walks in the countryside around Marienbad, especially in the protected Slavkov Forest.

The cast-iron colonnade at Marienbad, completed in 1889

THREE GUIDED WALKS

RAGUE OFFERS some good opportunities for walking. In the centre of the city, many streets are pedestrianized and the most important sights are confined to quite a small area (see pp14–15). Here are three guided walks of varied character. The first passes through a main artery of the city, from the Powder Gate on the outskirts of the Old Town to St Vitus's Cathedral in Prague Castle, crossing the wonderful Charles Bridge at its mid-point. This is the Royal Coronation Route, followed for

House sign in Celetná Street
(See Royal Route Walk pp174–5)

centuries by Bohemian kings. Away from the busy centre, the second of the walks takes in the peace and tranquility of one of Prague's loveliest parks. Petřín Park is especially rewarding, also, for its spectacular views of the city. The final walk is in Vyšehrad. This is a peaceful, ancient fortress which is steeped in history and atmosphere, and the route includes a visit to the resting place of some of Prague's most famous citizens. The views from Vyšehrad of the Vltava and Prague Castle are unparalleled.

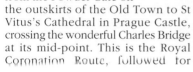

Charles Bridge at sunrise *(See the Royal Route Walk pp174–5)*

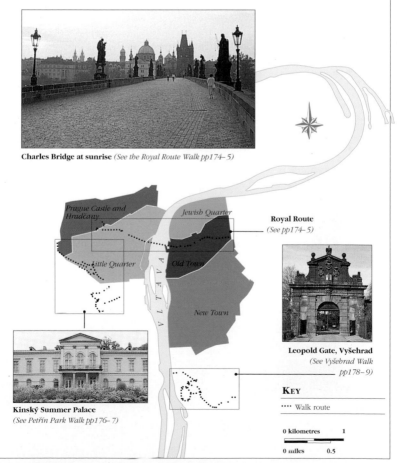

Prague Castle and Hradčany

Jewish Quarter

Royal Route
(See pp174–5)

Little Quarter

Old Town

VLTAVA

New Town

Leopold Gate, Vyšehrad
(See Vyšehrad Walk pp178–9)

Kinský Summer Palace
(See Petřín Park Walk pp176–7)

KEY

···· Walk route

0 kilometres 1

0 miles 0.5

◁ **View of the New Town from Petřín Park with the Church of St Lawrence in the foreground**

A 90-Minute Walk along the Royal Route

THE ROYAL ROUTE ORIGINALLY linked two important royal seats; the Royal Court – situated on the site of the Municipal House and where the walk starts – and Prague Castle, where the walk finishes. The name of this walk derives from the coronation processions of the Bohemian kings and queens who passed along it. Today, these narrow streets offer a wealth of historical and architecturally interesting sights, shops and cafés, making the walk one of Prague's most enjoyable. For more details on the Old Town, the Little Quarter and Hradčany turn to pages 60–79; 122–41 and 94–121 respectively.

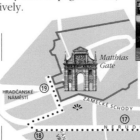

Figural *sgraffito* covers the façade of the Renaissance House at the Minute

History of the Royal Route

The first major coronation procession to travel along this route was for George of Poděbrady (*see p26*) in 1458. The next large procession took place in 1743, when Maria Theresa was crowned with great pomp – three Turkish pavilions were erected just outside the Powder Gate. September 1791 saw the coronation of Leopold II. This procession was led by cavalry, followed by mounted drummers, trumpeters and soldiers and Bohemian lords. Some 80 carriages came next, carrying princes and bishops. The most splendid were each drawn by six pairs of horses, flanked by servants with red coats and white leather trousers, and carried the ladies-in-waiting.

The last great coronation procession along the Royal Route – for Ferdinand V – was in 1836 with over 3,391 horses and four camels.

From the Powder Gate to Old Town Square

At Náměstí Republiky turn towards the Municipal House (*see p64*) and walk under the Gothic Powder Gate ① (*see p64*). Here, at the city gates, the monarch and a large retinue of church dignitaries, aristocrats, and foreign ambassadors were warmly welcomed by leading city representatives. The gate leads into one of Prague's oldest streets, Celetná (*see p65*). It was here the Jewish community and the crafts guilds, carrying their insignia, greeted their king.

The street is lined with Baroque and Rococo houses. At house No. 36 was the Mint ②. It moved here after the mint at Kutná Hora (*see p168*) was occupied

by Catholic troops in the Hussite Wars (*see pp26–7*). It minted coins from 1420 to 1784. The House of the Black Madonna ③ contains a museum of Czech Cubist art (*see p65*). Revellers would watch processions from the taverns, At the Spider ④ and At the Vulture ⑤.

House at the Black Madonna ③

At the end of Celetná Street is the Old Town Square ⑥ (*see pp66–9*). Here, the processions halted beside Týn Church ⑦ (*see p70*) for pledges of loyalty from the university. Keep to the left of the square, past No. 17, At the Unicorn ⑧, then No. 20, Smetana House, where the composer began a music school in 1848. Proceed to the Old Town Hall ⑨ (*see pp72–4*).

The distinct Baroque façade of the House at the Golden Well in Karlova Street ⑪

Matthias Gate

HRADČANSKÉ NÁMĚSTÍ ⑲

ZÁMECKÉ SCHODY   THUNOVSKÁ

⑰   NERUDOVA   LETENSKÁ

⑱   MALOSTRANSKÉ NÁMĚSTÍ ⑮   12-22   VOJAN SAD

⑯   MOSTECKÁ   JOSEFSKÁ   MÍŠEŇSKÁ

TRŽIŠTĚ

PROKOPSKÁ   LÁZEŇSKÁ

⑭   Little Quarter Towers

Here, the municipal guard and a band waited for the royal procession and city dignitaries cheered from the temporary balcony around the hall.

Along Karlova Street and across Charles Bridge

Walk past the sgraffitoed façade of the House at the Minute and into Malé náměstí ⑩, where merchants waited with members of the various religious orders. Bear left off the square, then turn right into

good omen. But only a few months later he died. Walk under the Old Town Bridge Tower ⑫ and over Charles Bridge ⑬ and then under the Little Quarter Towers ⑭ (see pp136–9).

The Little Quarter

The walk now follows Mostecká Street. On entering the Little Quarter the mayor handed the city keys to the king and the artillery fired a salute. At the end of this street is Little Quarter Square ⑮ (see p124) and the Baroque

Sculpture of Moor by Ferdinand Brokof on Morzin Palace

turn sharp right and walk up the Castle ramp, which leads you to Hradčanské Square. The route ends at the Castle's Matthias Gate (see p43) ⑲. The procession ended with the coronation held at St Vitus's Cathedral.

The Old Town from Charles Bridge ⑬

gallery-filled Karlova Street. Beyond Husova Street is an attractive Baroque house, At the Golden Well ⑪. Further on is the 16th-century Clementinum (see p79), where the clergy stood. You then pass into Knights of the Cross Square (see p79). When Leopold II's procession passed through here the clouds lifted, which was considered to be a

church St Nicholas's ⑯ (see pp128–9). The procession passed the church to the sound of its bells ringing.

Leave this picturesque square by Nerudova Street ⑰ (see p130). Poet and writer Jan Neruda, who immortalized hundreds of Little Quarter characters in books like *Mala Strana Tales*, grew up and worked at No. 47, The Two Suns ⑱. Cross the street,

KEY

•••	Walk route
☆	Good viewing point
Ⓜ	Metro station
▥	Tram stop
—	Hunger wall

0 metres	300
0 yards	300

TIPS FOR WALKERS

Starting point: Náměstí Republiky.
Length: 2.4 km (1.5 miles).
Getting there: Line B goes to Náměstí Republiky metro station. At Hradčany you can get tram 22 back into town.
Stopping-off points: Rest beneath the sunshades of the outdoor cafés on Old Town Square or Karlova Street in the summer. On Malostranské náměstí you can enjoy the restaurant Square and in Karlova the café Clementin (at Hotel Clementin).

Coronation procession passing through the Knights of the Cross Square

A Two-Hour Walk through Petřín Park

Part of the charm of this walk around this large and peaceful hillside park are the many spectacular views over the different areas of Prague. The Little Quarter, Hradčany and the Old Town all take on a totally different aspect when viewed from above. The tree-covered gardens are dotted with châteaux, pavilions and statues and crisscrossed by winding paths leading you to secret and unexpected corners. For more on the sights of Petřín Hill see pages 140–41.

One of the gateways in the Hunger Wall ⑤

Actress Hana Kvapilová's statue, near Kinský Summer Palace ①

Kinský Square to Hunger Wall

The walk starts at náměstí Kinských in Smíchov. Enter Kinský Garden through a large enclosed gateway. This English-style garden was founded in 1827 and named after the wealthy Kinský family, supporters of Czech culture in the 19th century.

Take the wide cobbled and asphalt path on your left to the Kinský Summer Palace ①. This 1830s pseudo-classical building was designed by Jindřich Koch and its façade features Ionic columns terminating in a triangular tympanum. Inside the building is a large hall of columns with a triple-branched staircase beautifully decorated with statues. The Ethnographical Museum is housed here; however, it is closed at present for reconstruction.

Next to the museum is a 1913 statue of the actress Hana Kvapilová.

About 50 m (150 ft) above the palace is the lower lake ②, where a small waterfall trickles into a man-made pond. Keep going up the hill until you reach the Church of St Michael ③, on your left. This 18th-century wooden folk church was moved here from a village in the Ukraine.

Follow the path up the hill for about 20 m (60 ft), then go to the top of the steps to a wide asphalt path known as the Observation Path for its beautiful views of the city. Turn right and further on your left is the small upper lake ④ with a 1950s bronze statue of a seal at its centre. Keep following the Observation Path; ahead of you stands a Neo-Gothic gate. This allows you to pass through the city's old Baroque fortifications.

Hunger Wall to Observation Tower

Continue along the path to the Hunger Wall ⑤ *(see pp140–41)*. This was a major part of the Little Quarter's fortifications; the wall still runs from Újezd

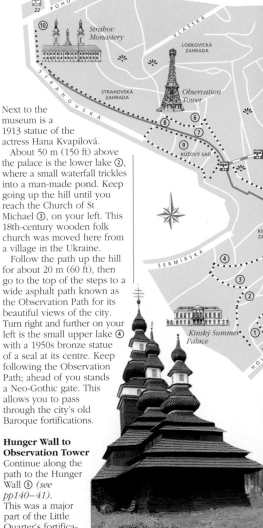

Church of St Michael ③

Street across Petřín Hill and up to Strahov Monastery. Passing through the gate in the wall brings you to Petřín Park. Take the wide path to the left below the wall and walk up the hill beside the wall until you cross the bridge which spans the funicular railway *(see p141)*. Below on your right you can see the

Sunbathers on Petřín Hill

Nebozízek restaurant *(see p202)* famed for its views. On either side of the path are small sandstone rockeries. Most are entrances to reservoirs, built in the 18th and 19th centuries, to bring water to Strahov Monastery; others are left over from the unsuccessful attempts at mining the area. Walk up to the summit of the hill. On your right is the Mirror Maze ⑥ *(see p140)*. Facing the maze is the 12th-century St Lawrence's Church ⑦ *(see pp140–41)*, renovated in 1740 in the Baroque style.

KEY

••• Walk route

Good viewing point

Tram stop

Funicular railway

— Hunger wall

0 metres   300

0 yards   300

Observation Tower to Strahov Monastery

A little further on stands the Observation Tower ⑧ *(see p140)*. This steel replica of the Eiffel Tower in Paris is 60 m (200 ft) high. Opposite the tower is the main gate of the Hunger Wall. Pass through, turn left and follow the path to the Rose Garden ⑨.

The garden was planted by the city of Prague in 1932, and features a number of attractive sculptures. When you look down to the far end of the garden you can see The Observatory *(see p140)*. This was rebuilt from a municipal building in 1928 by the Czech Astronomical Society and was then modernized in the 1970s. It now houses a huge telescope and is open in the evenings to the public.

Returning to the Observation Tower, follow the wall on the left, passing some chapels of the Stations of the Cross dating from 1834. Then pass through a gap in the Hunger Wall, turn right, and walk past a charming Baroque house. About 50 m (150 ft) beyond this, you pass through another gap in the Hunger Wall on your right. Turn left into a large orchard above Strahov Monastery ⑩ *(see pp120–21)* for spectacular views of the city. Leave by the same hole in the wall that you came in by, turn right, and walk downhill along the wall, through the orchard and past tennis courts

Sgraffitoed façade of the Calvary Chapel next to the Church of St Lawrence ⑦

to the Strahov Monastery courtyard. You can catch tram 22 from here, or linger in the peaceful monastery grounds. If you feel energetic you can walk back down the hill.

TIPS FOR WALKERS

Starting point: náměstí Kinských in Smíchov.
Length: 2.7 km (1.7 miles). The walk includes steep hills.
Getting there: The nearest metro station to the starting point is Anděl. Trams 6, 9 and 12 go to náměstí Kinských (Kinský Square).
Stopping-off points: There is a restaurant, Nebozízek, half way up Petřín Hill and during the summer a few snack bars are open at the summit of the Hill near the Observation Tower.

Hradčany and the Little Quarter from the summit of Petřín Hill

A 60-Minute Walk in Vyšehrad

ACCORDING TO ANCIENT LEGEND, Vyšehrad was the first seat of Czech royalty. It was from this spot that Princess Libuše is said to have prophesied the future glory of the city of Prague *(see pp20–21)*. However, archaeological research indicates that the first castle on Vyšehrad was not built until the 10th century. The fortress suffered a turbulent history and was rebuilt many times. Today, it is above all a peaceful place with parks and unrivalled views of the Vltava valley and Prague. The fascinating cemetery is the last resting place of many famous Czech writers, actors, artists and musicians.

Decorative sculpture on the Baroque Leopold Gate ⑤

The ruin of Libuše's Baths on the cliff face of Vyšehrad Rock ⑩

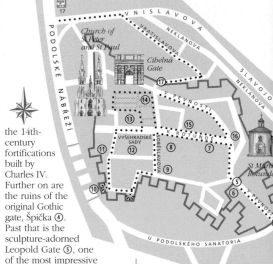

V Pevnosti

From Vyšehrad metro ① make your way up the steps facing the metro exit to the Congress Centre Prague ② straight ahead. Walk west along its large granite terrace, go down the incline and straight ahead into the quiet street Na Bučance. Cross the road, turn right at the end, and you find yourself on V Pevnosti, facing the brick walls of the original Vyšehrad Citadel. Ahead of you is the west entrance to the fortress, the mid-17th-century Tábor Gate ③. Past this gate on the right are the ruins of

the 14th-century fortifications built by Charles IV. Further on are the ruins of the original Gothic gate, Špička ④. Past that is the sculpture-adorned Leopold Gate ⑤, one of the most impressive parts of these 17th-century fortifications. It adjoins the brick walls ⑥ that were widened during the French occupation of 1742.

K rotundě to Soběslavova Street

Turn right out of the gate and just after St Martin's Rotunda, turn left into K rotundě. A few metres on your left, almost concealed behind high walls, is the New Deanery ⑦. Situated at the corner of K rotundě and Soběslavova streets is the Canon's House ⑧. Turn left down Soběslavova to see the excavations of the foundations of the

Basilica of St Lawrence ⑨. This was built by Vratislav II, the first Bohemian king, in the late 11th century, but was destroyed by the Hussites *(see pp26–7)* in 1420. About 20 m (65 ft) past the basilica, turn right on to the fortified walls for a stunning view of Prague.

KEY

••• Walk route

☼ Good viewing point

Ⓜ Metro station

🚋 Tram stop

— Castle wall

0 metres	200
0 yards	200

18th-century engraving by I G Ringle, showing Vyšehrad and the Vltava

Vyšehrad Rock

The wooded outcrop of rock on which Vyšehrad was built drops in the west to form a steep rock wall to the river – a vital defensive position. On the summit of the rock are the Gothic ruins of the so-called Libuše's Baths ⑩. This was a defence bastion of the medieval castle. To the left of the bastion is a grassy patch where the remains of a 14th-century Gothic palace ⑪ have been found.

The elaborate memorial to the composer Antonín Dvořák in Vyšehrad Cemetery ⑭

Vyšehrad Park

The western part of Vyšehrad has been transformed into a park. Standing on the lawn south of the Church of St Peter and St Paul are four groups of statues ⑫ by the 19th-century sculptor Josef Myslbek. The works represent figures from early Czech history – including the legendary Přemysl and Libuše (see pp20–21). The statues were originally on Palacký Bridge, but were damaged during the US bombardment of February 1945. After being restored, they were taken to Vyšehrad Park. The park was the site of a Romanesque palace, which was connected to the neighbouring church by a bridge. Another palace was built here in the reign of Charles IV (see pp24–5).

The Church of St Peter and St Paul

This twin-spired church ⑬ dominates Vyšehrad. It was founded in the latter half of the 11th century by Vratislav II and was enlarged in 1129. In the mid-13th century it burned down and was replaced by an Early Gothic church. Since then it has been redecorated and restored many times in a variety of styles. In 1885, it was finally rebuilt in Neo-Gothic style, the twin steeples being added in 1902. Note the early-12th-century stone coffin, thought to be of St Longinus, and a mid-14th-century Gothic panel painting *Our Lady of the Rains* on the altar in the third chapel on the right.

Vyšehrad Cemetery and the Pantheon

The cemetery ⑭ was founded in 1869 as the burial place for some of the country's most famous figures, such as Bedřich Smetana (see p79). Access is through a gate at the front. On the east side of the cemetery is the Slavín (Pantheon) – built in 1890 for the most honoured citizens of the Czech nation, including the sculptor Josef Myslbek.

Leave the cemetery by the same gate and return down K rotundě. On your left is the Devil's Column ⑮, said to be left by the devil after losing a wager with a priest. At the end is St Martin's Rotunda (see p44) ⑯, a small Romanesque church built in the late 11th century and restored in 1878. Turn left, walk downhill to Cihelná (Brick) Gate ⑰, built in 1741 and home to a small museum that houses six of the original statues from Charles Bridge. Go down Vratislavova Street to Výtoň tram stop on the Vltava Embankment.

The Neo Gothic Church of St Peter and St Paul ⑬

Statue of Přemysl and Princess Libuše by Josef Myslbek in Vyšehrad Park ⑫

TIPS FOR WALKERS

Starting point: Vyšehrad metro station, line C.
Length: 1.5 km (1 mile).
Getting there: The walk starts at Vyšehrad metro station and ends at Výtoň tram stop. Trams 3, 17 and 19 go back to the city centre.
Stopping-off points: Relax in the park next to the church of St Peter and St Paul. There is a café in front of the Basilica of St Lawrence and more outdoor cafés in the summer.

TRAVELLERS'
NEEDS

WHERE TO STAY

INCE THE "VELVET REVOLUTION" of 1989, Prague has become one of the most visited cities in Europe. Thanks to investment in new hotels, helped by huge injections of foreign capital, Prague has developed enough accommodation to meet every tourist need. Many old hotels have been rebuilt, while others have been fully re-vamped. Most of the renovated hotels are as smart as any in Europe – and they are often just as expensive. Unfortunately there is little scope for the budget traveller.

Doorman at the exclusive Palace hotel (see p189)

The few cheap hotels tend to be old-fashioned places in the centre of the city, or smaller, pension-type hotels located in the suburbs. We have inspected over 100 hotels in every price bracket in Prague, and on pages 186–9 we recommend 30 of those that offer especially good value. A cheap alternative is to stay in a flat or a room in a private home, which is usually booked by an agency (see p184). Hostels and campsites offer other budget options (see p185).

The Ungelt hotel (see p187)

WHERE TO LOOK

AS PRAGUE is such a small city, it is best to stay near the centre close to all the main sights, restaurants and shops. Most hotels are found around Wenceslas Square. Here you are at the hub of everything, and the prices of some (but not all) of the hotels reflect this. Another popular area is the nearby Náměstí Republiky, but the best area is around Old Town Square, a few minutes' walk from Charles Bridge. Hotels here include large, international establishments, old-fashioned Czech places, and some small, much more exclusive hotels.

To the south, in the New Town, there are a few cheaper hotels only a few metro stops from Old Town Square. But the area is less picturesque and some of the streets suffer from heavy volumes of traffic.

For a view of the river Vltava, stay in the Jewish Quarter, although most hotels here are new and expensive. There are also a few botels (floating hotels) moored along the embankments away from the city centre. They are a bit cheaper, but the small cabins are very cramped and uncomfortable, and most of the boats would benefit from some renovation.

Over Charles Bridge, in the Little Quarter, you will find a handful of interesting hotels in delightful surroundings, but there are far fewer by Prague Castle in Hradčany. Further north of this area, there are some large and particularly unappealing hotels. The city's suburbs too, have a number of rather nondescript places a few of these being new. These have some good

facilities, but are often as expensive as their equivalents in the centre with the added inconvenience of travelling time and cost – the metro stops at midnight and taxis can become expensive.

HOW TO BOOK

TO RESERVE a room you can book online or send a letter by fax (the best deals are often done online; a popular website is www.HRS.com). It is important to receive written confirmation of your booking by letter or fax in advance, something that will save you time and trouble when you arrive. Most hotel receptionists speak English, so you can always ring them for advice, otherwise ask your tour operator for help;

Pool-side bar at the luxury Praha Renaissance (see p187)

a number of UK operators specialize in Prague *(see p184)*. When arriving by car, park in the hotel garage or ask at reception about secure parking in the area.

FACILITIES

F OLLOWING THE large investment in many of Prague's hotels, most rooms now have en suite WC and shower or bath, telephone and TV, which may also offer video and satellite channels. Many hotels offer a reasonably-priced laundry service, and the larger hotels usually have 24-hour room service and mini bars. Guests are expected to vacate rooms by midday, but most hotels are happy to keep luggage safe if you are leaving later. Foreign-owned hotels sometimes import managers, but the Czech staff generally speak good English so you should encounter few communication problems.

DISCOUNT RATES

T HE PRICE STRUCTURE for hotels in Prague is fairly flexible. One way to get a cheap rate is to turn up at the hotel and negotiate, although this practice is being phased out. The popular seasons are Christmas, New Year and Easter, when rooms are often hard to find. For cheap rooms in summer it is worth looking at student houses. Most of these have two bedrooms and a kitchen on the same floor, plus a small shop selling hot and cold drinks.

HIDDEN EXTRAS

A LL HOTELS include tax (currently at 19%) and service charges in their tariff, but do check these details when you book. Telephone charges can be a shock when you receive your bill so be aware of the mark-up rate. All telephone boxes in the city take phone cards and many take credit cards; phone cards are much cheaper than using cash *(see p224)*. Some expensive hotels charge an extra fee for

The Paříž is a national monument *(see p187)*

breakfast, others include a continental breakfast, but hot dishes cost extra. Buffet-style continental breakfasts are popular, and usually offer fresh fruit, cereals, yogurt, muesli, cold meat and cheese, and juice, jugs of coffee and tea.

Tipping is now common and is expected in many hotels. As in most countries, single travellers receive no favours. There are few single

The modern Hilton hotel dominates the area *(see p189)*

rooms, particularly in newer hotels, and a supplement is charged for single occupancy of a double room; expect to pay about 70–80% of the standard rate.

DISABLED TRAVELLERS

W HEELCHAIR accessibility to hotels on pages 187–9 represents each hotel's own assessment. For information on accommodation for the disabled, write to the Czech Association of Persons with Disabilities *(see p226)*, or contact the Embassy of the Czech Republic in your country.

TRAVELLING WITH CHILDREN

C HILDREN are accommodated by most hotels, either in family rooms or with extra beds, but Prague is not geared to their needs. Hotel breakfasts offer plenty of choice, and although all the fresh milk is pasteurized, hotels also provide long life milk. Few places offer high-chairs or baby-sitters. It is worth asking if there are discounts, or if children can stay free in parents' rooms.

DIRECTORY

UK AGENCIES

British Airways Holidays
London Road,
Crawley, West Sussex
RH10 2XA.
[C] 0870 442 3820.
[W] www.britishairways.com/holiday

Čedok Travel
Suite 22–23,
Morley House,
314–322 Regent Street,
London W1B 3BG.
[C] 020 7580 3778.
[W] www.cedok.co.uk/prague

Cresta Holidays
Tabley Court,
32 Victoria St,
Altrincham,
Cheshire WA14 1E2.
[C] 0870 16 10 900.
[W] www.cresta holidays.co.uk

Crystal Holidays
Kings Place,
Wood Street,
Kingston-upon-Thames,
Surrey KT1 1JY.
[C] 0870 160 90 30.
[W] www.crystal holidays.co.uk

Czech Tourist Centre
16 Frognal Parade,
Finchley Road,
London NW3 5HG.
[C] 020 7794 3263/4. [W]
www.czechtourism.com

Osprey Holidays
Broughton Market,
Edinburgh EH3 6NU.
[C] 0870 56 05 605.
[W] www.osprey-holidays.co.uk

Page & Moy Ltd.
136 & 140 London Road,
Leicester LE2 1EN.
[C] 0870 01 06 460.
[FAX] 0870 01 06 449.
[W] www.page-moy.co.uk

Prospect Music and Art Tours
36 Manchester Street,
London W1M 5PE.
[C] 020 7486 5704.
[FAX] 020 7486 5868.
[W] www.prospect tours.com

Thomson Tour Operations Holiday Shop
Albert House,
Tindall Bridge, Edward St,
Birmingham B1 2RA.
[C] 0121 252 3669.
[FAX] 0121 236 7030.

Travelscene
Travelscene House
11–15 St Ann's Road,
Harrow, Middlesex
HA1 1LQ.
[C] 020 8427 8800.
[FAX] 020 8861 5083.
[W] www.travelscene.co.uk

US AGENCIES

Central Europe Holidays
Suite 1402, 50 E. 42nd St
New York, NY 10017.
[C] 212 490 33 13.
[FAX] 212 490 76 94.
[W] www.tourdeal.com

Friends of Czech Greenways
Suite 1B, 515 Avenue I
Brooklyn, NY 11230.
[C] 718 258 54 68.
[FAX] 718 258 56 32.
[W] www.praguevienna greenways.org

FLATS AND ROOMS IN PRIVATE HOMES

IN UK

The Czechbook
Jopes Mill, Trebrownbridge,
Nr. Liskard,
Cornwall PL14 3PX.
[C] & [FAX] 01503 240 629.
[@] agnes.michael@czechbook.com
[W] www.czechbook.com

Regent Holidays
15 John Street,
Bristol BS1 2HR.
[C] 01179 211 711.
[FAX] 01179 254 866.
[W] www.regent-holidays.co.uk

Rosie Jackson Travel
57 Queens Road,
London SW14 8PH.
[C] 020 8878 0088.
[FAX] 020 8878 0464.
[@] rosie@rosiej.demon.co.uk.
[W] www.rosiejackson travel.com

IN PRAGUE

Akasi
Jungmannovo náměstí 9.
Map 3 C5.
[C] 22 22 42 354.
[FAX] 22 42 37 235.

American Express Travel Service
Václavské náměstí 56.
Map 3 C5.
[C] 22 22 10 106.
[W] www.american express.com

Autoturist Travel Agency
Londýnská 62. **Map** 6 F4.
[C] 22 25 12 053.
[W] www.autoturist.cz

AVE Ltd
Hlavní nádraží (main station). **Map** 4 E5.
[C] 22 42 23 226.
[FAX] 22 42 30 783.
[W] www.avetravel.cz

Čedok
Na Příkopě 18. **Map** 4 D4.
[C] 22 41 97 616.
[W] www.cedok.cz

Estec
Vaníčkova 5, Prague 6.
[C] 25 72 10 410.
[W] www.estec.cz

Hotel Line Accommodation
Žalovská 435, Prague 8.
[C] 60 44 88 096.
[W] www.hotelline.cz

Pragotur
Za Poříčskou branou 7.
Map 4 D3.
[C] 22 17 14 130.
[W] www.prague–info.cz

Prague Information Service (PIS)
Na příkopě 20.
Map 3 C4.
[C] 22 17 14 130.
[W] www.pis.cz

Staroměstské náměstí 1.
Map 3 B3.
[C] 22 17 14 130.
[W] www.pis.cz

Hlavní nádraží (main station).
Map 4 E5.
[C] 22 17 14 130.
[FAX] 22 17 14 127.
[W] www.pis.cz

e.travel.cz
Ostrovní 7. **Map** 3 B5.
[C] 22 49 90 990.
[W] www.e.travel.cz

Top Tour
Revoluční 24. **Map** 4 D2.
[C] 22 48 13 172.
[W] www.toptour.cz

Travel Agency of České Dráhy
V Celnici 6. **Map** 3 C4.
[C] 22 42 25 849.
[W] www.cdrail.cz

HOSTELS

CKM Youth Agency
Mánesova 77. **Map** 6 E1.
[C] 22 27 21 595.
[W] www.ckm-praha.cz

Dlouhá
Dlouhá 33. **Map** 3 C3.
[C] 22 48 26 662.
[W] www.travellers.com

Koleje a Menzy
Opletalova 38. **Map** 4 D5.
[C] 22 49 30 010.
[W] www.kam.cuni.cz

CAMPING

Aritma Džbán
Kemp Džbán 3, Vokovice.
[C] [FAX] 23 53 59 007.
[W] www.dzban.cz

Kotva Braník
U ledáren 55, Braník.
[C] 24 44 61 712.

Troja
Trojská 157, Troja.
[C] 28 38 50 487.
[@] autocamp-trojska@iol.cz

DISABLED TRAVELLERS

Czech Association of Persons with Disabilities
Karlínské náměstí 12,
Prague 8.
[C] 22 48 15 915.
[@] puszdp@braill.net.cz

Embassy of the Czech Republic
26 Kensington Palace Gardens,
London W8 4QY.
[C] 020 7243 1115.
[W] www.mzv.cz/london

Pension Páv, in a quiet street of a historic neighbourhood (see p188)

PRIVATE ROOMS AND SELF-CATERING APARTMENTS

OVER THE PAST few years, the number of private rooms to rent in Prague has grown enormously. Although cheap and popular, they may be some distance from the centre. Private rooms in homes start at about Kč600 per person per night, usually with breakfast. There are also self-contained apartments – a fairly central one-bedroom apartment costs about Kč1,600 per night. Most agencies that offer private rooms also rent out apartments (see Directory opposite).

To book a room or apartment, tell the agency exactly what you want, for how many, when and in which area. The agency will suggest places. Find out the exact location

and the nearest metro before accepting; if you are in Prague, see it yourself. Make sure you receive written or faxed confirmation of a booking to take with you. On arrival in Prague, pay the agency in cash; they give you a voucher to take to the room or apartment (sometimes you can pay the owner directly). If the agency requires advance payment by banker's draft or Eurocheque, go direct to the accommodation with your receipt. Agencies may ask for a deposit on bookings from abroad, or charge a registration fee payable in Prague.

HOSTELS

THERE ARE ALSO many hostels in Prague, and the CKM Youth Agency in the New Town provides up-to-date information on availability. Useful websites include www.hoteldiscount.cz, www.bed.cz, and www.travellers.cz.

CAMPING

MOST CAMPSITES in or near Prague are closed from November to the start of April. They are very cheap with basic facilities, but are well served by transport. The largest site is at Troja (see pp164–5), 3 km (1.5 miles) north of the centre. Aritma Džbán, 4 km (2.5 miles) west, is open all year for tents, and Kotva Braník is 6 km (4 miles) south of the city on the banks of the Vltava. For details contact the PIS (see Directory opposite).

USING THE LISTINGS

The hotels on pages 187–9 are listed according to area and price category. The symbols summarize the facilities at each hotel.

all rooms have bath and/or shower, unless otherwise indicated
[1] single-rate rooms available
rooms for more than two people available, or an extra bed can be put in a double room
[24] 24-hour room service
[TV] television in all rooms
non-smoking rooms available
rooms with good views
air-conditioning in all rooms
gym/fitness facilities
swimming pool in hotel
business facilities: message-taking service, fax machine for guests, desk and telephone in all rooms and a meeting room within the hotel
children's facilities: cots
wheelchair access
lift
hotel parking available
gardens/grounds
bar
restaurant
tourist information point
credit and charge cards accepted:
AE American Express
DC Diners Club
JCB Japanese Credit Bureau
MC Mastercard/Access
V Visa

Price categories for a standard double room per night, including breakfast, tax and service:
Ⓚ Kč up to 4,000
ⓀⓀ Kč4–5,000
ⓀⓀⓀ Kč5–6,000
ⓀⓀⓀⓀ Kč6–7,000
ⓀⓀⓀⓀⓀ over Kč7,000

The smartly refurbished City Hotel Moran (see p188)

Choosing a Hotel

THE HOTELS IN THIS GUIDE have been selected across a wide range of price categories for the excellence of their facilities, location or character. The chart below lists the hotels in price categories within each particular area, starting with the Old Town and moving on to hotels further outside the city centre. For map references, see pages 244–9.

	CREDIT CARDS	NUMBER OF ROOMS	PARKING OR GARAGE	RESTAURANT	BAR

OLD TOWN

ATLANTIC Ⓚ | AE DC MC V JCB | 60 | | ● | ■
Na poříčí 9, 110 00 Praha 1. **Map** 4 D3. ☎ 22 48 11 084. ⅁ 22 48 12 378.
A few minutes' walk from Náměstí Republiky, this hotel is well placed for exploring the city. Reconstructed in 1988–9, it is neat and modern, if lacking in character, and the bedrooms are comfortable. There is a restaurant and a bistro cum bar. 🖧 ① ♨ 📺 ♿ ↻

CENTRAL Ⓚ | AE JCB MC V | 68 | | | ■
Rybná 8, 110 00 Praha 1. **Map** 3 C2. ☎ 22 48 12 041. ⅁ 22 32 84 04.
An old-style hotel, with reasonable prices, the lobby and reception have had a cursory face-lift, but this fades as you climb the stairs. The bedrooms, though old-fashioned, are clean. The bathrooms are immaculate.
🖧 ① ♨ ↻

CLEMENTIN ⓀⓀⓀ | AE MC V | 9 | | | ■
Seminářská 4, 110 00 Praha 1. **Map** 3 B4. ☎ 22 22 21 798. ⅁ 22 22 21 768.
ⓌⓌ www.clementin.cz
Located at the crossroads of ancient and modern Prague, this Hotel is an ideal starting point for discovering and enjoying the city. It is housed in the narrowest building in Prague and dates to 1360. Shoe-cleaning and internet services are provided. 🖧 ① ♨ 24 📺 ▤ ↻ ❀

ÉLITE ⓀⓀⓀⓀ | AE DC MC V | 79 | ■ | ● | ■
Ostrovní 32, 110 00 Praha 1. **Map** 3 B5. ☎ 22 49 32 250. ⅁ 22 49 30 787.
ⓌⓌ www.hotelelite.cz
The Élite is housed in a building which dates from the late 14th century. Its cosy atmosphere is aptly augmented by a stylish grill club on the ground floor (it offers excellent Mediterranean and Argentinian food) and by a cocktail bar providing jazz and Latino music. An open atrium contains a day-bar with a small garden. 🖧 ① ♨ 24 ✂ 📺 ▤ ♿ ↻ ✂ ❀ ⛾ ❂

METEOR ⓀⓀⓀⓀ | AE DC MC V | 88 | | ● | ■
Hybernská 6, 110 00 Praha 1. **Map** 4 D3. ☎ 22 41 92 130. ⅁ 22 42 13 005.
ⓌⓌ www.hotel-meteor.cz
Though part of the international Best Western group, the Meteor still has a cosy, old-fashioned feel. Some parts are slightly scruffy, but most of it has been well modernized. Many of the bedrooms are on the small side. In the cellar there is a nice restaurant. 🖧 ① ♨ 📺 ↻ ⛾

UNGELT ⓀⓀⓀⓀ | AE MC V | 9 | | ● | ■
Štupartská 7, 110 00 Praha 1. **Map** 3 C3. ☎ 22 48 28 686. ⅁ 22 48 28 181.
ⓌⓌ www.ungelt.cz
Tucked away in a quiet street behind the Old Town Square, this elegant hotel has an air of exclusivity. The accommodation is in suites, simply but stylishly fitted out – some rooms feature magnificent wooden ceilings. The restaurant is simple and there is a shady terrace. 🖧 ♨ 24 📺 ❀ ⛾ ❂

FOUR SEASONS HOTEL ⓀⓀⓀⓀⓀ | AE DC MC V | 162 | ■ | ● | ■
Veleslavínova 2a, 110 00 Praha 1. **Map** 3 A3. ☎ 22 14 27 000. ⅁ 22 14 26 000.
ⓌⓌ www.fourseasons.com
A luxury hotel close to the Charles Bridge, there are a variety of rooms and suites to choose from. Stunning views over the Vltava. 🖧 ♨ 24 📺 ⛏ ❀ ⛾ ❂

PAŘÍŽ ⓀⓀⓀⓀⓀ | AE DC MC V | 98 | ■ | ● | ■
U Obecního domu 1, 110 00 Praha 1. **Map** 4 D3. ☎ 22 21 95 195. ⅁ 22 42 25 475.
ⓌⓌ www.hotel-pariz.cz
This Neo-Gothic building with Art Nouveau elements was built by the celebrated architect Jan Vejrych, and was declared a historic monument in 1984. The rooms have been well modernized in international style and everything is in pristine condition. 🖧 ① ♨ 24 📺 ❀ ⛾ ↻ ❂

<table>
<tr><td>
Price categories for a standard double room per night in high season, including breakfast, tax and service:
Ⓚ Kč up to 4,000
ⓀⓀ Kč4–5,000
ⓀⓀⓀ Kč5–6,000
ⓀⓀⓀⓀ Kč6–7,000
ⓀⓀⓀⓀⓀ over Kč7,000
</td></tr>
</table>

CREDIT CARDS
Indicates which credit cards are accepted: AE American Express; DC Diners Club; MC MasterCard/Access; V Visa.

PARKING OR GARAGE
The hotel provides a private car park or garage on site or close by for hotel guests. Some hotels may charge for use.

RESTAURANT
Hotel restaurant or dining room usually open to non-residents unless otherwise stated.

BAR
This is not necessarily recommended.

JEWISH QUARTER

	Credit Cards	Number of Rooms	Parking or Garage	Restaurant	Bar
HOTEL ROTT ⓀⓀⓀⓀ Malé náměstí 4/138, 110 00 Praha 1. **Map** 3 B3. 📞 22 41 90 901. **FAX** 22 42 16 761. 🌐 www.hotelrott.cz This quiet hotel near the Staroměstské náměstí is the only hotel in the Czech Republic which offers interactive Grundig TV communication. Each room also has a safety deposit.	AE V JCB	82	●		
HOTEL JOSEF ⓀⓀⓀⓀⓀ Rybná 20, 110 00 Praha 1. **Map** 3 C3. 📞 22 17 00 111. **FAX** 22 17 00 999. 🌐 www.hoteljosef.com This modern hotel is wonderfully equipped and is less than fifteen minutes' walk from Wenceslas Square. Breakfast is served all morning, and there is a gym on the top floor.	AE DC MC V JCB	82	●		
INTERCONTINENTAL ⓀⓀⓀⓀⓀ Náměstí Curieových 43–45, 110 00 Praha 1. **Map** 3 B2. 📞 29 66 31 111. **FAX** 22 48 10 071. 🌐 www.prague.interconti.com An imposing 1970s building set on the bank of the Vltava, this hotel has health and fitness facilities and a swimming pool. There is nothing particularly Czech about the place, but it is a good example of a five-star international hotel. Many of the rooms have lovely views.	AE DC MC V JCB	364	●		■
MAXIMILIAN ⓀⓀⓀⓀⓀ Haštalská 14, 110 00 Praha 1. **Map** 3 C2. 📞 22 53 03 111. **FAX** 22 53 03 110. 🌐 www.maximilianhotel.com Exquisitely furnished rooms with oversized beds are the order of the day at the Maximilian. Each room has an electronic safe, a fax machine, and classical drapes from Venice.	AE DC MC V	71	■		■

LITTLE QUARTER

	Credit Cards	Number of Rooms	Parking or Garage	Restaurant	Bar
KAMPA ⓀⓀⓀ Všehrdova 16, 118 00 Praha 1. **Map** 2 E5. 📞 25 73 20 404. **FAX** 25 73 20 262. 🌐 www.euroagentur.cz A 17th-century armoury, the Kampa is minutes from Charles Bridge, tucked away in a peaceful side street surrounded by gardens. In the large reception hall, a bar and restaurant are combined under a huge Baroque vaulted ceiling. The furnishings are simple and bedrooms are clean.	AE DC MC V	83	●		
POD VĚŽÍ ⓀⓀⓀⓀ Mostecká 2, 110 00 Praha 1. **Map** 2 F3. 📞 25 75 32 041. **FAX** 25 75 32 069. 🌐 www.podvezi.com In the heart of the historical centre, this is a delightful, family-run hotel. Pod Věží offers a peaceful ambience, underlined by the charming roof garden and by the sidewalk café, which is open all day. A generous breakfast is included in the price.	AE DC MC V JCB	12	●		
U PÁVA ⓀⓀⓀⓀ U lužického semináře 32, 110 00 Praha 1. **Map** 2 F3. 📞 25 75 33 573. **FAX** 25 75 30 919. Located in a quiet part of the Little Quarter, U Páva provides a stylish stay. Historical features are enhanced by traditional dark wooden furniture, crystal chandeliers and attractive rugs. Personal touches give it an individual feel, and the bedrooms are spacious and comfortable.	AE MC V	11	■		■
U TŘÍ PŠTROSŮ ⓀⓀⓀⓀⓀ Dražického náměstí 12, 118 00 Praha 1. **Map** 2 F3. 📞 25 75 32 410. **FAX** 25 75 33 217. 🌐 www.upstrosu.cz Just beside Charles Bridge, the hotel "At The Three Ostriches" began life as the home of Jan Fux, a dealer in ostrich feathers (*see p134*). It is one of the best known hotel/restaurants in Prague. Family run, the place has an intimate atmosphere. The bedrooms have been recently refurbished.	AE MC V	18	■	●	■

| Price categories for a standard double room per night in high season, including breakfast, tax and service: Ⓚ Kč up to 4,000 ⓀⓀ Kč4–5,000 ⓀⓀⓀ Kč5–6,000 ⓀⓀⓀⓀ Kč6–7,000 ⓀⓀⓀⓀⓀ over Kč7,000 | CREDIT CARDS Indicates which credit cards are accepted: AE American Express; DC Diners Club; MC MasterCard/Access; V Visa. PARKING OR GARAGE The hotel provides a private car park or garage on site or close by for hotel guests. Some hotels may charge for use. RESTAURANT Hotel restaurant or dining room usually open to non-residents unless otherwise stated. BAR This is not necessarily recommended. |

	CREDIT CARDS	NUMBER OF ROOMS	PARKING OR GARAGE	RESTAURANT	BAR

NEW TOWN

AXA Ⓚ
Na poříčí 40, 110 00 Praha 1. Map 4 E3. *22 48 12 580.* FAX *22 42 14 489.*
W www.hotelaxa.com
This old-style hotel is slightly dispiriting, yet reasonably priced and central. The rooms have been renovated and there is a swimming pool.

| AE DC MC V | 131 | | ● | ■ |

EVROPA Ⓚ
Václavské náměstí 25, 110 00 Praha 1. Map 4 D5. *22 42 28 117.* FAX *22 42 24 544.*
W www.evropahotel.cz The Evropa is Prague's most beautiful hotel, with superb Art Nouveau decor. The dining room boasts stunning glasswork and the café/bar is the most famous in Prague (*see p146*). 🛏 30.

| AE DC MC V | 85 | | ● | |

LUNÍK Ⓚ
Londýnská 50, 120 00 Praha 2. Map 6 E2. *22 42 53 974.* FAX *22 42 53 986.*
W www.hotel-lunik.cz Located in a quiet street lined with trees, the hotel is in immaculate condition. There is simple but smart decor throughout with whitewashed walls and good quality wooden furnishings.

| AE JCB MC V | 35 | | | ■ |

PENSION PÁV Ⓚ
Křemencova 13, 110 00 Praha 1. Map 5 B1. *22 49 33 760.* FAX *22 49 33 080.*
@ pav@vol.cz
Situated in a tranquil street in a historic part of Prague, this hotel is a compact place with a few rooms and apartments. These are simple but stylish. The pension has its own cosy bar and a reasonable restaurant.

| | 8 | | | |

HARMONY ⓀⓀ
Na poříčí 31, 110 00 Praha 1. Map 4 E3. *22 23 20 720.* FAX *22 23 10 009.*
The Harmony is in pristine condition after complete reconstruction. A compact place, it is run by young, friendly staff. Two small restaurants, one with tables on the pavement, give a choice of cuisine.

| AE DC MC V | 60 | | ● | ■ |

ADRIA ⓀⓀⓀⓀ
Václavské náměstí 26, 110 00 Praha 1. Map 4 D5. *22 10 81 111.* FAX *22 10 81 300.*
W www.hoteladria.cz
The Adria is bright and chic with an entrance on Wenceslas Square. Clever use of glass and mirrors make the reception seem bigger than it is and with plenty of gleaming brass the impression is light and up-beat. The bedrooms are bright and cheery and smartly furnished.

| AE DC MC V JCB | 66 | ■ | ● | ■ |

CITY HOTEL MORÁŇ ⓀⓀⓀⓀ
Na Moráni 15, 120 00 Praha 2. Map 5 A3. *22 49 15 208.* FAX *22 49 20 625.*
W www.hotel-moran-prague.hotels.ly/
This hotel has been beautifully decorated in an understated style with white-washed walls with soft green carpets, plush sofas and chairs on pale marble floors. A smart café/restaurant and bar overlooks the street.

| AE DC MC V | 57 | ■ | ● | ■ |

PRAHA RENAISSANCE ⓀⓀⓀⓀ
V celnici, PO Box 726, 110 00 Praha 1. Map 4 E3. *22 18 22 100.* FAX *22 18 22 333.*
W www.renaissancehotels.com
The gleaming glass front of this new hotel takes over one corner of Náměstí Republiky. The luxurious bedrooms include soft furnishings, plump bedcovers and fluffy bathrobes. There is a choice of restaurants, a beer hall and health club.

| AE DC MC V JCB | 309 | ■ | ● | ■ |

CARLO IV ⓀⓀⓀⓀⓀ
Senovážné náměstí 13, 110 00 Praha 1. Map 4 E4. *22 45 93 111.* FAX *22 42 23 960.*
W www.boscolohotels.com
This luxurious, magnificently decorated hotel (shimmering marble floors, intricate hand-painted frescos in a Neo-Classical building) is in the heart of the city.

| AE DC MC V JCB | 153 | ■ | ● | ■ |

JALTA PRAHA

ⓀⓀⓀⓀⓀ

Václavské náměstí 45, 110 00 Praha 1. **Map** 4 D5. ☎ *22 28 22 111.* FAX *22 42 13 866.*
An old-fashioned hotel, the Jalta Praha is on Wenceslas Square. Parts of the hotel have undergone some reconstruction: the main restaurant redesigned and bedrooms have been refurbished. The rooms are comfortable, good-sized and attractively decorated. 🛏 ① 🏋 24 TV 🛳 🚲 🍴 🛗 🍷 📶 🌐 🔧

AE	89	■	●	■
DC				
MC				
V				
JCB				

PALACE

ⓀⓀⓀⓀⓀ

Panská 12, 110 00 Praha 1. **Map** 4 D4. ☎ *22 40 93 111.* FAX *22 42 21 240.*
W www.palacehotel.cz
Located on a quiet side street near Wenceslas Square, this hotel reopened in 1989 after a complete refurbishment, the mixture of styles – modern, Art Nouveau and traditional – with lashings of brass, glass, mirrors and fake flowers, may not be to everyone's taste, but the hotel succeeds in providing any luxury guests may require. 🛏 ① 24 TV 🍷 🛳 📶 🍴 🛗 📶

AE	124	■	●	■
DC				
MC				
V				
JCB				

FURTHER AFIELD

ANNA

Ⓚ

Budečská 17, Praha 2. ☎ *22 25 13 111.* FAX *22 25 15 158.* W www.hotelanna.cz
Housed in an elegant Neo-Classical building with Art Nouveau interiors, the Hotel Anna is only a ten-minute walk from Wenceslas Square.
🛏 ① 🏋 TV 🍷 🛳 🛗 📶

AE	24	■		
MC				
V				

BELVEDERE

Ⓚ

Milady Horákové 19, 170 00 Praha 7. ☎ *22 01 06 254.* FAX *23 33 74 471.*
W www.belvedere-hotel.com
Just one metro stop from Florenc, this area buzzes with shops, cafés and restaurants. Although there is nothing special about the hotel itself, it is clean, neat, fairly central and moderately priced. The rooms are simple but comfortable, with modern shower rooms. The hotel's bar/café opens on to the street. 🛏 ① 🏋 24 TV 🍷 🛳 🍴 🛗 📶 🌐 🔧

AE	142	■	●	■
DC				
MC				
V				
JCB				

CAROL

Ⓚ

Kurta Konráda 547 / 12, 190 Praha 9. ☎ *26 63 11 316.* FAX *28 48 19 475.* W www.carol.cz
This hotel is Dutch owned, and the atmosphere is relatively relaxed for Prague. Bedrooms feature minimalist decor, but are immaculate and comfortable. The only disadvantage is the distance from the city centre.
🛏 ① 🏋 24 TV 🍴 🛗 📶 🔧

AE	40	■	●	■
DC				
MC				
V				
JCB				

ESPRIT

Ⓚ

Lihovarská 1098, 190 00 Praha 9. ☎ *28 48 10 273.* FAX *28 48 19 597.*
W www.hotel-esprit.cz
Espirit's breakfast-room/bar/restaurant is cheerfully decorated and kept pristine. The well-kept bedrooms are simple but smart with pine furniture and whitewashed walls. The hotel's only drawback is its distance from the centre: a ten-minute walk from the last stop on metro B line. Avoid booking through a travel agent, as it will double the price. 🛏 ① 🏋 🛳 📶 🔧

AE	63	■	●	■
V				

CORINTHIA TOWERS

ⓀⓀⓀⓀⓀ

Kongresová 1, 140 69 Praha 4. ☎ *26 11 91 218.* FAX *26 12 11 673.* W www.corinthia.cz
Situated beside the Vyšehrad metro stop, the Corinthia Towers is only a few minutes from the city centre. Built in 1988 as a modern high-rise filled with glass, brass and marble, it has an impressive health centre and a beautiful indoor swimming pool. The good-sized bedrooms are well decorated and comfortable. 🛏 🏋 24 TV 🍷 🛳 🍴 🛳 🛗 📶 🔧

AE	551	■	●	■
DC				
MC				
V				
JCB				

DIPLOMAT PRAHA

ⓀⓀⓀⓀⓀ

Evropská 15, 160 00 Praha 6. ☎ *22 43 94 111.* FAX *22 43 94 215.* W www.diplomat-hotel.cz
This hotel is located right at the end of metro line A, but is only 12 minutes from the city centre. It opened in 1990 and still feels very new. Very efficiently run by Austrians, the hotel offers excellent facilities including a nightclub, numerous restaurants, shops, and even a whirlpool in the health club. It is popular with tour operators, and is very comfortable. 🛏 ① 🏋
TV 🍷 🛳 🍴 🛗 🚲 🛗 📶 🌐

AE	382	■	●	■
DC				
MC				
V				
JCB				

PRAHA HILTON

ⓀⓀⓀⓀⓀ

Pobřežní 1, 186 00 Praha 8. **Map** 4 F2. ☎ *22 48 41 111.* FAX *22 48 42 378.*
W www.hilton.com
French-owned and designed, it is the biggest hotel in the country, and despite the huge size, it does have a certain style. The bedrooms are all tastefully decorated with all the comforts you would expect to find in a large international hotel. 🛏 ① 🏋 24 TV 🍷 🛳 🍴 🛳 🚲 🛗 📶 🌐 🔧

AE	800	■	●	■
DC				
MC				
V				
JCB				

RESTAURANTS, CAFÉS AND PUBS

RESTAURANTS in Prague, just like the economy, seem to be getting better. For 40 years state-licensed eating and drinking establishments had little incentive to experiment or improve. But attitudes are rapidly changing. Fuelled by the booming tourist industry, new restaurants are opening constantly, many of them foreign-owned, offering the discerning eater an ever-increasing choice. The restaurants described in this

The Good Soldier Švejk at U Kalicha (see p154)

section reflect the change, though many only serve a limited range of standard Western dishes as well as staple Czech meals. *Choosing a Restaurant* on pages 198–9 summarizes the key features of the restaurants and cafés, listed by area. Full listings can be found on pages 198–203 and information on pubs, beer halls and bars appears on page 204–205. Compared to Western prices, eating out in Prague is still cheap.

TIPS ON EATING OUT

BECAUSE OF the huge influx of tourists, eating out has changed in character. The lunch hour is still early – between 11am and 1pm, and for most Czechs the normal time for the evening meal is around 7pm. However, many of the restaurants stay open late and it is possible to get a meal at any time from 10am until 11pm. Kitchens close 30 minutes to one hour earlier than stated closing times.

During spring and summer, the large numbers of visitors tend to put a strain on many of Prague's more popular restaurants. To be certain of a table, especially in the very well-known restaurants, it is advisable to book in

advance. The city centre is full of restaurants, and there are several off the normal tourist track. Prices also tend to be lower the further you go from the centre.

PLACES TO EAT

THE IMPORTANCE of a stylish yet comfortable setting, and food which is inspired rather than just prepared, is slowly beginning to trickle down to Prague's better and more innovative restaurants. The places which follow this maxim are generally the best.

One of the simplest places to eat is the sausage stand, a utilitarian establishment which is very common in Central Europe. It offers Czech sausages, which can either be eaten standing at

Modern Czech restaurant

the counter or taken away cold. For a late-night meal your best bet is often a snack bar *(bufet)*.

For greater comfort, head for a café *(kavárna)*. Cafés range from loud, busy main street locations to quieter bookstore establishments. All have fully stocked bars and serve a variety of food from simple pastries and sandwiches to full-blown meals. Opening hours differ widely, but many open early in the morning and are good for a quick, if not quite a Western-style, breakfast.

A restaurant may be called a *restaurace* or a *vinárna* (one that sells wine). The best are those geared to non-Czech clientele. While usually cheap by Western standards, they are pricier than Czech places, but in return offer better service and higher quality food.

Plain Czech food is normally available at the local beer hall or pub *(pivnice)*, though the emphasis there is normally on drinking rather than eating.

Diners enjoying their meal at U Kalicha (see p203)

Tourists eating at the outdoor cafés in the Old Town Square

READING THE MENU

NEVER JUDGE a restaurant by the standard of its menu translations – mistakes are common in every class of restaurant. Many menus still list the weight of meat served (a relic of communist rationing). Bear in mind that most main courses come with potatoes, rice or dumplings. Salads and other side dishes must be ordered separately. (*See pp194–5 for What to Eat in Prague.*)

Restaurant sign

THINGS TO BEWARE OF

IN SOME RESTAURANTS OR BARS the waiter may bring nuts to your table. Yes, they are for you to eat, but at a price equal to, or higher than, an appetizer. You will not insult

Fine dining amid stained-glass Art Deco splendour

anybody by telling the waiter to take them away. The same applies to appetizers brought round by the waiter.

Check your bill carefully, because extra charges are often added – this is quite a common practice in Prague. However, legitimate extra costs do exist. Cover charges range from Kč10–25 and such basic items as milk, ketchup, bread and butter might be charged for. Finally, a 19% tax, normally included in the menu. Severe cases of food poisoning are rare in Prague, but mild cases are more common. Avoid stands selling food in the street, as the ingredients are exposed to bacteria and may not be cooked thoroughly. In general, restaurants in Prague have a high standard of hygiene, equal to the rest of Europe.

ETIQUETTE

YOU DON'T HAVE to wait to be seated in snack bars and smaller eateries. It is also quite normal for others to join your table if there is any room. No restaurant has an official dress code, but people tend to dress up when dining in up-market restaurants.

PAYMENT AND TIPPING

THE AVERAGE PRICE for a full meal in the centre of Prague is about Kč360. In some restaurants the waiter may write your order on a piece of paper and then leave it on your table for the person who comes around when you are ready to pay. Levels of service vary, but generally a 10% tip is appropriate. Add the tip to the bill, do not leave the money on the table.

More and more restaurants now accept major credit cards, but always ask before the meal to make sure. Traveller's cheques are not accepted.

VEGETARIANS

EVEN VEGETARIANS are well catered for in Prague. Fresh vegetables are available throughout the year, including winter, and numerous restaurants offer vegetarian and vegan options (*see pp198–203*). Nevertheless, even when a dish is described as meatless, it's always worth double-checking.

DISABLED

RESTAURANTS do not cater specifically for the disabled. The staff will almost always try to help, but Prague's ubiquitous stairs and basements will defeat all but the most determined.

Prague's Best: Restaurants and Cafés

T HE VARIETY AND NUMBER of places to eat and drink in Prague has increased considerably in recent years. But despite a massive influx of discerning diners, some of the restaurants may disappoint visitors with their uninspired cuisine. The following restaurants, chosen from the listings on pages 200–4, will guide you to sample tasty, interesting meals while relaxing in venues which not only provide a pleasant atmosphere, but also offer reasonably priced, good quality food.

U Tří pštrosů
High-quality and traditional Czech dishes are found at this exclusive restaurant. (See p202.)

Peklo
The 12th-century beer cellars and delicious Italian fare make this well worth a visit. (See p201.)

Prague Castle and Hradčany

Little Quarter

Nebozízek
The spectacular view over Prague from this café terrace ensures the popularity of this establishment.
(See p201.)

U Malířů
This converted 16th-century house has a good reputation for its exquisite French dishes, in an atmosphere of discreet luxury. The murals and painted ceilings add to the romantic mood.
(See p201.)

Chez Marcel
This is a little corner of Paris in the heart of Prague's Jewish Quarter. (See p199.)

U Červeného kola
Steaks and mouth-watering desserts are a speciality in this quiet restaurant, tucked away in a side street near St Agnes's Convent. (See p200.)

Opera Grill
French nouvelle cuisine *is served in an intimate and exclusive atmosphere.* (See p200.)

Jewish Quarter

Old Town

New Town

0 metres 300
0 yards 300

La Perle de Prague
La Perle de Prague serves haute cuisine in an elevated setting at the top of the stylish "Ginger and Fred" building. (See p203.)

Hotel Evropa Café
A pause for coffee is a good way to enjoy this beautiful Art Nouveau hotel. (See p202.)

What to Eat in Prague

CZECH COOKERY IS VERY SIMILAR to Austrian – lots of meat (usually pork or beef) served with dumplings, potatoes or rice, in a sauce. Meat, poultry, fish, cabbage and potatoes are all prepared simply and without strong spices; meat tends to be fried, roasted, or oven-baked in stock. On special occasions, game is usually the main course: venison, boar steaks or quails. Standard dishes tend to be served in copious quantities, and main courses are virtually meals in themselves. The most common dish is pork served with dumplings and sauerkraut (vepřové, knedlíky a zelí). Dumplings are traditionally served with most hot dishes and gravy. Vegetable portions can be small, although there has been a slight increase in the consumption of fresh vegetables in recent years. Salads are variable in quality. Hot soups are the traditional start to a meal, and range from broth with liver dumplings to cabbage soup with sausage.

"Stuffed eggs" are a popular appetizer

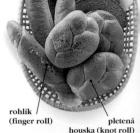

žitný chléb (rye bread)

rohlík (finger roll)

pletená houska (knot roll)

chléb and pečivo (breads)
An assortment of breads is served with most meals.

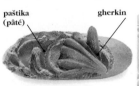

uzený losos (smoked salmon)

paštika (pâté)

gherkin

sardinka (sardines)

tvaroh s ředkvičkami (cream cheese with radishes)

klobásy (grilled sausages)

párky (frankfurters)

mustard

Chlebíčky
These open sandwiches arranged on sliced baguette (French bread) can be found in any Lahůdky (delicatessen) and Bufet (snack bar) in Prague. They are popularly served to guests in Czech homes. Ham, fish, salami, roast beef, egg and cheeses are used, often with mayonnaise or garnished with a gherkin (nakládaná okurka). Unfortunately western-style fast food is encroaching on this snack's popularity.

Klobásy and párky
Klobásy are grilled sausages; párky are boiled frank-furters (hot dogs). Both are sold with mustard (hořčice) from street stalls and in special sausage shops.

Plněná šunka
An appetizer of stuffed ham, filled with a mix of whipped cream and coarsely grated horseradish, which gives it a kick.

Polévka
Simple vegetable soups – pea, potato, cauliflower, cabbage or tomato – are popular starters.

Hovězí polévka s játrovými knedlíčky
Liver dumplings in beef broth is a warming soup for all seasons.

Pečená kachna
Roast duck with bacon dumplings (špekové knedlíky) and red sauerkraut is a popular main course.

Uzené
Smoked pork is mostly served with slices of potato dumplings (bramborové knedlíky) and white sauerkraut.

Vepřový řízek
Breaded and fried pork steak (schnitzel) is usually accompanied by hot potatoes or a cold potato salad. It often has a salad garnish and a slice of lemon.

**Houskové knedlíky
(sliced bread
dumplings)**

**Brusinky
(cranberries)**

**Hovězí
(beef)**

Salát
In winter, salads are often pickled; in summer, they are simply-dressed mixtures of tomato, lettuce, cucumbers and peppers.

Svíčková na smetaně
Pot-roasted fillet of beef (svíčková) is served in a rich, creamy, slightly sweet vegetable sauce (na smetaně) and is garnished with either cranberries or a dollop of whipped cream.

Jablkový štrúdel
Thin apple slices are wrapped in a light pastry case. Other strudel fillings include cherries or cream cheese.

Ovocné knedlíky
Fruit dumplings, in this case švestkové (plum), are served with melted butter, icing sugar and ground poppy seeds.

Vdolek
This round yeast pastry is served with redcurrant or plum jam and whipped cream.

Palačinky
Crêpe pancakes can be filled with ice cream and/or stewed fruit or jam, and coated in sugar, chocolate or almonds.

What to Drink in Prague

'Golden Tiger' beer mat

Czech beers are famous around the world, but nowhere are they drunk with such appreciation as in Prague. The Czechs take their beer (*pivo*) seriously and are very proud of it. Pilsner and its various relations originate in Bohemia. It is generally agreed that the best Pilsners are produced close to the original source – and all the top producers are not far from Prague. Beers can be bought in cans, in bottles, and best of all, on draught. Canned beer is made mostly for export, and no connoisseur would ever drink it. The Czech Republic also produces considerable quantities of wine, both red and white, mainly in Southern Moravia. Little of it is bottled for export. Mineral water can be found in most restaurants; Mattoni and Dobrá voda (meaning good water) are the two most widely available brands.

Gambrinus, legendary King of Beer, and trademark of a popular brand of Pilsner

Traditional copper brew-kettles in Plzeň

PILSNER AND BUDWEISER

The best-known czech beer is Pilsner. Clear and golden, with a strong flavour of hops, Pilsner is made by the lager method: top-fermented and slowly matured at low temperatures. The word "Pilsner" (which is now a generic term for similar lagers brewed all over the world) is derived from Plzeň (in German, Pilsen), a town 80 km (50 miles) southwest of Prague, where this type of beer was first made in 1842. The brewery that developed the beer still makes Plzeňské pivo as well as the slightly stronger Plzeňský prazdroj (original source), which is better known by its German name Pilsner Urquell. A slightly sweeter beer, Budweiser Budvar (which is no relation to the American beer of the same name), is brewed 150 km (100 miles) south of Prague in the town of České Budějovice (in German, Budweis).

Budweiser logo

Pilsner Urquell logo

This higher percentage refers to the original gravity, not the alcohol content

10 %

Velkopopovické ®

pivo

e 0,5 l
MIN. TRVANLIVOST

02 11 99

SVĚTLÉ

4,0% obj.
OBSAH ALKOHOLU

ČSN 56 60... Obj. využit. energ. 1550 kJ/l

Světlé means light   Alcohol content

Reading a Beer Label

The most prominent figure on the label (usually 10% or 12%) does not refer to the alcohol content. It is a Czech measure of original gravity, indicating the density of malt and other sugars used in the brew. The percentage of alcohol by volume is usually given in smaller type. The label also states whether it is a dark or a light beer.

BEER AND BEER HALLS

Staropramen	**Gambrinus**	**Velkopopovický kozel**	**Budweiser Budvar**	**Plzeňský prazdroj (Pilsner Urquell)**

THE REAL PLACE TO ENJOY Czech beer is a pub or beer hall (*pivnice*). Each pub is supplied by a single brewery (*pivovar*), so only one brand of beer is available, but several different types are on offer. The major brands include Plzeňské and Gambrinus from Plzeň, Staropramen from Prague, and Velkopopovické from Velké Popovice, south of Prague. The usual drink is draught light beer (*světlé*), but a number of beer halls, including U Fleků (*see p155*) and U Kalicha (*see p154*) also serve special strong dark lagers (ask for *tmavé*). Another type you may encounter is *kozel,* a strong light beer like a German *bock.*

A half litre of beer (just under a pint) is called a *velké* (large), and a third of a litre (larger than a half pint) is called a *malé* (small). The waiters bring beers and snacks to your table and mark everything you eat and drink on a tab. In some pubs (*see p205*) there is a tacit assumption that all the customers want to go on drinking until closing time, so don't be surprised if more beers arrive without your ordering them. If you don't want them, just say no. The bill is totted up when you leave.

People enjoying a drink in one of Prague's beer gardens

WINES

CZECH WINE PRODUCERS have not yet emulated the success of other East European wine-makers. The main wine-growing region is in Moravia, where most of the best wine is produced for local consumption. Some wine is also made in Bohemia, around Mělník, just north of Prague. The whites are made mostly from Riesling, Müller-Thurgau or Veltliner grapes (*polosuché* is demi-sec and *suché* is sec). Rulandské (Pinot) is an acceptable dry white. The reds are slightly

Rulandské, white and red

better, the main choices being Frankovka and Vavřinecké. In the autumn, a semi-fermented young, sweet white wine called *burčák* is sold and drunk across the capital.

CZECH SPIRITS AND LIQUEURS

IN EVERY RESTAURANT and pub you'll find Becherovka, a bitter-sweet, amber herbal drink served both as an aperitif and a liqueur. It can also be diluted with tonic. Other local drinks include Borovička, a juniper-flavoured spirit, and plum brandy or Slivovice. The latter is clear and strong and rather an acquired taste. Imported spirits and cocktails are more expensive.

Becherovka

Choosing a Restaurant

THESE RESTAURANTS have been selected across a wide price range for their good value or exceptional cuisine; they are listed area by area, starting with the Old Town and moving on to restaurants further outside the city. The entries appear alphabetically within each price category, and any special features are indicated by the coloured bars or symbols below.

	CREDIT CARDS	FIXED-PRICE MENU	CZECH SPECIALITIES	ATTRACTIVE LOCATION	LATE OPENING
OLD TOWN					
BOHEMIA BAGEL Ⓚ Masná 2. **Map** 3 C3. 📞 24 81 25 60. The best breakfast deal in Prague is available until late in the morning at this always-busy bagel shop and café. High-speed internet connections are also provided at very reasonable rates. It's become so popular that a second Bohemia Bagel has opened across the Vltava at Újezd 16. ★ 🅥		●			
COUNTRY LIFE Ⓚ Melantrichova 15. **Map** 3 B4. 📞 224 213 366. This is part of the international group of vegetarian restaurants, but few can compete with its picturesque setting. It gets crowded at lunchtimes by vegetarians and omnivores alike, hungry for their pizzas, salads and soups. 🅥 ● *Sat, Sun.*					
KLUB ARCHITEKTŮ Ⓚ Betlémské nám 5A. **Map** 3 B4. 📞 224 401 214. This hidden gem is tucked away in a warren of tunnels and arches, reached through a courtyard near the Bethlehem Chapel. The servings are hearty, and, unusually for inexpensive Prague dining, the menu includes a goodly vegetarian selection. 🅥	AE DC MC V	●	■	●	
DAHAB ⓀⓀ Dlouhá 33. **Map** 3 C3. 📞 22 00 00 00. Right in the heart of the Old Town, Dahab is perhaps the only place in Prague where you can puff on a hookah pipe after your meal. This combination of tea room, patisserie, café and restaurant, has a nice selection of Middle Eastern dishes, including several vegetarian options. 🅥	AE DC MC V JCB				■
JAMES JOYCE ⓀⓀ Liliová 10. **Map** 3 B4. 📞 24 24 87 93. The James Joyce was the first Irish pub in Prague, and it's home to hearty meals including Irish breakfasts, 'door stopper' sandwiches and what most expatriates would still say is the best Irish stew in Prague. ★	AE MC V				
PATRIOT X ⓀⓀ V Celnici 3. **Map** 4 D3. 📞 224 235 158. This is a Czech restaurant, café and bar which, quite distinctively, takes a Scandinavian 'less is more' approach to décor, yet keeps the portions traditionally ample. The café is upstairs, while the restaurant and bar are downstairs. It has a terrace with nice views.	AE DC MC V				
RED, HOT AND BLUES ⓀⓀ Jakubská 12. **Map** 3 C3. 📞 22 31 46 39. Located in what were the Czech king's stables some 500 years ago, this place is renowned for good, home-town New Orleans and Creole cooking: chilli, chowder, burgers with all the trimmings, and étouffé. There's live jazz or blues on most nights. 🅥 🎵 🍴	AE MC V				
RESTAURANT LA PROVENCE ⓀⓀ Štupartská 9. **Map** 3 C3. 📞 222 324 801. It's well worth the trip down the winding staircase from the lively Banana Bar to this reasonably priced French provincial restaurant. The menu includes country favourites like rabbit and duck, and the cluttered, rustic décor has a charm all its own. 🅥	AE DC MC V JCB				■
RYBÍ TRH (FISH MARKET) ⓀⓀ Týnský dvůr 5. **Map** 3 C3. 📞 224 895 447. Rybí Trh may have had a smart new facelift recently, but you can still choose from salt or freshwater fish, lobsters and oysters, which are either kept in their aquariums or freshly imported and stored on ice. An interesting wine list includes many new world wines. 🍷 🍴	AE DC MC V JCB				

	CREDIT CARDS	FIXED-PRICE MENU	CZECH SPECIALITIES	ATTRACTIVE LOCATION	LATE OPENING

Price categories
These have been calculated to represent the cost of an average three-course meal for one, including half a bottle of wine, and all unavoidable charges:
Ⓚ under Kč250
ⓀⓀ Kč250–450
ⓀⓀⓀ Kč450–650
ⓀⓀⓀⓀ over Kč650

CREDIT CARDS
Indicates which credit cards are accepted: AE American Espress; DC Diners Club; MC MasterCard/Access; V Visa.

FIXED-PRICE MENU
A good value menu is offered, usually with three courses.

CZECH SPECIALITIES
Typical Czech fare is served.

ATTRACTIVE LOCATION
In an unusual or historic setting, or has a beautiful view.

LATE OPENING
Last orders are taken on or after 10:30pm.

TAVERNA TOSCANA ⓀⓀ
Malé náměstí 11/22. **Map** 3 B4. 📞 21 61 15 35.
This is actually a two-in-one deal: number 11 is a trattoria-style restaurant, offering antipasti, salads, pasta, risotto and meat dishes, while a few doors away at number 22 is one of Prague's best pizzerias.
AE MC V — LATE OPENING: ■

U MODRÉ RŮŽE (THE BLUE ROSE) ⓀⓀ
Rytířská 16. **Map** 3 B4. 📞 224 225 873.
There's something for everyone on the Czech and international menu of this upscale but underground restaurant, with beef, lamb, game, seafood and vegetarian dishes. The setting is certainly unique, in beautifully restored 15th-century catacombs. 🎵 Ⓥ
AE DC MC V JCB — ATTRACTIVE LOCATION: ●

CHEZ MARCEL ⓀⓀⓀ
Haštalská 12. **Map** 3 C2. 📞 22 23 15 676.
Chez Marcel is a touch of France in the centre of Prague. This is where business people and students alike come for regional *plats du jour*, as well as steak *au poivre*, fresh mussels and the best French fries in the city.
🍷 ★ 🔧

DON GIOVANNI ⓀⓀⓀ
Karolíny Světlé 34/208. **Map** 3 A4. 📞 22 22 20 60.
This, the first upscale Italian restaurant in Prague (after 1989), was named after the Opera which Mozart débuted a few blocks away in the National Opera House. The seafood selection includes lobster and crab, fresh from the in-house aquarium. ★ Ⓥ
AE DC MC V JCB — ATTRACTIVE LOCATION: ●

PRAVDA ⓀⓀⓀ
Pařížská 17. **Map** 3 B2. 📞 22 32 62 03.
A wonderful blend of old and new with elegant gilt-and-white dining rooms and wai ters in chic uniforms, Pravda will tempt the adventurous with its Asian- and Scandinavian-inspired fare. This includes relatively expensive seafood dishes like Cajun crawfish and poached cod. ★
AE DC MC V — LATE OPENING: ■

RESTAURACE STOLETÍ ⓀⓀⓀ
Karolíny Světlé 21. **Map** 3 A4. 📞 222 220 008.
Arched ceilings, sepia prints and old china all evoke a gentler era in this quiet, intimate restaurant. The menu is inspired by the famous of yesteryear; for example, you can order a Marlene Dietrich (stuffed avocado with whipped Roquefort and marzipan) or an Al Capone (roast chicken leg with hot salsa and papaya).
AE MC V

REYKJAVIK ⓀⓀⓀ
Karlova 20. **Map** 3 A4. 📞 2222 12 18.
This is an Icelandic restaurant which serves dependably good seafood favourites such as *frutti di mare*, shrimp cocktails and Icelandic salmon – in this case grilled *á la Norvegienne*. The service is unobtrusively efficient and it's a pleasantly cosy nook on a cold winter's day. ★ 🍷
AE DC MC V — ATTRACTIVE LOCATION: ●

TRATTORIA VECCHIA MODENA ⓀⓀⓀ
Michalská 6 Stare' Město. **Map** 3 B4. 📞 224 225 836.
Located close to Old Town Square, this typical Italian restaurant serves regional food from the Emiglia and Romagna in a friendly atmosphere. Highly recommended is the homemade pasta, prepared fresh everyday, and a superb cold buffet.
★ 🍷 Ⓥ 🍷 🔧
AE MC V — FIXED-PRICE MENU: ● — LATE OPENING: ■

---

7 ANGELS ⓀⓀⓀⓀ
Jilská 20. **Map** 3 B4. 📞 224 234 381.
There has been a restaurant on this spot since the 13th century, but whatever the changes of management have been since then, 7 Angels remains one of the most charming small dining rooms in Central Europe. The house specialty is traditional Bohemian cuisine. 🎵 ★
AE MC V — CZECH SPECIALITIES: ■

<table>
<tr><td colspan="2">

Price categories
These have been calculated to represent the cost of an average three-course meal for one, including half a bottle of wine, and all unavoidable charges:
Ⓚ under Kč250
ⓀⓀ Kč250–450
ⓀⓀⓀ Kč450–650
ⓀⓀⓀⓀ over Kč650

</td></tr>
</table>

CREDIT CARDS
Indicates which credit cards are accepted: AE American Espress; DC Diners Club; MC MasterCard/Access; V Visa.

FIXED-PRICE MENU
A good value menu is offered, usually with three courses.

CZECH SPECIALITIES
Typical Czech fare is served.

ATTRACTIVE LOCATION
In an unusual or historic setting, or has a beautiful view.

LATE OPENING
Last orders are taken on or after 10:30pm.

	CREDIT CARDS	FIXED-PRICE MENU	CZECH SPECIALITIES	ATTRACTIVE LOCATION	LATE OPENING
BELLEVUE ⓀⓀⓀⓀ 18 Smetanovo nábřeží 2. **Map** 3 A5. 22 22 14 49. Situated by the river, Bellevue has a stunning view of the castle. The interior is an Art Deco triumph, all inlaid wood walls and marble floors. The menu includes Antipodean delicacies such as *carpaccio* with New Zealand lamb. ★	AE DC MC V JCB			●	
FLAMBÉE ⓀⓀⓀ Husova 5. **Map** 3 B4. 224 248 512. They're proud of their famous guests at Flambée – everyone from Madeline Albright to Pink Floyd – as well as their numerous awards for cuisine and décor. Suitably sumptuous dishes include fresh lobster, terrine of pheasant and steak of young bullock on glassée of Foie Gras. ▪ ♪	AE DC MC V JCB	●			■
LE SAINT-JACQUES ⓀⓀⓀ Jakubská 4. **Map** 3 C3. 222 322 685. Le Saint-Jacques is managed by a French proprietor who is as attentive as his cuisine is sumptuous. Try any fish dish from the constantly evolving menu. A pianist and violinist serenade patrons every night.	AE DC MC V JCB				
OPERA GRILL ⓀⓀⓀⓀ Karolíny Světlé 35. **Map** 3 A4. 22 22 05 18. There are only seven tables in the Opera Grill, which gives it the feel of a private dining room – but this also means it's a good idea to book ahead. The menu features international dishes, such as lamb, pasta and steak. ★ ♪	AE MC V	●			

JEWISH QUARTER

	CREDIT CARDS	FIXED-PRICE MENU	CZECH SPECIALITIES	ATTRACTIVE LOCATION	LATE OPENING
ORANGE MOON ⓀⓀ Rámová 5. **Map** 3 C2. 22 32 51 19. Immensely popular since its opening, Orange Moon bucks the local propensity for mildly spicy food by having its dishes listed on the menu with a one, two or three red pepper rating. That's spicy, very spicy or burning. Ⓥ	AE MC V	●			
U SÁDLŮ ⓀⓀ Klimentská 2. **Map** 4 D2. 24 81 38 74. Who can decry the kitsch aspects of a medieval-themed restaurant when it's done with such aplomb? Every dish has a thematic name, including several under the heading 'Meat from an Apocalyptic Piglet!' Cheerful staff.	DC MC V		■		
BAROCK ⓀⓀⓀ Pařížská 24. **Map** 3 B2. 223 292 21. An eclectic and excellent range of Thai and Japanese cuisine is served by efficient staff in this perennially fashionable restaurant. But it's not merely a trendy venue; the food really is up to international standards. ★ Ⓥ	AE DC MC V				■
JEWEL OF INDIA ⓀⓀⓀ Pařížská 20. **Map** 3 B2. 24 81 10 10. Here the specialty is Mughal cuisine from Northern India, although to the uninitiated it will appear to be very much like any other Indian restaurant. Favourites include samosas, pakoras, chicken masala, and rogan josh. Ⓥ	AE MC V				
KING SOLOMON ⓀⓀⓀⓀ Široká 8. **Map** 3 B3. 24 81 87 52. The light, pleasant interior of the King Solomon extends to its winter garden. All the food is impeccably prepared and presented, complemented by Kosher wines from the Czech Republic and beyond. They also deliver special Shabbat meals to hotels throughout Prague. ★ Ⓥ ● *Fri–Sat.*	AE MC V	●			
U ČERVENÉHO KOLA (AT THE RED WHEEL) ⓀⓀⓀⓀ Anežská 2. **Map** 3 C2. 24 81 11 18. Step behind the cloister of St Agnes's (see pp92–3) to find this elegant restaurant with plush carpets, antique clocks and softly upholstered seats. Steaks are the house speciality. There is also a garden room. ★ ▦	AE DC MC V JCB				

Prague Castle and Hradčany

Palffy Palace Restaurant ⓚⓚⓚⓚ
Valdštejnská 14. **Map** 2 E2. **☎** 57 53 14 20.
Enter at Valdstenjska 14, then climb the stone staircase to this wonderfully alternative restaurant, in what feels like an aristocrat's private rooms. Melodies seep from a musical academy on the premises, providing perfect accompaniment to a regularly changing menu. ★ ▦

AE MC V ● ■ ●

Peklo (Hell) ⓚⓚⓚⓚ
Strahovské nádvoří 1. **Map** 1 B4. **☎** 220 516 652.
Peklo is near the Strahov Monastery, which belongs to the order of the Premonstratensians. They've been keeping wine in the cellars here since the 14th century. The restaurant offers fine Czech and international cuisine and a fabulous array of wines. ▯ ★ ● *Sun.*

AE DC MC V JCB ■

Little Quarter

Bazaar ⓚⓚ
Nerudova 40. **Map** 2 D3. **☎** 257 535 050.
This is a sprawling complex of bars and dining rooms, serving slightly overpriced Mediterranean cuisine against a backdrop of lavishly eccentric décor. The upper terrace, however, affords one of the best views of central Prague. �V ▦

AE DC MC V JCB ● ■

Hungarian Grotto ⓚⓚ
Tomášská 12. **Map** 2 E3. **☎** 257 532 344.
The land of Tokay, Bull's Blood, goulash and paprika has inspired this reasonably priced, romantically rustic cellar restaurant with a pleasant outdoor courtyard. To add to the atmosphere, the premises are supposedly haunted by a cuckolded baker from the 17th century.

AE MC V JCB ●

Mount Steak ⓚⓚ
Josefská 1. **Map** 2 E3. **☎** 257 53 26 52.
Very much for real meat-lovers, this restuarant offers over 60 different steaks, including boar, venison, kangaroo, shark and ostrich. It also has a bar. ▯ ★ �V ▯

AE DC MC V JCB ● ■

U Černého Orla (At the Black Eagle) ⓚⓚ
Malostranské náměstí 14. **Map** 2 E3. **☎** 57 53 32 07.
The quiet, cosy atmosphere makes this place a haven from the busy Malá Strana area outside. The food is traditional Czech, well-prepared and generously served. Leave room for an excellent dessert. ★

AE MC V ■

David ⓚⓚⓚ
Tržiště 21. **Map** 2 E3. **☎** 57 53 31 09.
It's a steep incline up a cobblestone lane to David, but foodies will find it worth the exertion. The gourmet set lunch is a serious two to three hour affair, with an interesting selection of Czech, European and New World wines. ▯ ★

AE DC MC V JCB ●

Koto ⓚⓚⓚ
Mostecká 20. **Map** 2 E3. **☎** 257 532 922.
Prague now has at least a dozen sushi bars, a far cry from the days when sausages and dumplings reigned. This was the first, and it remains one of the best, with Japanese staff and a reasonably priced menu. ▯

AE DC MC V JCB ●

Nebozízek (Little Auger) ⓚⓚⓚ
Petřínské sady 411. **Map** 2 D5. **☎** 257 31 53 29.
During spring and summer months the outdoor patio is very popular, affording wonderful views of Prague. Inside, it is cosy and elegant. The menu is diverse, with seafood, Chinese and Czech dishes, steaks and more. ★ ▦

AE DC MC V ■

Kampa Park ⓚⓚⓚⓚ
Na Kampě 8b. **Map** 2 F4. **☎** 257 532 685.
This upscale restaurant nestled on the banks of the Vltava was badly damaged in the floods of 2002. It has been completely restored, and the walls are once again covered with photos of its famous visitors. The European 'fusion' cuisine includes several vegetarian dishes. ★ ▦ �V

AE DC MC V JCB ● ●

U Malířů (At the Painter's) ⓚⓚⓚⓚ
Maltézské náměstí 11. **Map** 2 E4. **☎** 257 530 318.
There has been a restaurant on this spot since 1543. Even back then, U Malířů received high praise: King Rudolf II's food tasters gave it three Royal stars. Expect high quality traditional and contemporary French cuisine. ▯ ★

AE DC MC V JCB ●

Price categories
These have been calculated to represent the cost of an average three-course meal for one, including half a bottle of wine, and all unavoidable charges:
Ⓚ under Kč250
ⓀⓀ Kč250–450
ⓀⓀⓀ Kč450–650
ⓀⓀⓀⓀ over Kč650

CREDIT CARDS
Indicates which credit cards are accepted: AE American Express; DC Diners Club; MC MasterCard/Access; V Visa.

FIXED-PRICE MENU
A good value menu is offered, usually with three courses.

CZECH SPECIALITIES
Typical Czech fare is served.

ATTRACTIVE LOCATION
In an unusual or historic setting, or has a beautiful view.

LATE OPENING
Last orders are taken on or after 10:30pm.

	CREDIT CARDS	FIXED-PRICE MENU	CZECH SPECIALITIES	ATTRACTIVE LOCATION	LATE OPENING
U MODRÉ KACHNIČKY (AT THE BLUE DUCKLING) ⓀⓀⓀⓀ Nebovidská 6. **Map** 2 E4. 57 32 03 08. The hand-painted walls of this restaurant are surely Prague's best display of modern Art Nouveau. It's also a carnivore's heaven, with a terrific selection of game, meat, and salmon. Portions are generous by any standard.	AE DC MC V				
U TŘÍ PŠTROSŮ (AT THE THREE OSTRICHES) ⓀⓀⓀⓀ Dražického náměstí 12. **Map** 2 E3. 57 53 24 10. The dining room of The Three Ostriches is reminiscent of a Bavarian hunting lodge, but the cuisine is 100 percent bona-fide Czech. Adventurous diners may wish to try their ostrich specialities of goulash and roulade 'Prague style'. ★ Ⓥ	AE DC MC V JCB	●	■	●	
VALDŠTEJNSKÁ HOSPODA (WADSTEIN INN) ⓀⓀⓀⓀ Valdštejnské nám 7. **Map** E 23. 257 531 759. The Waldstein Inn, as it sounds, was once a typical local pub, but renovations and redecorations have exposed the original features of this 15th-century building, such as ceilings and stonework. The menu of Czech favourites has an emphasis on game.					

NEW TOWN

	CREDIT CARDS	FIXED-PRICE MENU	CZECH SPECIALITIES	ATTRACTIVE LOCATION	LATE OPENING
BUFFALO BILL'S Ⓚ Vodičkova 9. **Map** 5 C1. 224 948 624. Quite the sensation when it opened 10 years ago on this busy thoroughfare, Buffalo Bill's still draws locals, expatriates and tourists alike with its mixture of 'Tex Mex' dishes and its range of ribs and wings from the American grill. Definitely child-friendly.	AE DC MC V JCB				
CAFÉ IMPERIAL Ⓚ Na Poříčí 15. **Map** 4 D3. 23 16 012. This high-ceilinged café is laden with beautiful, original Art Deco tilework. This is affordable elegance, however, with light breakfasts, lunches, suppers and snacks all served in the atmosphere of a continental coffeehouse. ★	AE DC MC V				■
HOTEL EVROPA CAFÉ Ⓚ Václavské náměstí 25. **Map** 3 C5. 224 228 117. The café that put the V back into Evropa is an Art Nouveau classic, even if it is now slightly shabby around the edges. Ask for a look at the restaurant, which was used as the model for the dining room on the Titanic. ★ 🛗	AE MC V			●	
CAFÉ RESTAURANT LOUVRE ⓀⓀ Národní třída 20. **Map** 3 B5. 224 930 912. An excellent place for breakfast, Café Restaurant Louvre has been in business since the early 1900s. As well as a full restaurant menu of Czech and European fare, they have an excellent selection of cakes and pastries. There's also a smart billiards room on the premises. Ⓥ	AE DC MC V JCB			●	
DON JUAN ⓀⓀ Na struze 7. **Map** 5 A1. 224 930 182. The Flamenco guitar playing softly in the background of Don Juan's candlelit dining rooms sets the scene for a range of classic Spanish dishes. The seafood, such as Squid Andalusian style, is particularly memorable. Photographs of bullfighting greats adorn its walls. 🎵	AE MC V				
RADOST FX CAFÉ ⓀⓀ Bělehradská 120. **Map** 6 E2. 224 254 776. Good vegetarian food is a rarity in Prague, but the food here is so good that many non-vegetarians come here for business and working lunches. Beyond the restaurant is a bar serving lethal absinthe cocktails and an art gallery. Downstairs is Prague's most upmarket disco, home to extravagant theme parties. ★ Ⓥ	ⓀⓀ				■

RESTAURANT MARIE TERESIE ⓚⓚ
Na Příkopě 23. **Map** 3 C4. 📞 224 229 869.
A fluorescently lit shopping arcade is left behind on entering this spacious cellar restaurant, named after an Austrian Habsburg Princess. The fare is traditional Czech, served with a silver service flourish.

AE MC V ● ■

U FLEKŮ ⓚⓚ
Křemencova 11. **Map** 5 B1. 📞 224 934 019.
This cavernous brewery and restaurant with its many rooms and lounges is thought to have been founded in 1499. There's even been an on-site brewery since the 1900's. The food is upmarket Czech pub fare. 🏠

AE DC MC V JCB ■

CASABLANCA ⓚⓚⓚ
Na Příkopě 10. **Map** 3 C4. 📞 24 21 05 19.
This is an authentic Kosher Moroccan restaurant within the Savarin Palace. The Mediterranean- and African-influenced cuisine is served by charming staff. The best selection of kefta, harira, couscous and pastilla in Prague. 🅅 🏠

AE DC MC V JCB ● ● ■

EL GAUCHO ⓚⓚⓚ
Václavské náměstí 11 – Kenvelo Centre. **Map** 3 C5. 📞 221 629 410.
Step downstairs from a mini mall and into a surprisingly genuine Argentine restaurant. Steaks are cooked on an authentic 'Asado' grill, waiters are dressed as gauchos, and there is a good selection of South American wines. ★

AE DC MC V JCB ● ■

LE BISTROT DE MARLÉNE ⓚⓚⓚ
Plavecká 4. **Map** 5 A4. 📞 24 92 07 43.
The rustic interiors of this well-established French bistro recently gave way to a more chic and sleek look, but the high standards of cooking and presentation remain. The wine list is notable for its quality more than its quantity. 🅅

AE MC V

U KALICHA (AT THE CHALICE) ⓚⓚⓚ
Na bojišti 12–14. **Map** 6 D2. 📞 296 189 600.
The look of this restaurant, including its cartooned walls, is based on the famous Czech novel *The Good Soldier Švejk*. Author Jaroslav Hašek was a frequent visitor and set some of his novel's pivotal scenes here. Traditional Czech cuisine is available at prices aimed at western tourist budgets. 🎵

AE DC MC V JCB

LA PERLE DE PRAGUE ⓚⓚⓚⓚ
Rašín Building, Rašínovo nábřeží 80. **Map** 5 A2. 📞 221 984 160.
Situated on the 7th floor of the Rašín Building, with views of the Vltava and Prague Castle, this is a reasonably priced upscale French restaurant. The wine menu is quite extensive, and there is a well-stocked cocktail bar. 🍷 ★

AE DC MC V JCB ●

FURTHER AFIELD

GOVINDA VEGETARIAN CLUB ⓚ
Soukenická 27. 📞 24 81 66 31.
At this Hare Krishna club, tea room and restaurant, there is no menu as such, simply the dishes of the day for less than a 100 korunas. However, patrons have to sit on the floor to eat at the low tables. 🅅

●

AMBIENTE ⓚⓚ
Mánesova 59. **Map** 6 E1. 📞 222 727 851.
This eclectic restaurant, which features everything from American South-western to Italian cuisine, is most renowned for its salads, and indeed they serve probably the best Caesar salad in Prague. 🅅

AE DC MC V JCB

KRÁSNÁ ŘEKA ⓚⓚ
Anglická 6. **Map** 6 E2. 📞 24 21 81 54.
This is still the best Chinese restaurant in Prague, although with small portions, you may decide to order an additional main course. The dishes range from tofu to duck, and there is a variety of vegetarian options. 🅅

DC MC V JCB

TAJ MAHAL ⓚⓚ
Škrétova 10. **Map** 6 E1. 📞 24 22 55 66.
On a small street behind the National Museum is this Indian restaurant popular with Prague's expatriate community. The menu is quite extensive, and its oriental décor and sitar player add to the exotic atmosphere. 🏠 🎵

AE MC V ●

STŘELECKÝ OSTROV ⓚⓚⓚ
Střelecký ostrov 336. **Map** 2 F5. 📞 224 934 026.
The chic interior and unusual setting – on an island on the river Vltava – gives this restaurant a special ambience. The terrace offers fine views and the menu draws together Czech and international cuisine. 🍷 🎵 🏠

AE MC V ● ■ ●

Pubs, Beer Halls and Bars

THERE IS A VARIETY OF drinking establishments in Prague, to suit practically every taste. Indeed, the drinking scene has certainly diversified since the velvet revolution, with theme bars competing with more traditional establishments. One of the charms of Prague is that it's possible to stroll around the Old Town in the small hours and find places to drink and fraternise with Czechs and expatriates alike. If you sit at an empty table, don't be surprised if others join you. In traditional Czech pubs a waiter will automatically bring more beer as soon as you appear close to finishing, unless you indicate otherwise. In Prague, it pays to expect the unexpected: in some supposedly upmarket places, the waiters' attitude can be surly and unhelpful, while in the humblest pub you may find service to be efficient and courteous.

TRADITIONAL PUBS AND BEER HALLS

TRADITIONALLY, CZECH pubs either serve food or are large beer halls dedicated to the mass consumption of beer. *Hostinec* and *hospoda* indicate a pub with food, whereas a *pivnice* serves only beer, but over time the distinctions have faded. Recommended for the brave, **U Zlatého tygra** (the Golden Tiger) is a loud Czech literati pub, wall-to-wall with, mostly male, regulars. This is where Vaclav Havel took Bill Clinton to show him local beer culture. **U Fleků** has brewed its unique beer, Flekovské, since 1499. For authenticity, and Budvar, try **U Medvídků** which is not far away from the National Theatre *(see pp156–7)* and the Old Town Square. The traditional *hospoda* scarcely comes more so than **U Pinkasů**, hidden behind Wenceslas square in a quaint little courtyard. The **Hospoda u Goldexu** shares its kitchen with a restaurant, and the food is good. A spacious former chapel, **U Betlémské kaple** serves fish dishes and cold beer from Velké Popovické. **Pivovarský dům** brews its own beer, and is a slightly more up-market take on the usual Czech pub.

COCKTAIL BARS

PRAGUE NOW HAS almost more cocktail bars than you could shake a swizzle stick at, but these are some that stand out. On Pařížská,

Prague's Fifth Avenue, you'll find **Bugsy's**. This bar has even printed their own cocktail bible, though towards the end of the week it does become somewhat overtaken by burly men in long coats. That fate has yet to befall the neighbouring **Barock**, a cocktail bar and restaurant with a noticeably chic clientele. Nearby **Tretters** is a new addition to the scene, which combines smart looks with a slightly more down-to-earth attitude.

IRISH PUBS AND THEME BARS

PRAGUE NOW HAS theme bars in all shapes and sizes, with still the most common being the ubiquitous Irish pub. **Caffreys** is one of Prague's most popular – and pricier – Irish bars, located off the Old Town Square. **Rocky O'Reilly's** is the biggest Irish pub in town, and a rollicking place, while **Scarlett O'Hara's** is a quiet alternative. The **James Joyce** is but a stone's throw from Charles Bridge, and is probably Prague's most up-market Irish pub. Its neighbour is possibly the only Irish-Cuban hybrid pub anywhere, the noisy and fun **O'Che's**.

There are Cuban dancers at the **Tendr Club**, while **La Casa Blu** is a South American bar which is frequently home to a carnival type atmosphere. **Prace** is another world away; homage is paid to the good old, bad old days of Stalin and communism, festooned with relics from that bygone era.

BOHEMIAN HANGOUTS

NOT ONLY IN the geographical heart of Bohemia, these bars also represent the unconventional side of Prague city life. The almost always busy **Chapeau Rouge** is one of the most famous, not to say notorious, drinking dens in the Old Town, host to a parade of visitors and locals. The large, red velvet drinking emporium that is the **Marquis de Sade** also epitomizes that spirit, built as it is in a 19th-century brothel. Over the Vltava in the Castle district you'll find **U Malého Glena** which translates roughly to Glen's house, and is one of the longest surviving expatriate bars in the city. Not far away is **Jo's Bar & Garáž**, which has also stood the test of time as an ex-pat hangout. It's a small, cavernous pub, Mexican eatery and disco, and becomes quickly packed. Over in Žižkov is the large converted cinema and cultural centre that is **Akroplis**, home to an ever-changing programme of live music and DJs.

SPORTS BARS

SPORTS BARS HAVE taken off in Prague, with places like **Legends**, a long, polished cellar bar with a deck of TV screens. **Jágr's Sports Bar** is also for sports enthusiasts, owned as it is by Czech ice hockey hero Jaromír Jágr.

CAFÉ SOCIETY

THE CITY IS EMBEDDED in café society, ranging from old-fashioned smoky joints to cafés within bookstores, boutiques and billiard halls. Some are restaurants, others focus on drinking, but all serve alcohol. **Lávka** has the finest setting in the city. Situated at the foot of the Charles Bridge, it offers a spectacular view of the castle. Places to see and be seen, are **Dolce Vita** in the Jewish Quarter and **Slavia**, recently reopened by the river opposite the National Theatre. For a perfect meeting place, try the **Café Milena** opposite the clock tower in the old town square.

DIRECTORY

TRADITIONAL PUBS AND BEER HALLS

Hospoda u Goldexu
Vinohradská 25.
Map 6 E1.
(224 211 806.

Konvikt Pub
Bartolomějská 11.
Map 3 B5.
(224 231 971.

Lávka
Novotného lávka 1.
Map 3 A4.
(222 222 156.

Parukářka
Vrch Sv. Kříže, Sabinrva 10,
Praha 3. (0606 93 17 18.

The Beer House
PIVOVARSKÝ DŮM
Lípová 15, Praha 2.
Map 5 C2.
(296 216 666.

The Black Bull
U ČERNÉHO VOLA
Loretánské nám1.
Map 1 B3.
(254 04 65.

The Golden Tiger
U ZLATÉHO TYGRA
Husova 17.
Map 3 B4.
(222 221 111.

The Shot Out Eye
U VYSTŘELENÉHO OKA
U Božích bojovníků 3.
(62 78 714.

The Thirsty Dog
ŽIZNIVÝ PES
Elišky Krásnohorské 5.
Map 3 B2.
(222 310 039.

U Betlémské kaple
Betlémské náměstí 2.
Map 3 B4.
(224 211 879.

U Fleků
Křemencova 11.
Map 5 B1.
(224 934 019.

U Kalicha
Na Bojišti 12–14.
Map 6 D3.
(296 189 600.

U Kocoura
Nerudova 2.
Map 2 D3.
(257 530 107.

U Medvídků
Na Perštýně 7.
Map 3 B5.
(224 211 916.

U Pinkasů
Jungmannovo náměstí
15/16.
Map 3 C5.
(224 222 965.

COCKTAIL BARS

Alcohol Bar
Dušní 6.
Map 3 B2.
(224 811 744.

Bar Bar
Všehrdova 17.
Map 2 E5.
(257 312 246.

Barock
Pařížská 24.
Map 3 B2.
(22 32 92 21.

Bugsy's
Pařížská 10.
Map 3 B2.
(22 32 99 43.

From Dusk til Dawn
OD SOUMRAKU DO ÚSVITU
Týnská 19.
Map 3 C3.
(224 808 250.

Tretters
Kolkovně 3.
Map 3 C5.
(24 81 11 65.

Ultramarin
Ostrovní 32.
Map 3 B5.
(224 932 249.

IRISH PUBS AND THEME BARS

Caffreys
Staroměstské 608/10.
Map 3 B3.
(24 82 80 31.

James Joyce
Liliová 10.
Map 3 B4.
(224 248 793.

La Casa Blu
Kozí 15.
Map 3 C2.
(24 81 82 70.

Molly Malone's
U obecního dvora 4.
Map 4 D3.
(24 81 88 51.

O'Che's
Liliová 14.
Map 3 C3.
(222 221 178.

Rocky O'Reilly's
Štěpánská 32.
Map 3 A5.
(22 23 10 60.

Scarlett O Hara's
Mostecká 21.
Map 2 E3.
(57 53 26 49.

Tendr Club
Pařížská 6.
Map 3 B2.
(24 81 36 05.

Work
PRÁCE
Kamenická 9.
(220 571 232.

BOHEMIAN HANGOUTS

Akropolis
Kubelikova 27.
Map 2 E5.
(296 330 911.

Chapeau Rouge
Jakubská 2.
Map 3 C3.
(22 32 62 42.

Duende
Karolíny Světlé 30.
Map 3 A4.
(222 221 255.

Jo's Bar & Garáž
Malostranské nám 7.
Map 2 E3.
(57 53 33 42.

Marquis de Sade
Templová 8.
Map 3 C3.
(24 81 75 05.

Paradise Bar
Jilská 18.
Map 3 B4.
(224 21 55 99.

U Malého Glena
Karmelitská 23.
Map 2 E4.
(57 53 17 17.

SPORTS BARS

Jágr's Sports Bar
Václavské nám. 56.
Map 3 C5.
(224 248 793.

Legends
Týn 1.
Map 3 C3.
(24 89 54 04.

Zlatá hvězda
Ve smečkách 12.
Map 6 D1.
(22 21 01 24.

CAFÉ SOCIETY

Dolce Vita
Široká 15.
Map 3 B3.
(22 32 91 92.

Café Medúza
Belgická 17.
Map 6 F3.
(222 515 107.

Café Milena
Staroměstské nam 22.
Map 3 B3.
(221 632 602.

Hotel Evropa Café
Václavské náměstí 25.
Map 3 C5.
(224 228 117.

Slavia
Smetanovo nábř 2.
Map 3 A5.
(224 220 957.

SHOPS AND MARKETS

FOLLOWING THE TRANSITION to a market economy, and the Czech Republic's entry into the European Union, the number of shops and the range of goods available in Prague has increased enormously. A number of leading US and West European firms have established businesses in the city, and the quality of goods manufactured in the Czech Republic has improved considerably. Most of Prague's **Bohemian crystal** best shops are conveniently located in the city centre, especially in and around Wenceslas Square. Many of these areas have been pedestrianized, making for leisurely window-shopping, although they can get rather crowded. There are a number of department stores which sell an eclectic range of Czech and Western items. For a different shopping experience, the few traditional markets in the city offer everything from fresh fruit and vegetables to imported Russian caviar, toys, clothes, furniture, Czech crafts, electrical spare parts and even second-hand cars.

OPENING HOURS

MOST OF PRAGUE'S shops are open from 8am to 6pm Monday to Friday and until noon on Saturdays (supermarkets are open later). However, they are often more flexible than that, as many shops rely almost entirely on tourists for their trade. The more expensive gift shops have adapted their opening hours to the needs of their Western customers, often opening at 10am and closing much later in the evening.

Food stores open earlier, most of them at 7am – reflecting the early working day of many locals – and close at around 7pm. Some shops also take a break for lunch, which can vary from any time between noon and 2pm. Department stores and the big shopping centres also open early but tend to close later, often around 8pm.

All the shops are at their most crowded on Saturdays and for stress-free shopping it's often better to wander around the shops during the week. Prague's markets are generally open early every morning weekday but have varied closing times.

One of the many antique shops in Bridge Street in the Little Quarter

HOW TO PAY

MOST STAPLE GOODS, such as food, are cheaper than comparable items in the West. However, with more and more multinationals, such as Boss and Pierre Cardin, moving into the city, prices are slowly starting to rise.

The total price of goods should always include Value Added Tax (this is 19% of the total price, depending on what is being sold), although all food is exempt from this. Cash payments can only be made in Czech crowns, although major credit cards are accepted (see p222). Global Refund is a programme for non-EU residents that allows tax-free shopping for purchases exceeding Kč1,000. When you make a purchase at a shop displaying the Global Refund sign, ask at the cash till for a tax-free cheque. On leaving the country, show your items, receipts and cheques to customs officials, who will stamp the cheques, and you will get your VAT back. For more details, go to the Global Refund website (www.globalrefund.com).

SALES AND BARGAINS

FOLLOWING THE examples of the Western stores, sales are becoming more popular. As a result, it is now quite normal for clothes to be sold off cheaper at the end of each season. There is also an increasing number of post-Christmas sales in the shops found around Old Town Square, Wenceslas Square, Na příkopě and 28. října.

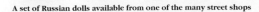

A set of Russian dolls available from one of the many street shops

If you want fresh vegetables, fruit, meat or other perishable goods, buy them at the beginning of the day, when the best quality goods are still on sale. There is no point in waiting till the end of the day in the hope of getting bargains, as is the case in Western shops that reduce prices to get rid of perishable items.

DEPARTMENT STORES

THERE ARE about ten of these open at present, although more are being planned for the future.

The best-known department store, **Kotva** (The Anchor), lies in the centre of the city. It was built in 1975 and its four storeys offer a wide range of Western goods, particularly fashion and electronics, with the bonus of an underground car park. But compared to Western department stores, Kotva has a smaller selection of goods than you may be accustomed to – with the exception of food such as smoked meats, for example. Prices for some of the more luxurious items on sale, such as perfumes, can often be equivalent to Western ones.

Another popular store is **Tesco**. This has a good selection of Czech and western products. The city's oldest department store is **Bílá Labut'** (The White Swan) in Na poříčí. It was opened shortly before the occupation of Czechoslovakia in 1939 and was the first building in Prague to have an escalator.

Two figurines decorate the façade of a chemist in the Old Town

It has since been refurbished, and now specializes in furniture and interior accessories.

MARKETS AND MALLS

PRAGUE'S MARKETS offer a vast range of goods in a friendly atmosphere where bargaining is all part of the fun. The largest market in the city, **Prague Market**, is in Holešovice. It was converted from a former slaughterhouse. The market now sells fresh fruit and vegetables, all kinds of poultry as well as fish, textiles, flowers, electronics and even second-hand cars and vehicle parts. These are all sold in several large halls and in outdoor stalls. The market is generally open from Monday to Friday, 6am to 5pm. In Havelská, right in the centre of the city, is the small **Havel Market**, which mainly sells fresh fruit and vegetables.

Other well-known markets in Prague include the **Smíchov Market** and a small one in the street V kotcích. Remember that some of the goods sold at all these markets, especially the mass of clothes and shoes, can be of very poor quality. Nevertheless, they are an excellent place to hunt for a bargain.

There is an increasing number of western-style shopping malls in Prague, which are more popular and often much better than the old department stores, offering better value and a greater range of high-quality goods. **Vinohrady Pavilion** has been reopened as a shopping mall, following extensive modernization, as has **Koruna Palace** and the **Myslbek** shopping arcade. More recently opened arcades include **Flora Palace** (Palác Flora: take the metro to Flora) and **Andel**, and there is also a **Carrefour** (both metro Anděl).

STREET STALLS

STREET STALLS and wandering street vendors are not officially allowed to operate in most areas of Prague. A number of vendors are permitted to sell souvenirs around Charles Bridge. Street stalls are allowed near the entrance to the Old Jewish Cemetery in the Jewish Quarter, and they also line the Old Castle Steps from Malostranská metro station up to the castle's eastern gate.

A second-hand bookshop in Karlova Street

What to Buy in Prague

THE INCREASINGLY LARGE selection of goods available in Prague's shops means that everyday items, such as food, books, camera film and toiletries are easily available, and you may find that imported clothing is a better buy here. Prague's more traditional products, such as Bohemian crystal, china, wooden toys and antiques make great souvenirs, and there are still some real bargains to be picked up. Increasingly popular are the more unusual goods which are sold by many of Prague's street shops. These include Soviet army medals, Red Army uniforms, Russian dolls, wooden puppets, ceramics and a wide selection of jewellery. In general, prices are far lower than in the West.

GLASS AND CHINA

BOHEMIAN GLASS and china have always been ranked among the finest in the world. From huge, decorative vases to delicate glass figures, the vast selection of glass and china items for sale is daunting.

Crystal, glass, and china can be quite different depending on where they are made. Some of the best glass and china in Bohemia is produced at the Moser glassworks at Karlovy Vary and sold at the **Karlovy Vary China** shop and **Moser**. The large Crystalex glassworks at Nový Bor and Poděbrady produce some of the most highly-decorated glass, sold at **Crystal**. Other shops which sell a good selection of glass and china include **Bohemia Crystal, Dana-Bohemia**, and two outlets called **Glass**. However, prices are starting to reflect the increasing popularity of a number of the rarer items and bargains are harder to find. Remember that many of the modern pieces are just as lovely and much cheaper. Because of the fragile nature of the goods, many shops will pack anything you buy there. But if you go for a more expensive piece, it is worth looking into insurance before you leave Prague.

ANTIQUE SHOPS

ANTIQUES IN PRAGUE have always been considered a good buy, as prices are still generally lower than in the West. Antique shops that are well worth a look at include

Dorotheum and **Starožitnosti. Antique Clocks** sells exactly what it says and **Military Antiques** is a haven for all army fanatics. For goods over Kč1,000, check with the shop whether you will need a licence to export them. However, watch out for an increasing number of fakes which are now appearing on the market.

Prague also has several *bazar* shops which stock a range of items at cheaper prices. Items are often unusual and good bargains can be found. **Bazar B & P** is a small, popular shop full of second-hand goods. For furniture bargains **Bazar nábytku** is well worth a visit.

TRADITIONAL CRAFTS

THE TRADITIONAL manufacture of high-quality and hand-crafted goods still survives. The variety of the products available in the shops – hand-woven carpets, wooden toys, table mats, beautifully-painted Easter eggs, baskets, figurines in folk costumes, and ceramics – are all based on Czech and Moravian folk crafts and then enriched with modern elements. You can buy them from many market stalls as well as a fair number of shops. **Czech Traditional Handi-crafts** offers a huge choice of hand-carved decorative items. Other arts and crafts shops include **Pottery Tupesy**. A number of street vendors around Old Town Square also sell a range of handmade items including jewellery and puppets.

BOOKS

THERE ARE numerous book-shops in Prague, but most of the books sold are in Czech. Foreign-language books are available in the specialist bookshops in the city centre.

One of the main bookshops is **U Černé Matky Boží**. Here you'll find a range of English-language books (including Czech works which have been translated into English) as well as a fair number of German and French editions. Another well-stocked outlet is the **Big Ben Bookshop**. Maps and guides to Prague in English can be bought at **Academia**. Other specialist bookshops include **Palác knih**, **Kanzelberger**, **Arbes Bookshop** and **Fišer's Bookshop**.

Prague also has second-hand bookshops – look in Golden Lane and Karlova Street – which stock some English-language books, and they all offer the visiting bibliophile hours of enjoyable browsing. **Antikvariát Makovský & Gregor** is one of the best.

FOOD AND DELICATESSENS

PRAGUE'S SUPERMARKETS are well stocked with the basic foodstuffs *(see p207)*. For something special, there are a few delicatessens. **Delicacies-lahůdky** is a small shop with meat and fish counters. A specialist food shop, selling smoked sausage, cheeses and other local delicacies, is **Jan Paukert**. For freshly baked bread visit the bakers around Wenceslas Square and Karmelitská Street. **Paneria** shops sell a good selection of patisseries and sandwiches.

PHARMACIES

MOST PHARMACIES in Prague stock all modern medi-cines, but a prescription from a Czech doctor is needed to buy them. Check listings for addres-ses *(see directory for 24-hour pharmacies)*. Toiletries can be bought at a drugstore.

DIRECTORY

DEPARTMENT STORES

Anchor
KOTVA
Náměstí Republiky 8.
Map 4 D3.
22 48 01 111.

Tesco
Národní 26. **Map** 3 B5.
22 42 27 971.

White Swan
BÍLÁ LABUŤ
Na Poříčí 23.
Map 4 D3.
22 48 11 364.

MARKETS AND MALLS

Flora Palace
PALÁC FLORA
Vinohradská 151.
Map 6 F1.

Havel Market
Havelské náměstí.
Map 3 C4.

Koruna Palace
Václavské náměstí 1.
Map 3 C5.
22 42 19 526.

Prague Market
Bubenské nábřeží 306.
Prague 7.
22 08 00 945.

Smíchov Market
Náměstí 14. října 15.
Map 3 C4.
25 73 21 101.

Vinohradský Pavilion
Vinohradská 50. **Map** 6 F1.
22 20 97 111.

GLASS AND CHINA

Bohemia Art Crystal
ČESKÝ KŘIŠTÁL
Železná 14.
22 42 27 118.
One of several branches.

Crystal
Karlova 5.
Map 3 A4.
22 22 20 064.
One of several branches.

Dana-Bohemia
GLASS, CHINA, CRYSTAL
Národní 43. **Map** 3 A5.
22 42 14 655.
One of several branches.

Glass
SKLO
Malé náměstí 6.
Map 3 B4.
22 42 29 221.
Staroměstské
náměstí 26–27.
Map 3 C3.
22 42 29 755.

Karlovy Vary China
KARLOVARSKÝ PORCELÁN
Pařížská 2.
Map 3 B2.
22 48 11 023.

Moser
Na příkopě 12. **Map** 3 C4.
22 42 11 293/
22 42 28 686.
www.moser-glass.com

ANTIQUE SHOPS

Antique Clocks
STAROŽITNOSTI UHLÍŘ
Mikulandská 8.
Map 3 B5.
22 49 30 572.

A.D. Starožitnosti
Skořepka 8, Prague 1.
Map 3 B4.
22 42 34 696.

Bazar B & P
Nekázanka 17.
Map 4 D4.
22 42 10 550.

Bazar nábytku
Libenský ostrov.
26 60 29 310.

Dorotheum
Ovocný trh 2.
Map 3 C4.
22 42 22 001.
www.dorotheum.cz

Military Antiques
Charvátova 11.
Map 3 C5.
29 62 40 088.
One of several branches.

Starožitnosti
náměstí Kinských 7.
25 73 11 245.
www.antique-shop.cz

GIFTS AND SOUVENIRS

Czech Traditional Handicrafts
Karlova 26. **Map** 3 A4.
22 11 11 064.
Řetězová 10. **Map** 3 B4.
22 22 20 433.

Hračky Traditional Toys
Pohořelec 24. **Map** 1 B3.
06 03 51 57 45.

Pottery Keramika Tupesy
Truhlářská 9. **Map** 4 D3.
22 31 11 56.

BOOKS

Antikvariát Makovský & Gregor
Kaprova 9.
Map 3 B3.
22 23 28 335.

Arbes Bookshop
ARBESOVO KNIHKUPECTVÍ
Štefánikova 26.
Prague 5.
25 73 29 171.

Big Ben Bookshop
Malá Štupartská 5.
Map 3 C3.
22 48 26 565.

Fišer's Bookshop
FIŠEROVO KNIHKUPECTVÍ
Kaprova 10.
Map 3 B3.
22 23 20 733.

Kanzelberger
Václavské náměstí 4.
Map 4 D5.
22 42 19 214.

Knihkupectuí Academia
Václavské náměstí 34.
Map 4 D5.
22 42 23 511.

Palác knih
Václavské náměstí 41.
Map 4 D5.
22 42 16 201.

U Černé Matky Boží
Celetná 34.
Map 3 C3.
22 42 11 155.

FOOD AND DELICATESSENS

Bakeshop
Kozí 1. **Map** 3 C2.
22 23 20 195.

Delicacies-lahůdky
ZLATÝ KŘÍŽ
Jungmannova 34.
Map 3 C5.
22 11 91 801.

Jan Paukert
Národní 17. **Map** 3 B5.
22 42 14 968.

Paneria Pekařstvi
Valentinská 10/20.
Map 3 B3.
22 48 27 912.
www.paneria.cz
One of several branches.

PHARMACIES

It is not usual for pharmacies to have individual names, so look out for **Léky** (drugs) or **Lékárna** (pharmacy).

Národní 35. **Map** 3 B5.
22 42 30 086.

Palackého 5. **Map** 3 C5.
22 49 46 982.
Open 24 hours.

Václavské náměstí 64.
Map 3 C5.
22 22 11 423.

Lékárna u Anděla
Stefanikova 6, Prague 5.
25 73 20 918.
Open 24 hours.

ENTERTAINMENT IN PRAGUE

S INCE THE VELVET REVOLUTION, Prague's entertainment programme has become increasingly varied. Whether you prefer opera to jazz or mini-golf to a football match, the city has plenty to offer. Movie buffs can choose from many of the latest Hollywood blockbusters, a lot of them in English with subtitles. For the adventurous, mime and fringe theatre are both thriving. Prague has a great musical tradition, which includes symphony orchestras, opera, musicals, jazz and folk music. Concerts are performed throughout the year, in venues which range from Baroque palaces to public parks and gardens. Even if you don't speak Czech, you can still enjoy the city's cultural offerings. Some plays can be seen in English, and for many types of entertainment, music, dance and sport, a knowledge of the language isn't necessary at all.

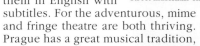

Street musicians entertaining the crowds

PRACTICAL INFORMATION

T HE BEST PLACE to look for information about what's on and where in Prague is in the English-language newspaper *The Prague Post (see p219)*. This provides details of the best entertainment and cultural events which will be of interest to an English-speaking audience. Those events that are in English or have translation facilities are marked. Other sources of information are the leaflets and City Guides given out at the ticket agencies in the city, like **Ticketpro** or **PIS** *(see p211)*, as well as the many weekly alternative newspapers. These are generally printed in Czech, English and German. You can also use the free booklets *Přehled* and *The Month in*

Members of the Opera Mozart *(see p214)* **performing** *Così Fan Tutte*

Prague printed in English and available from any **PIS** office. For a comprehensive rundown of events, buy *Culture in Prague*, a detailed monthly publication listing information on a variety of local exhibitions, concerts and theatre.

BOOKING TICKETS

T ICKETS CAN be bought in advance from the box office at most venues. You can also book tickets in advance by writing to, or ringing, the venue. Remember that many of the city's box offices may not have any English speakers available. Tickets for the opera or for the National Theatre can also be booked online; visit www.opera.cz or www.narodni-divadlo.cz respectively. The more popular events tend to become heavily booked up in advance by tour groups – particularly during the summer – and by season-ticket holders. However, standby tickets are usually available about an hour before the show. If this isn't practical and you want to be sure of a

PUPPET THEATRE

Puppetry has a long tradition in Prague and is still strongly represented. The most famous puppet show in the city is held at the **Spejbl and Hurvínek Theatre** *(see p214)*. The show revolves around Daddy Spejbl and his reprobate son Hurvínek. Other puppet theatres include the **National Marionette Theatre** *(see p214)*, which uses all-string marionettes featured in regular performances for children at weekends. The **Theatre in the Old Town** *(see p214)* and the **Puppet Empire** *(see p214)* also put on puppet shows occasionally. Check listings magazines *(see p218)*.

Theatre puppets

ticket on a particular day, it is better to buy your tickets at a booking agency. The drawback to using agencies is that commission on these tickets can be high, sometimes doubling the original price. Your hotel receptionist may also be able to get you tickets.

TICKET PRICES

TICKET PRICES are very cheap compared to Western prices, except for certain performances, most notably during the Prague Spring Festival (see p50). Prices range from around Kč100 for a small fringe production or puppet theatre to up to Kč1,500 for a performance by an internationally famous orchestra. Paying by credit card is rarely acceptable.

TICKET TOUTS

THERE HAS BEEN a recent spate of counterfeit tickets on sale, especially for the larger rock concerts. To be safe, always buy your tickets at reputable agencies or at the venue itself.

LATE-NIGHT TRANSPORT

PRAGUE'S METRO (see p234) stops running shortly after midnight, while the normal bus and tram service ends around 11:30pm. Then the city's extensive night bus and tram service takes over. Timetables are displayed at each stop. Night trams and buses

The Neo-Classical Estates Theatre (Stavovské divadlo)

are regular and efficient and it is likely that there will be a tram or bus stop near your hotel. Taxis provide the most certain form of late-night transportation, but beware of unscrupulous drivers trying to overcharge you (see p237).

Sparta Stadium (see p215)

Try to walk a little way from the theatre before you hail a cab; the fare will probably be a lot cheaper. Ask your hotel before you go out what the best transport options are.

MUSIC FESTIVALS

THE MOST famous music festival of all is the Prague Spring Music Festival (see p50), held between May and June. Hundreds of international musicians come to Prague to take part in the celebrations. Other music festivals include the Mozart Festival (see p51), held in the summer, the Prague Autumn Music Festival (see p52) and the International Jazz Festival (see p52), held in the autumn.

A view of the Rudolfinum auditorium (see p214)

BOOKING AGENTS

Bohemia Ticket International
Malé Nàměsti 13. **Map** 3 B4.
[22 42 27 832.
Na Příkopě 16. **Map** 4 D4.
[& FAX 22 42 15 031.
W www.ticketsbti.cz

Lucerna
Štěpánská 61. **Map** 5 C1.
[22 42 12 003.

Pragotur
Staroměstské nám.1. **Map** 3 B3.
[22 17 14 128/130.
FAX 22 17 14 127.

Prague Information Service (PIS)
Staroměstské náměstí 1. **Map** 3 B3.
[12 444.
Na Příkopě 20. **Map** 4 D4.
[12 444.
W www.pis.cz

Prague Tourist Centre
Rytířská 12. **Map** 3 C4.
[& FAX 22 42 12 209.
W www.ptc.cz

Ticketpro
Salvátorská 10. **Map** 3 B3.
[29 63 28 888.
FAX 29 63 29 999.
W www.ticketpro.cz

Top Theatre Tickets
Žatecká 1. **Map** 3 B3.
[22 48 19 322.
FAX 22 48 19 324.

Týnská Galerie
Staroměstské náměstí 14. **Map** 3 B3.
[22 23 14 936.

Variety of Entertainment

Prague has always been known for its artistic heritage. Theatre has played an important role in the city's cultural development, and recently the range of entertainment has expanded considerably. Many new theatre groups have emerged, especially more experimental ones. In general, the theatre season runs from September to June. During the summer, open-air performances are given in Prague's gardens and parks. The city also has a strong musical tradition, including great musicians and performers such as Mozart, Smetana and Dvořák. For those who prefer to dance till dawn, relax to the sound of jazz or take in a movie: you'll find plenty to entertain you in this inexpensive city.

English-Language Performances

Many theatres in Prague have started to stage a number of English-language productions – especially in the summer months. Even if the play is not performed in English, many theatre venues have installed simultaneous translation facilities. For more details, check in the listings magazines (see p219).

Major Theatres

Prague's first permanent theatre was built in 1738, but the city's theatrical tradition dates from the Baroque and Renaissance periods.

The **National Theatre** (see p156) is Prague's main venue for opera, ballet and plays. The neighbouring New Stage is another important venue. It is also the main stage for the multi-media **Laterna Magika** company, which is one of Prague's best-known theatre groups as well as being at the forefront of European improvisational theatre.

Other major theatres in the city include the "stone theatres". These gained importance during the 19th century and include the **Vinohrady Theatre**, the **Estates Theatre** (see p65) – one of the most respected in Prague – and the **Prague Municipal Theatre**, an acting company whose plays appear in turn at the **ABC Theatre**, the **Comedy Theatre** and the **Rokoko Studio of Drama**. The **Kolowrat Theatre** is based in the Kolowrat Palace.

Fringe Theatres

These originated during the 1960s and won renown for their fight against the status quo. The groups are still very innovative and largely experimental. They perform in small theatres, and many of Prague's best actors and actresses have developed their skills while working for some of these companies.

Fringe theatres include: the **Dramatic Club**, well known for its supporting ensemble; the **Ypsilon Studio**, with one of the finest acting companies in the city; **Theatre Na Fidlovačce**, stages a mix of musicals and straight drama; the large **Theatre Below Palmovka**, renowned for its mix of classical and modern plays and the **Theatre in Celetná**. One of Prague's most spectacular theatrical and music venues is **Křižík's Fountain**, at the Exhibition Ground, where classical concerts are held and full orchestras perform to stunning lightshows. The **Semafor Theatre** is the home of the very popular comedian, Jiří Suchý.

Pantomime, Mime and "Black Theatre"

Some of the most popular theatre entertainment in Prague is Black Theatre (where black-clad actors move objects against a dark stage without being seen – a stunning visual spectacle), pantomime and mime. None of three requires any understanding of Czech and all are strongly represented. **Jiří Srnec's Black Theatre** is one of the major venues for black theatre performance.

Dance

In Prague, opera and ballet companies traditionally share the **National Theatre**, where the permanent ballet company is based. You can also watch ballet at the **Estates Theatre** and at the **Prague State Opera**. Musicals tend to be popular in Prague, and these are performed by some of the modern dance groups.

Classical Music

The main concert venues for classical music are the **Rudolfinum** (see p84) and the Smetana Hall, found in the **Municipal House** (see p64). Other permanent concert halls include the **Atrium in Žižkov**, a converted chapel, the **Clementinum** and the imposing **Congress Centre Prague**. **Bertramka** is another venue with the added attraction of being the place where Mozart stayed when he was in Prague.

Music in Churches and Palaces

Concerts performed in the numerous churches and palaces around Prague are extremely popular. Many of these buildings are closed to the public, so this is the only chance to see inside them. Major churches include the **Church of St James** (see p65); the **Church of St Nicholas** (see p128) in the Little Quarter; the **Church of St Nicholas** (see p70) in the Old Town; the **Church of St Francis** in Knights of the Cross Square (see p79); **St Vitus's Cathedral** (see p100) and **St George's Basilica** (see p98). Among the other venues included are the **National Museum** (see p147); the **Lobkowicz Palace** (see p99) and the **Sternberg Palace** (see p112). It's worth checking the listings magazines (p219) for the specific dates and times of concerts.

OPERA

DURING THE 20th century, opera has become very popular in Prague, and there are now two major opera companies in the city. One company performs solely in the **National Theatre** *(see pp156–7)* and the other in the **State Opera**. The latter presents all its performances in the language in which they were written, usually Italian, while the National Theatre has more Czech translations of the operas. The **Music Theatre in Karlin** puts on classical operettas and musicals only. More innovative pieces are staged by the **Hudební Fakulta**.

NIGHTCLUBS

EVEN THOUGH nightlife in Prague is not as extensive as in other European capitals, it is rapidly catching up. Since 1989 there have been great changes, so that now visitors have a wider choice of nightclubs, discos and cabaret.

The biggest club in the city is the **Lucerna Bar** which offers a varied programme in an unusual basement ballroom in the beautiful but run down Lucerna building. The **Praga Variety** has a disco and revue programme and is one of Prague's more popular venues. The **Eden-Palladium Dance Club** is the largest disco in Prague. **Zlatý Strom** offers techno/house together with 70's, 80's and 90's dance tunes until 5am in a medieval cellar setting. The trendier clubs include **Radost FX**, where the city's most affluent are attracted by a constant diet of techno/house and plush decor, together with **Obvodní Kulturní dům Vltavská**.

ROCK AND POP CLUBS

LOVERS OF ROCK MUSIC are well served in Prague. There are a large number of popular rock venues, generally small clubs and cafés, which host a variety of different groups. There is a thriving indigenous scene –

Prague's own rock bands play both their own compositions as well as cover versions of more famous numbers, many singing in English. Higher-profile, more internationally renowned Western bands also play in Prague occasionally. The **Rock Café**, and the **Uzi rock-bar**, both very popular venues, offer regular concerts followed by discos. Other venues include the **Futurum Rock Club**, open to the early hours; the **Junior Club na Chmelnici**, whose indie bands begin at 7:30pm. For lovers of nostalgia, **Classic Club** plays an hour of the most popular 1960s classics.

JAZZ

THE ROOTS OF JAZZ in Prague can be traced not only to the American tradition but also to the pre-war heyday of Prague's famous jazz players, such as Jaroslav Ježek. Prague's many jazz clubs play all forms, from Dixieland to swing. One of the leading and most popular jazz venues in the city is the **Jazz Club Reduta**, which has daily jazz concerts at around 9pm. The popular **Metropolitan Club** holds late-night concerts until 3 or 4am. At the **Agharta Jazz Centrum**, you can hear a high standard of playing while eating in its café. **U Malého Glena** has regular live blues, jazz and funk, while **Malostranská beseda** is the venue for more traditional jazz. For serious enthusiasts, the International Jazz Festival *(see p52)* during October attracts talent.

ETHNIC MUSIC

A SMALL NUMBER of clubs and bars in Prague offer ethnic music. The **Palác Akropolis** hosts diverse daily performances in an atmospheric converted 20's theatre building. A variety of bands can be seen from around the world in an atmospheric setting, at the **House of Culture**.

GAY AND LESBIAN VENUES

PRAGUE'S FEW gay venues tend to cater mainly for men, though the buds of a lesbian scene are just beginning to peep through; *Amigo* magazine will give you up-to-date listings. The **A Club** has become very much the headquarters of the lesbian scene. Other popular gay places include **Drake's Club, Villa Mansland, Club Angel**, the disco **Gejzeer**, and the cellar bar **Friends**.

CINEMAS

ALTHOUGH PRAGUE doesn't have all the latest Hollywood blockbusters, more than 80 per cent of the films shown are recent US productions and a third of them have Czech subtitles. The listings magazines *(see p219)* show which films are on and in what language. Most major cinema screens are situated around Wenceslas Square, including **Hvězda, Lucerna, Slovanský Dům** and **Blaník**; others are listed in the directory *(see p215)*. The **Bio Konvikt Ponrepo** cinema shows old films. For a cinema restaurant, visit **Evald**.

SPORTING VENUES

IN CENTRAL PRAGUE, sports facilities are not extensive, so you may have to travel a little further out if you feel like some exercise. Golf, mini-golf or tennis are on offer at the **Motol**, the **Exhibition Ground** *(see p162)* and **Štvanice Island**. Swimming pools are also further out, including two at **Divoká Šárka** and **Kobylisy**. There are beautiful natural lakes at **Lhotka** and **Šeberák** and a whole range of water sports is now on offer at **Hostivař Reservoir** and **Imperial Meadow**.

The main spectator sports are soccer and ice hockey. Sparta Praha, the top soccer team, play at **Sparta Stadium** in Letná, while ice hockey matches are held in the sports hall at the Exhibition Ground.

DIRECTORY

THEATRES

Dramatic Club
ČINOHERNÍ KLUB
Ve Smečkách 26.
Map 6 D1.
📞 29 62 22 123.
🌐 www.cinoherniklub.cz

Estates Theatre
STAVOVSKÉ DIVADLO
Ovocný trh. **Map** 3 C3.
📞 22 42 15 001.
🌐 www.narodni-
divadlo.cz

**Jiří Srnec's Black
Theatre**
ČERNE DIVADLO
JIŘÍHO SRNCE
U Lékárny 597,
15600 Prague 5.
📞 25 79 21 835.

Kolowrat Theatre
DIVADLO KOLOWRAT
(IN ESTATES THEATRE)
Ovocný trh. **Map** 3 C3.
📞 22 49 01 448.
🌐 www.narodni-
divadlo.cz

Křižík's Fountain
KŘIŽÍKOVA FONTÁNA
Výstaviště, Prague 7.
📞 22 01 03 280/295.
🌐 www.krizikova
fontana.cz

Laterna Magika
Národní 4. **Map** 3 A5.
📞 22 49 14 129.
🌐 www.laterna.cz

National Theatre
NÁRODNÍ DIVADLO
Národní 2. **Map** 3 A5.
📞 22 49 01 448.
🌐 www.narodni-
divadlo.cz

**National
Marionette Theatre**
NÁRODNÍ DIVADLO
MARIONET
Žatecká 1.**Map** 3 B3.
📞 22 48 19 322.

**Prague Municipal
Theatre,
ABC Theatre**
MĚSTSKÁ DIVADLA
PRAŽSKÁ, DIVADLO ABC
Vodičkova 28. **Map** 3 C5.
📞 22 42 15 943.
🌐 www.ecn.cz/abc

**Prague Municipal
Theatre,
Comedy Theatre**
MĚSTSKÁ DIVADLA
PRAŽSKÁ, DIVADLO
KOMEDIE
Jungmannova 1. **Map** 5 B1.
📞 22 42 22 734.
🌐 www.divadlokomedie.cz

**Prague Municipal
Theatre,
Rokoko Studio
of Drama**
MĚSTSKÁ DIVADLA
PRAŽSKÁ, DIVADLO
ROKOKO
Václavské náměstí 38.
Map 4 D5.
📞 22 42 12 837.
🌐 www.rokoko.cz

Puppet Empire
ŘÍSE LOUTEK
Žatecká 1. **Map** 3 B3.
📞 22 23 24 562.
🌐 www.riseloutek.cz

Reduta Theatre
DIVADLO REDUTA
Národní 20. **Map** 3 B5.
📞 22 49 12 246.

Semafor Theatre
Divadlo Semafor,
Křižíkova 10.
Map 4 F3.
📞 22 18 68 151.

**Spejbl and
Hurvínek Theatre**
DIVADLO SPEJBLA A
HURVÍNKA
Dejvická 38.
📞 22 43 12 380.
🌐 www.spejbl-hurvinek.cz

**Theatre in
Celetná**
DIVADLO V CELETNE
Celetná 17. **Map** 3 C3.
📞 22 23 26 843.

**Theatre below
Palmovka**
DIVADLO POD
PALMOVKOU
Zenklova 34, Prague 8.
📞 26 63 11 708.
🌐 www.vol.cz/palmovka

**Theatre in the
Old Town**
DIVADLO V DLOUHÉ
Dlouhá 39. **Map** 3 C3.
📞 22 48 26 807.
🌐 www.divadlovdlouhe.cz

**Theatre Na
Fidlovačce**
DIVADLO NA FIDLOVAČCE
Křesomyslova 625.
Map 6 E5.
📞 26 12 15 722.
🌐 www.fidlovacka.cz

Vinohrady Theatre
DIVADLO NA
VINOHRADECH
Náměstí Míru 7.
Map 6 F2.
📞 22 42 54 813.
🌐 www.dnv-praha.cz

Ypsilon Studio
STUDIO YPSILON
Spálená 16. **Map** 3 B5.
📞 22 49 47 119.
🌐 www.ypsilonka.cz

MUSIC VENUES

Academy of Music
HUDEBNÍ FAKULTA AMU
Malostranské náměstí 13.
Map 2 E3.
📞 25 75 34 206.

Atrium in Žižkov
ATRIUM NA ŽIŽKOVĚ
Čajkovského 12, Prague 3.
📞 22 27 21 838.

Bertramka
BERTRÁMKA MUZEUM
W A MOZARTA
Mozartova 169, Prague 5.
📞 25 73 18 461.

Church of St James
KOSTEL SV. JAKUBA
Málá štupartská. **Map** 3 C3.

**Church of St
Nicholas (Old Town)**
KOSTEL SV. MIKULÁŠE
Staroměstské náměstí.
Map 3 B3.

**Church of
St Nicholas**
KOSTEL SV. MIKULÁŠE
Malostranské náměstí.
Map 2 E3.

**Church of
St Francis**
KOSTEL SV. FRANTIŠKA
Křižovnické náměstí.
Map 3 A4.

**Church of
Sts Simon and Jude**
KOSTEL SV. ŠIMONA
A JUDY
Dušní ulice. **Map** 3 B2.

Clementinum
ZRCADLOVÁ SÍŇ
KLEMENTINA
Mariánské náměstí 10.
Map 3 B3.

Lobkowicz Palace
LOBKOVICKÝ PALÁC
Jiřská 1, Pražský hrad.
Map 2 E2.
📞 25 75 34 578.

**Music Theatre
in Karlín**
HUDEBNÍ DIVADLO V
KARLÍNĚ
Křižíkova 10. **Map** 4 F3.
📞 26 11 71 111.

**Congress Centre
Prague**
KONGRESOVÉ CENTRUM
PRAHA
5. května 65, Prague 4.
📞 26 11 71 111.
🌐 www.kcp.cz

National Museum
NÁRODNÍ MUZEUM
Václavské náměstí 68.
Map 6 D1.
📞 22 44 97 111.

Prague State Opera
STÁTNÍ OPERA PRAHA
Wilsonova 4. **Map** 6 E1.
📞 22 42 27 266.
🌐 www.opera.cz

Rudolfinum
RUDOLFINUM –
DVOŘÁKOVA SÍŇ
Alšovo nábřeží 12.
Map 3 A3.
📞 22 48 93 111.

St George's Basilica
BAZILIKA SV. JIŘÍ
Jiřské náměstí, Pražský hrad.
Map 2 E2.

St Vitus's Cathedral
KATEDRÁLA VÍTA
Pražský hrad. **Map** 2 D2.

Sternberg Palace
ŠTERNBERSKÝ PALAC
Hradčanské náměstí 15.
Map 1 C3.
📞 23 32 50 068.

NIGHTCLUBS

Disco Kobra
Zlatnická 4. **Map** 4 E2.
📞 22 23 29 157.

Diskotéka Zlatý Strom
Karlova 6.
Map 3 A4.
(22 22 20 441.

Eden-Palladium Dance Club
U Slavie 1.
(27 27 36 306.

Karlovy Lázně
Novotného lávka, Praha 1.
Map 3 A4.
(22 16 35 408.

Lucerna Bar
Vodičkova 36.
Map 5 C1.
(22 42 17 108.

Obvodní Kulturní dům Vltavská
Bubenská 1.
(22 08 79 683.
w www.vltavska.cz

Praga Variety
VATIETE PRAGA
Vodičkova 30.
Map 3 C5.
(22 42 22 100.

Radost FX
Bělehradská 120.
Map 6 E2.
(22 42 54 776.
w www.radostfx.cz

ROCK AND POP CLUBS

Classic Club
Pařížská 4.
Map 3 B3

Futurum Rock Club
Zborovská 7.
Map 2 F5
(25 73 28 571.

Klub Lávka
Novotného lávka 1.
Map 3 A4.
(22 22 22 156.
w www.lavka.cz

Meloun
Michalská 12. **Map** 3 B4.
(22 42 30 126.
w www.meloun.cz

Rock Café
Národní 20. **Map** 3 B5.
(22 49 33 945.

Roxy
Dlouhá 33. **Map** 3 C3.
(22 48 26 296.
w www.roxy.cz

Uzi rock-bar
Legerova 44. **Map** 6 D2.
(29 00 03 275.

JAZZ CLUBS

Agharta Jazz Centrum
Krakovská 5. **Map** 6 D1.
(22 22 11 275.
w www.AGARTHA.cz

Jazz Club Reduta
Národní 20.
Map 3 B5.
(22 49 12 246.

Malostranská Beseda
Malostranské náměstí 21.
Map 2 E3.
(25 75 32 092.

Metropolitan Jazz Club
Jungmannova 14.
Map 3 C5.
(22 49 47 777.

U Malého Glena
Karmelitská 23.
Map 2 E4.
(25 75 31 717.
w www.malyglen.cz

ETHNIC MUSIC

House of Culture
OBVODNÍ KULTURNÍ
DŮM VLTAVSKÁ
Bubenská 1.
(22 08 79 683.
w www.vltavska.cz

Palác Akropolis
Kubelíkova 27.
(29 63 30 913.
w www.palacakropolis.cz

GAY AND LESBIAN CLUBS

A Club
Milíčova 25.
(22 27 81 623.

Club Angel
Kmochova 8.
(25 73 16 127.
w www.clubangel.praha.cz

Drake's Club
Zborovská 50, Praha 5.
(25 73 26 828.

Friends
Náprstkova 1. **Map** 3 A4.
(22 16 35 408.

Gejzeer
Vinohradská 40. **Map** 6 F1.
(22 25 16 036.
w www.gejzeer.cz

Kafírna U Českého Pána
Kozí 13. **Map** 3 C2.
(22 23 28 283.

Villa Mansland
Štěpničná 9/11, Praha 8.
(22 16 35 408.

CINEMAS

Bio Konvikt Ponrepo
Bartolomějská 11.
Map 3 B5.
(22 42 37 233.

Blaník
Václavské náměstí 56.
Map 6 D1.
(22 40 32 172.

Budějovická Broadway
Budějovická 1667,
Praha 4.
(26 13 82 297.

Evald
Národní 28. **Map** 3 B5.
(22 11 05 225.
w www.evald.cinemart.cz

Hvězda
Václavské náměstí 38.
Map 4 D5.
(22 42 16 822.

Kotva
Náměstí Republiky 8.
Map 4 D3.
(22 48 11 482.

Lucerna
Vodičkova 36.
Map 3 C5.
(22 42 16 972.

Multiplex Cinema Nový Smíchov
Plzeňská 8.
(25 71 81 212.

Perštýn
Na Perštýně 6.
Map 3 B3.
(22 16 68 432.

Praha
Václavské náměstí 17.
Map 4 D5.
(22 22 45 881.

Slovanský Dům
Na Příkopě 22.
Map 3 C4.
(25 71 81 212.
w www.stercentury.cz

SPORTING VENUES

Divoká Šárka
Prague 6.

Exhibition Ground
VÝSTAVIŠTĚ
Sports stadium, Prague 7.

Hostivař Reservoir
Prague 10.

Imperial Meadow
CÍSAŘSKÁ LOUKA
Prague 5.

Kobylisy
Prague 8.

Lhotka
Prague 4.

Motol
V Úvalu 84, Prague 5.

Šeberák
Prague 4.

Sparta Stadium
Milady Horákové,
Prague 7.

Štvanice Island
Ostrov Štvanice 1125,
Prague 7.

SURVIVAL
GUIDE

PRACTICAL INFORMATION

O VER THE LAST TEN YEARS, Prague has become more and more open to visitors. The city has responded well to the enormous influx of tourists, and facilities such as hotels, banks, restaurants and information centres have improved considerably. Even so, a little forward planning is always worthwhile. Reading up about a sight, checking it is open and how best to get there, can save a lot of time

A Martin Tour sightseeing bus

and inconvenience. Prague's transport system is straightforward and most of the city's sights are within walking distance. In general, prices are still considerably lower than in the West, but a few of the more up-market restaurants and hotels are priced according to Western rather than Czech wallets. Despite a small increase in petty crime, especially pick-pocketing, Prague is still safer than the majority of Western cities.

TOURIST INFORMATION

T HERE ARE a number of tourist information offices and specialized agencies. These can provide advice on anything from accommodation and travel to restaurants and guided tours.

Many employ English speakers and print English language publications. The efficient **Prague Information Service (PIS)** is the city's best tourist information point. It has three offices in the city centre and it provides visitors with maps, advice, listings *(see pp210–11)* and other types of information in English, German and Czech. To help you find your way around the city, **Kiwi** has a large selection of maps and guides in English.

Čedok street sign

TIPS FOR TOURISTS

I N PRAGUE, there are enough English speakers to make booking a room, buying a ticket or ordering a meal relatively simple. A smattering of German may also help, as many Czechs have a working knowledge of the language.

One of the best times to visit Prague is during the summer, although it can be

rather crowded. Other busy times of the year are Easter and major Catholic festivals *(see pp50–53)*. The main sights, such as the Old Town Square, are always packed during these periods, but the crowds give Prague a carnival atmosphere. Street entertainers, buskers and small street stalls spring up around the most popular attractions. If the crowds do get too . much, just turn off into one of the smaller streets and you are almost guaranteed peace and quiet. Bring a light raincoat for the summer and some warm, woolly clothes for the rest of the year.

OPENING HOURS

T HIS GUIDE lists the opening hours for the individual museums, galleries and churches. Most of the city's major sights can be seen throughout the year, but many of Prague's gardens and the castles outside the city are only open from 1 April to 31 October. Visiting hours are normally from 9am to 5pm, daily, but the final admission times can often be as much as an hour earlier. All museums and several castles arc also closed every Monday, so be sure to check before visiting them. The National Museum

Entry tickets for some of Prague's major tourist sights

is closed on the first Tuesday of the month and the Jewish Museum is closed on Friday afternoons and on Saturdays.

Opening hours of Prague's shops vary widely. Some businesses are open between 7am and 6pm, Monday to Friday, and 8am to noon on Saturdays. Some department stores *(see p208)* are open until 7pm on Saturdays and Sundays.

The main office of the Prague Information Service in the street Na příkopě

A horse-drawn carriage in the Old Town Square

Prague does not have any standard late-night shopping, although many of the more expensive tourist shops stay open until around 10pm. Banks open from 8am to 4pm, Monday to Friday. Restaurants, cafés and bars all have varied opening hours *(see pp188–9)*. Most of the city's bars open from 10am and as there are no licensing laws, often stay open until everyone leaves.

LISTINGS AND TICKETS

THERE ARE some 160 galleries and 40 museums scattered throughout the city, and to find out what's on it is best to look in a listings paper. The English-language newspaper *The Prague Post* gives detailed listings of most events and exhibitions. Available from newsstands in the city centre, it also give tips for the visitor and informative articles on Prague, its politics and its people. The **PIS** has a free monthly English-language listings book.

The price of entry tickets for museums varies widely, from Kč60 to around Kč300. Most churches are free, with a collection box at the door. Tickets for entertainment events can be bought from the booking agencies in the city, or at the venue itself. Some of Prague's hotels can get you tickets, or try a large travel agent in the centre.

SIGHTSEEING TIPS

A GOOD WAY to see Prague is to take a sightseeing tour. Many firms offer trips around Prague's major sights as well as outings to castles such as Karlstein and Konopiště

(see pp166–7). Tours usually start from Náměstí Republiky (Republic Square) and from the upper part of Václavské náměstí (Wenceslas Square). These trips can be expensive but prices vary, so it is worth checking what's on offer before you make a booking.The Jewish Museum *(see p87)* organizes trips around the Jewish Quarter. For those on a tight budget, **PIS** offers some of the cheapest tours.

A trip on tram No. 91, run by the Museum of Municipal Mass Transport, is one of the cheapest and best city centre tours. It starts off at the Exhibition Ground *(see pp176–7)* and travels around the Old Town, the New Town and the Jewish Quarter. It runs from Easter to the end of October every weekend and public holiday. Tickets can be bought on board. Sightseeing trips in horse-drawn carriages (fiacres) are run from the Old Town Square, and in summer, a "fun train" from Mostecká Street runs through some of the loveliest parts of Hradčany and the Little Quarter.

A street sign showing the services offered by Pragotur

INFORMATION CENTRES AND TOUR OPERATORS

Akasi
28.Října. **Map** 3 C5.
 22 22 43 067.
Na Příkopě 3–5. **Map** 3 C4.
 22 42 36 118.
FAX 22 42 37 235.

American Express
Václavské náměstí 56. **Map** 6 D1.
 22 42 19 992.
FAX 22 22 11 131.
W www.americanexpress.com

Best Tour
Václavské náměstí 27. **Map** 6 D1.
 28 48 14 141.
FAX 28 48 14 144.

Čedok
Na Příkopě 18. **Map** 3 C4.
 22 41 97 111/616.
FAX 22 22 44 421.

Tourist information centre

Rytířská 16. **Map** 3 C4.
 24 22 77 23.
W www.cedok.cz

Kiwi
Jungmannova 23. **Map** 3 C5.
 22 49 48 455.
FAX 22 62 45 555.

Martin Tour Praha
Štěpánská 61. **Map** 5 C1.
 22 42 12 473.
W www.martintour.cz

Pragotur
Staroměstské náměstí 1. **Map** 3 B3. 22 44 82 562. FAX 22 44 82 380. W www.prague-info.cz

Prague Information Service – PIS
Na Příkopě 20. **Map** 3 C4.
 12 444.
W www.pis.cz

Travelex
Národní 28. **Map** 3 B5.
 22 11 05 371.
FAX 22 49 49 002.

Personal Security and Health

COMPARED TO MANY Western cities, Prague is relatively safe. Though you may not need emergency help from the police, you should feel free to approach them at any time for advice of any kind; they are generally very helpful to the tourist population. If you should need emergency medical care during you stay in Prague, it will be given free. There is also a number of English-speaking services available, including health centres, pharmacies and dentists, as well as US and British information centres.

A Prague police sign

ADVICE FOR VISITORS

PRAGUE IS A SAFE and un-threatening city to walk around. Violent crimes against tourists in the city centre are rare. The main crime problems that affect tourists are petty pilfering from cars, hotels and pockets; violence with robbery is very unusual. Using your common sense should help you to avoid Prague's only real plague – its pick-pockets. The crowded summer months are a favourite time for these thieves. Always remember to keep your bag in sight and avoid carrying your passport, wallet and valuables in your back pocket or an open bag. Thieves do tend to operate around the popular sights, such as Charles Bridge, and

Municipal police badge

State police badge

many use diversionary tactics, one knocking into you while the other steals your belongings. It is very unlikely that anything stolen will ever be recovered. Never leave anything of value in your car. Car alarms have proved not to be a deterrent. Try and park your car in an underground car park, especially if you are driving a foreign make. Always take out adequate insurance before visiting Prague, as it is difficult to arrange once there. Report any thefts to the police for future insurance claims. Avoid getting drawn into a street card game known as shells. It is a classic con game.

Women may encounter a few stares and comments, but this is about as far as sexual harassment will go.

However, one place to try and avoid at night if you are a woman alone, is Wenceslas Square. Most men will assume you are one of the city's prostitutes. Unfortunately, Prague has too few reputable bars and cafés that stay open into the early hours. The words "non-stop" and "herna" are synonymous with shady characters; the latter are filled with slot-machines and gambling addicts. See our bars and cafés listings for recommended places *(see pp204–5)*

It is an unwritten law that you should carry your passport at all times and although you are unlikely to be asked to produce it, having it could save a lot of problems. Before you travel take photocopies of all essential documents as replacing them can be difficult and time-consuming.

THE POLICE AND SECURITY SERVICES

IN PRAGUE you will come across several kinds of policemen and women and members of various security services. Report any problems to a uniformed state police officer at a police station. The main stations are marked on the Street Finder maps *(see pp238–45)*. The state police carry guns and can arrest a suspect. They patrol the streets on foot or drive green and white patrol cars. The municipal police are the other main security force, have greater powers, and are divided into different sections. Traffic police ensure the smooth running of traffic and regulate parking, speeding and drink driving. Fines for illegal parking and speeding are huge. It is illegal to drive with any alcohol in your

A male state police officer

A municipal police officer

A female state police officer

A "black sheriff"

State police patrol car

Prague ambulance

bloodstream. Occasionally the police have a clamp down on drink driving and if you are caught, the penalties are severe. The traffic police are also responsible for car clamping and collecting the fines *(see pp232–3)*. Finally, if you have a traffic accident, you must immediately ring **Road Accidents**. It is against the law to move anything before the police get there. There are also a number of private security guards. These are often called "black sheriffs" (many of them actually wear black uniforms) and tend to guard banks and be used as security at football matches and so on. They are not armed.

HEALTH CARE

Pharmacy sign

HEALTH CARE in Prague is divided into state and private care. If you need emergency treatment it will be provided free of charge. But all non-essential treatment has to be paid for there and then. So make sure you have adequate medical insurance before you arrive in Prague and a credit card or enough traveller's cheques to pay – don't forget the receipt for your insurance claim.

Your hotel should be able to put you in touch with a local doctor, but if you need more prompt service, Prague's emergency services are on call 24 hours a day and you can call an ambulance if necessary. Hospitals with casualty units are marked on the Street Finder maps at the back of this book *(see pp238–45)*.

There are also 24-hour pharmacies (lékárna) *(see p209)* and a **First Aid/Emergency Dental Care Centre** giving advice and simple remedies. If you want an English-speaking doctor, visit **Fakultní Poliklinika** in the New Town, or else go to the **Diplomatic Health Centre** for foreigners at Na Homolce. You will need to take a passport and a means of payment if you use either of these.

Those with respiratory problems should be aware that between October and March, sulphur dioxide levels in Prague regularly exceed the World Health Organization's accepted levels – often by up to three times. With increasing car ownership and a lack of money for alternative fuels, this seems unlikely to decrease in the near future.

DIRECTORY

EMERGENCY NUMBERS

Ambulance
Rychlá lékařská pomoc
[155.

Police
Tísňové volání policie
[158.

Fire
Tísňové volání hasičů
[150.

Emergency Operator
[112 (in English).

MEDICAL CENTRES

Diplomatic Health Centre
Nemocnice Na Homolce
Roentgenova 2.
[25 72 72 144.
W www.homolka.cz

Fakultní Poliklinika
Karlovo nám 32. **Map** 5 B3.
[22 49 61 111.

First Aid/Emergency Dental Care
První pomoc zubní
Palackého 5. **Map** 3 C5. *(7pm–7am Mon–Fri, 24hrs Sat, Sun.)*
[22 49 46 981.

General Health Care Corporation
Krakovská 8. **Map** 6 D1.
M Muzeum.
[22 22 10 178.

24-hour Pharmacy
Štefánikova 6. M Anděl.
[25 73 20 918.
Palackého 5. **Map** 3 C5.
M Můstek, Národní třída.
[22 49 46 982.

GENERAL HELP

American Centre
Americké středisko
US Embassy, Tržiště 15. **Map** 2 E3.
[25 75 30 663.
W www.usembassy.cz

British Council
Britské kulturní středisko
Národní 10. **Map** 3 B5.
[22 19 91 111.
W www.britishcouncil.cz

Car Breakdown Service/Road Accidents
[1230, 1240, 1054.

Lost and Found
Ztráty a nálezy
Karoliny Světlé 5. **Map** 3 A5.
[22 42 35 085.

Money, Banks and Currency Exchange Offices

A bureau de change sign in Prague

COMPARED TO MANY European cities, Prague is a relatively cheap city to visit. Hundreds of banks and bureaux de change have been established, some staying open all night. For the lowest charges and, unfortunately, the longest queues, it is best to change money in a bank. Credit cards are becoming more and more accepted. Traveller's cheques can only be changed in banks.

BANKING

HUNDREDS OF private banks and bureaux de change have been opened in Prague since 1989. The large, modern banks – generally found in the city centre – all open between 8am and 5pm Monday to Friday. The banks may not close at lunch. There are always long queues at the exchange tills so make sure you get there well before closing time. Hundreds of Bureaux de change are found in tiny shops throughout the city. However, despite offering much better exchange rates than the banks, their commission charges are huge, often as high as 12% compared to the bank's 1–5%. But there is a minimum bank commission of Kč20–50. The main advantage of these exchange offices is their convenience. Many are open late every day, some offer a 24-hour service, and queues are rare.

Most of the larger hotels will also change foreign currency for you, but again commission rates may be very high. If you find you have some Czech currency left over from your stay, you can reconvert your money. All banks will reconvert your extra crowns for a small commission. Finally, never change your money on the

black market. As well as being illegal the rate is not any higher than banks or exchanges and it is likely you'll be given notes that are not legal tender.

There are also may ATM machines in the centre of Prague. Some of these are in the entrance to banks and are open even when the branch

An automatic teller machine for dispensing cash

is closed. They accept Mastercard, Visa and Eurocard, and information is in English, German, French or Czech.

CREDIT CARDS

PAYING BY credit card is becoming more popular. Even if a shop or restaurant window sports a credit card sign, do not assume they will take them as payment; always ask before you eat your meal. The cards most often accepted are: American Express, VISA, MasterCard and Access. Most banks will allow cash advances (up to your limit) on your card. Only a few restaurants, shops and hotels accept American Express.

Façade of the Československá Obchodní bank

DIRECTORY

BANKS

HVB-Bank
Revoluční 7. **Map** 4 D2.
(22 11 19 761.
FAX 22 11 19 762.
W www.HUB.cz

Česká Národní Banka
Na příkopě 28. **Map** 3 C4.
(22 44 11 111.
FAX 22 44 13 708.
W www.cnb.cz

Česká Spořitelna
Rytířská 29. **Map** 3 C4.
(22 41 01 111.
W www.csas.cz

Czechoslovak Commercial Bank
ČESKOSLOVENSKÁ OBCHODNÍ BANKA
Na příkopě 14. **Map** 3 C4.
(22 41 11 111.

Commercial Bank
KOMERČNI BANKA
Spálená 51. **Map** 3 B5.
(22 19 03 111.
W www.kb.cz
One of several branches.

Union Banka
Národní 24. **Map** 3 B5.
(22 49 34 122.
FAX 22 49 34 444.
W www.union.cz
One of several branches.

BUREAUX DE CHANGE

American Express
Václavské náměstí 56.
Map 3 C5.
(22 28 00 237.
FAX 22 22 11 131.
W www.aexp.com
One of several branches.

Čekobanka Chequepoint Rapid
Železná 2. **Map** 3 C4.
(24 82 64 65.
One of several branches.

Exact Change
Na Příkopě 12.
Map 4 D4.
(22 42 13 526.
One of several branches.

CASH AND TRAVELLER'S CHEQUES

CURRENCY COMES in Czech crowns and hellers. There are 100 hellers to the crown. It is legal to bring Czech currency into and out of the Czech Republic. Traveller's cheques are by far the safest alternative to carrying cash. It is recommended that you take well-known brands – American Express, Thomas Cook, for example – although it is unlikely that the major banks will refuse any. However, traveller's cheques are not accepted as currency by any shops or restaurants and must be changed at exchanges or banks. The American Express office *(see p225)* sells and cashes traveller's cheques. They don't charge commission for cashing their own cheques.

Banknotes
Czech banknotes are now in circulation in the denominations Kč20, Kč50, Kč100, Kč200, Kč500, Kč1,000, Kč2,000 and Kč5,000.

Coins
Coins come in the following denominations: 50 hellers; Kč1, Kč2, Kč5, Kč10, Kč20 and Kč50. All the coins have the Czech emblem, a lion rampant, on one side.

Kč5,000 note

Kč2,000 note

Kč1,000 note

Kč500 note

Kč200 note

Kč100 note

Kč50 note

Kč20 note

50 hellers

1 crown (Kč1)

2 crowns (Kč2)

5 crowns (Kč5)

10 crowns (Kč10)

20 crowns (Kč20)

50 crowns (Kč50)

Communications

THE CZECH telephone and postal service, Telecom, has undergone a major modernization programme. Digital phones have replaced the older coin-operated ones, and the postal service has become much more efficient. There were some problems in the transition, but the upgrading and improvements have been completed and few problems should be experienced.

USING PUBLIC TELEPHONES

ALTHOUGH THERE are plenty of public phones on street corners, you can also find them in post offices, where you have to leave a deposit, make the call, and then pay what you owe to the attendant. In hotels, you can usually get a direct line but commission charges on the calls are often exorbitant. Remember also that inter-national calls are extremely expensive, no matter what time of day you phone. But they are at least somewhat cheaper after 7pm, and also

on Saturdays and Sundays. The cheapest way to call abroad is via Telecom's Xcall service (ring 952 00).

There is an increasing number of modern phonecard telephones in Prague. You can buy the cards *(Telefonní karta)* for these phones from most tabáks and newsstands, and from post offices, supermarkets and petrol stations. Two very popular cards are Karta X, a pre-paid calling card which allows you to make national and international calls from any phone, and TRICK, a multifunctional card which can be used to pay for telephone calls and internet services.

On all phones in the country the dialling tone is a short note followed by a long one; the ringing tone consists of long regular notes, and the engaged signal has short and rapid notes.

PROBLEM NUMBERS

IF YOU HAVE problems getting through to a number in Prague, it is very likely that the number has changed due to the modernization of the phone system. To check, ring the directory enquiries number and ask for an English speaker.

INTERNET CAFÉS

THERE ARE SEVERAL internet cafés in Prague. On the whole, prices are modest, and the lines are reasonably fast for email access. One of the best is **Káva**, in the New Town. There is also one at the Trades Fair Palace *(see pp164–65).*

USING A COIN-OPERATED TELEPHONE

1 Lift the receiver and wait for the dialling tone.

2 Insert a 1, 2 or 5 crown coin in the slot.

3 The digital display shows how much credit is left. If you need to insert more money, the message *Vložte mince* appears.

4 When the words *Volte číslo* come up, dial the number then wait to be connected.

5 When you have finished speaking replace the receiver. Any coins that were unused are returned here. These phones do not give change.

Kč1   Kč2   Kč5   **Coins that can be inserted into coin-operated phones**

USING A PHONECARD TELEPHONE

1 Lift the receiver and wait for the dialling tone.

2 The message *Vložte tele-fonní kartu,* asks you to insert your card. The display also shows you how much credit you have left on your phonecard.

3 When the words *Volte číslo* appear, dial the number and wait to be connected.

By pressing this small button on the phone at any time during your call, you can have an English translation of the instructions.

Emergency numbers

4 The card is ejected automatically when it runs out of credit.

The multi-purpose TRICK phonecard

Post Offices

THERE IS A number of post offices in Prague *(see Street Finder on pp238–49)*. The best and largest one is the **Main Post Office** in Jindřišská, just off Wenceslas Square. It has a huge variety of services, including a large phone room where you can make international calls. This service operates from 7am to 11pm.

This post office has recently undergone a complete refurbishment, and is now astonishingly modern and straightforward to use, with easy-access information in English. Take a ticket when you enter the building and then follow the number on it to the correct booth, which will be indicated by an electronic display. Much to the delight of locals, the former long queues have at

Post Office sign

last been replaced by swift and efficient service.

A 24-hour service is also available at the post office in **Masarykovo Station**.

Sending a Letter

THE POSTAL SERVICE is now fast, but prices for all the post office services are expected to increase slightly in the future.

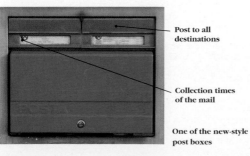

Post to all destinations

Collection times of the mail

One of the new-style post boxes

Reaching the Right Number

	Dial
• Internal (Czech) directory enquiries	1180
• Prague directory enquiries and the operator	1180
• International exchange and to make a collect call *(ask for an English-speaker)*	1181
• International call followed by the country code	00
• International directory enquiries	1181
• **In case of emergencies (Police)**	**158**
• **Emergency operator (English)**	**112**

Tobacconist's, where you can also buy stamps and phonecards

There is no first or second class mail in the Czech Republic, but the majority of letters usually arrive at their destination within a few days.

If you want to send something more valuable through the post, use the registered mail service, which is reliable and efficient. Aerogrammes abroad do not exist.

Postcards or letters can be posted in the many orange post boxes scattered around Prague. Both take around five working days to arrive in England and about a week to get to America.

Stamps can be bought from post offices, newsagents or tabáks – who will also tell you what stamps you need. All parcels and registered letters need to be handed in at a post office.

For emergency parcels and packages, you can use an international courier service, such as **DHL**.

Poste Restante

POST RESTANTE letters are delivered to the Main Post Office in Jindřišská Street. Go to window 28 (open Monday to Friday 6:30am to 8pm and Saturday 6:30am to 1pm) with your passport or other official identification. The **American Express** office will also hold mail and parcels for up to a month for anyone who is a registered card holder.

Useful Addresses

Main Post Office
Jindřišská 14. **Map** 4 D5.
22 11 31 111. 800 10 44 10 (general information).
Open 7am–8pm daily.
www.cpost.cz

Masarykovo Station Post Office
Hybernská 15. **Map** 4 E3.
22 42 19 714. **Open** 24hrs daily.

American Express
Václavské náměstí 56. **Map** 4 D5.
22 28 00 237. **FAX** 22 22 11 131.
www.aexp.com

DHL
Vaclavské náměstí 47. **Map** 4 D5.
800 103 000. **FAX** 22 15 12 424.
www.dhl.cz

Káva
Narodní 37. **Map** 3 B5. **Open** 7am–9pm daily (from 9am Sat & Sun).
www.kava-coffee.cz

Additional Information

Visitors enjoying tax-free shopping on Na Příkopě

DISABLED TRAVELLERS

FACILITIES FOR THE disabled are few and far between. Occasionally you will come across a ramp at the entrance to a building to allow the disabled easier access, but this is the exception rather than the rule. There are few organizations that campaign for the disabled and, unfortunately, those that do are currently hampered by both public inertia and a lack of funding.

Despite, this, these attitudes are slowly changing and, although transport around the city is a major problem, groups do now exist who can help you with advice, sightseeing tours, accommodation and getting around the city. Two of the best organizations to contact in advance of your trip are: the **Czech Association of Persons with Disabilities** and the **Prague Wheelchair Association**.

Czech Association of Persons with Disabilities
Karlínské náměstí 12.
Map 5 B2.
[22 48 16 976/22 48 15 915.

Prague Wheelchair Association
Benediktská 6.
Map 4 D3.
[22 48 27 210/22 48 26 078.
FAX 22 48 26 079.

CUSTOMS REGULATIONS AND IMMIGRATION

A VALID PASSPORT or, where applicable, an ID card is needed when entering the Czech Republic. Visitors are advised to contact the Czech embassy or consulate, or check details with their travel agent to confirm visa requirements before travelling. British and EU nationals must have a valid passport or identity card, but visas are not required (www.czechembassy.org.uk/consular.htm). Visitors from the United States, Canada, Australia and New Zealand need a valid passport with a minimum of 90 days remaining on it, and can stay for up to three months without a visa. Anyone wishing to stay longer than 30 days will need to register with the border police. Your hotel can usually arrange this for you. If you require a visa you can obtain one from your nearest Czech embassy or consulate.

For non-EU visitors, customs allowances per person are 2 litres (3.6 pints) of wine, 1 litre (1.8 pints) of spirits, 250 cigarettes or equivalent tobacco products. Goods under Kč3,000 in value can be imported duty-free.

You can take in as much foreign currency as you like, however, it is illegal to take more than Kč350,000 out of the Czech Republic. To export authentic antiques you need to obtain a special licence *(see Shopping pp206–7)*. VAT (value added tax) can be claimed back on items totalling Kč1,000 or more which are carried out of the country within 30 days of purchase.

STUDENT INFORMATION

IF YOU ARE ENTITLED to an International Student Identity Card (ISIC), it is worth getting one before travelling to Prague. Admission charges into most of Prague's major tourist sights are cheaper on production of a valid ISIC card. Students can also get cheaper coach travel, and while in the country, train travel. There are a couple of youth hostels in the centre of the city *(see Where to Stay, pp182–9)*. For further information about what is available contact the tour operator **Koleje a Menzy**.

Koleje a Menzy
Jednota Youth Hostel, Opletalova 38.
Map 4 D5. [22 49 30 010. FAX 22 49 30 361. W www.ruk.cuni.cz

NEWSPAPERS, TV, RADIO

PRAGUE HAS A number of newspapers including two weekly English-language ones, *The Prague Post* and *Prague Business Post*. They are both well produced and provide useful tips for visitors

The two English-language newspapers published in Prague

to the city as well as up-to-date and informative pieces on Prague, its people and politics. The former includes a good leisure supplement, *Night and Day*.

Most of the newsstands that are around Wenceslas Square and other popular tourist spots sell the main European papers and the *International Herald Tribune*. A wide selection of international papers is also available at the newsagent's in Jungmannova 5.

These days there is a larger choice of television in Prague than ever before. Western films are interspersed with well-made nature

A two-prong and a three-prong plug adaptor for use in Prague

programmes and classic Czech films. The stations also show many soap operas, like *Dallas*. Various satellite channels are also available, plus numerous programmes in English, including the daily news. Foreign films are often shown with optional Czech dubbing.

You can listen to the BBC World Service on 101.1FM, but one of the most popular radio stations is Europe II on 88.2MHz playing a blend of mainstream pop. Club VOA on 106.2FM has a similar mix of music with English news. Other stations include Radio I on 91.9MHz, Radio Golem on 90.3MHz and Radio Bonton on 99.7MHz. Reception can be very bad outside the city. You can also listen to the BBC on the Internet (www.bbc.co.uk/).

CONVERSION CHART

Imperial to Metric
1 inch = 2.54 centimetres
1 foot = 30 centimetres
1 mile = 1.6 kilometres
1 ounce = 28 grams
1 pound = 454 grams
1 pint = 0.6 litre
1 gallon = 4.6 litres

Metric to Imperial
1 millimetre = 0.04 inch
1 centimetre = 0.4 inch
1 metre = 3 feet 3 inches
1 kilometre = 0.6 mile
1 gram = 0.04 ounce
1 kilogram = 2.2 pounds
1 litre = 1.8 pints

ELECTRICAL ADAPTORS

THE ELECTRICITY SUPPLY in Prague is 220V AC and two-pin plugs are used. For British or US plugs, an adaptor is needed. Adaptors may not be easily found in Prague and it is wise to buy one before leaving home.

PRAGUE TIME

PRAGUE IS ON Central European time, which is Greenwich Mean Time (GMT) plus 1 hour. Summer time runs effectively from the end of March up until the end of October – this is GMT plus 2 hours.

RELIGIOUS SERVICES

Anglican
St. Clement's; Klimentská 5.
Map 4 D2. 📞 11am Sun.

Baptist
Baptist Church of Prague;
Vinohradská 68. **Map** 6 F1.
📞 60 46 34 677. 🕐 11am Sun.

Hussite Church
Church of St. Nicholas;
Staroměstské náměstí. **Map** 3 C3.
📞 22 42 15 402.
🕐 10:30am Sun.

Interdenominational
International Church;
Peroutkova 57.
📞 22 09 10 769.
🌐 www.volny.cz/jx-studio
🕐 (in English) 10:30am Sun.

Jewish
Old-New Synagogue (see pp88–9).
Jerusalem Synagogue;
Jeruzalémská 7. **Map** 4 E4.
🌐 www.kehilaprag.cz
✡ (in Hebrew) Sundown Fri;
9am Sat.

Methodist-Evangelical
Ječná 19. **Map** 5 C2.
📞 22 43 15 613, 25 75 30 020.
🌐 www.praguefellowship.cz
🕐 5:30pm Sun.

Roman Catholic
Services are held in many churches. Some are:
Church of the Infant Jesus of Prague, Karmelitská 9. **Map** 2 E4.
📞 25 75 33 646. 🌐 www. apha.cz 🕐 (in English) noon Sun.
Church of St. Thomas, Josefská 8.
Map 2 E3. 📞 25 75 32 675.
🕐 (in English) 11am Sun.

A Roman Catholic service

GETTING TO PRAGUE

PRAGUE IS LOCATED at the heart of Europe and – apart from the Czech Republic's lack of motorways – has good transport connections with the rest of the continent. There are direct flights every day from most of Europe's major cities and, via ČSA, from Newark, in the USA. However, there are no direct flights from Australia. International coach transport is efficient and cheap.

ČSA aircraft

But the journey is about 20 hours from London compared to an hour and a half by air. International rail transport is a popular method of travelling to Prague, but trains tend to get booked up early, especially in the summer. The main train station (Hlavní nádraží) is close to Wenceslas Square and the city centre and, except for the airport, other major points of arrival are also fairly central.

AIR TRAVEL

THERE ARE 40 international airlines which now fly to Prague airport. If you are flying from the United States, **Delta Air** operate scheduled flights from the east coast of America. But these are not direct flights – there is a stopover in Frankfurt. There are no Australian or New Zealand carriers flying to Prague, although you can fly **British Airways** with a stop in London. Other airlines include **Air France**, **KLM**, **Air Canada** and **Czech Airlines** (**ČSA**). It takes about one and a half hours to fly from London to Prague and about nine hours from the east coast of America – not including the stopover.

DISCOUNT FARES

BECAUSE OF the increasing popularity of Prague as a tourist destination, many new airlines are starting to fly to the city. Increased competition has led to a significant drop in the price of flights.

Charter flights have been introduced by a few agents. They are set to become more popular and it is well worth investigating their availability. Remember that these can be subject to last-minute changes and cancellations. Check the ads in the travel sections of major papers for special fares.

APEX (advanced purchase) tickets can be good buys, but they have stringent conditions attached to them. These include having to book your ticket at least a month in advance and severe penalties if you cancel your flight.

If you ring well in advance, airlines will quote you the standard fare, but the price may be lowered nearer the time if seats remain unsold – this is rarely the case in the summer months. Students, senior citizens and regular business travellers may all be able to get discounts. Children under two (who do not occupy a separate seat) pay 10% of

Porters at Ruzyně

the adult fare. Remember fares are more expensive in July and August. If you do manage to get a cheaper deal, ensure that you will get a refund if your agent goes out of business.

AIRLINE OFFICES

Air Canada
Ruzyně Airport. 22 48 10 181.
W www.aircanada.ca

Air France
Václavské náměstí 57. **Map** 3 D5.
16 62 662. W www.airfrance.com

British Airways
Ruzyně Airport. 22 21 44 444.
W www.britishairways.com

Czech Airlines (ČSA)
V Celnici 5. **Map** 4 D3.
22 01 04 111. W www.csa.cz

Delta Air Lines
Národní 32. **Map** 3 B5. 22 49 46 733. W www.delta-air.cz

KLM
Na Příkopě 21. **Map** 3 C4. 223 30 90 933. W www.klm.com

Lufthansa
Ruzyně Airport. 22 01 14 456.
W www.lufthansa.cz

The recently modernized interior of Ruzyně Airport

RUZYNĚ AIRPORT

PRAGUE'S ONLY international airport, Ruzyně, is 15 km (9 miles) northwest of the city centre. The 1936 airport is small, but modern, clean, efficient and functional. It was modernized during the 1960s and now offers all that you would expect from an international airport: 24-hour exchange facilities; car rental offices; a duty-free shop; post office and a left-luggage office.

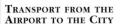

Sign for passport control

The airport was bought by Air France in 1992 and is presently undergoing further modernization, including the

The airport forecourt, from which buses and taxis can be taken into town

addition of a business class lounge. Other changes include a newly open catering facility. The quality of the food at the airport's restaurants and on ČSA flights has improved dramatically – a trained French chef has been employed to oversee all the preparation of both the traditional Czech and international dishes.

TRANSPORT FROM THE AIRPORT TO THE CITY

THE AIRPORT is linked to the city centre by a regular mini-bus service run by CEDAZ. For the return trip to the airport, these can be picked up at Náměstí Republiky and Dejvická metro stations. For a group of one to four people, the trip into town costs Kč350; for five to eight people it is Kč720. The buses can also take you to addresses outside the city, and can even be used to tour the

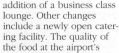

Sign for the CEDAZ airport bus at Náměstí Republiky metro station

Czech Republic. Whatever your destination, make sure to book the bus a couple of hours in advance. The buses can be ordered from 8am to 10pm daily. There is also a regular service to the airport from Dejvická metro (bus 119).

Alternatively, there is always a rank of taxis waiting in front of the terminal. Ask at the information booth about the price you should expect to pay for a taxi into town, and use it as a guide for the future.

CEDAZ
22 01 14 296 or 22 42 81 005.
FAX 22 01 14 286.
@ cedaz@cmail.cz

PRAGUE'S EUROPEAN AIR CONNECTIONS

Prague, situated at the centre of Europe, has good flight connections to most major European cities. It can be reached in less than two and a half hours on direct flights from all the airports marked on the map.

The spacious interior of the railway station, Masarykovo Nádraží

TRAVELLING BY TRAIN

Prague is connected by rail to all the major capitals of Europe. Rail travel can be an enjoyable, if rather slow, way to travel to and from Prague. International trains have dining cars and couchettes, and tickets are cheaper than air fares. The railways in the Czech Republic are run by the State (České Dráhy – ČD).

The façade of Hlavní nádraží

There are information offices at stations, and these usually have English speakers, so you shouldn't have any trouble booking a ticket. PIS and Čedok (see p219) will help you with timetables and prices. There are four types of train run by ČD. These are the rychlík (express) trains; the osobní (passenger) trains, which form a local service and stop at all stations, often travelling as slowly as 30 km/h (20 mph); the EX, or national express; and the EC (Eurocity) or international express. International trains are

the fastest, but get delayed at borders. Tickets can be bought in advance or on the day at stations or at the Travel Agency of České Dráhy (see p184), however, trains tend to get booked up quickly. If you do want to buy a ticket just before your train leaves, be warned that queues at ticket booths can be long. When you buy your ticket, specify exactly where and when you want to go, whether you want a single or return and what class of ticket you want. First class carriages exist on most trains and guarantee you a seat. In the timetable, an 'R' in a box by a train number means you must have a seat reserved on that train. An 'R' without a box means a reservation is recommended. If you are caught in the wrong carriage, you have to pay an on-the-spot fine.

TRAIN STATIONS

The biggest and busiest railway station in Prague is Hlavní nádraží (see p34) which is only a five-minute walk from the city centre. In the 1970s, the original Art Nouveau structure was enlarged and a modern departure hall now dominates

the whole terminal. The station is large, efficient and clean with a good-sized, inexpensive, 24-hr left-luggage office in the basement. The nearby luggage lockers are convenient and very cheap. There are also food stalls, bureaux de change and a number of booking and information services in the departure hall.

The other rail stations in the city are Masarykovo nádraží – Prague's oldest terminal, the newly-built and modern Holešovice Station and the smallest, Smíchov Station.

TRAVELLING BY COACH

Coach connections from Prague to many of the major European cities can be infrequent and are often very booked up. However, many of these coach routes are much cheaper, and often faster, than the slower trains. The city's main bus terminal is Florenc, situated on the eastern edge of the New Town.

A uniformed ČSD railway porter

During the summer months there are hundreds of coach trips to all the major coastal resorts in southern Europe. These get booked up quickly by Czechs, so buy your ticket in advance and be sure to reserve yourself a seat. International bus timetables are confusing; check with PIS (see p218) for more detailed information. Coach travel is cheap, but long-haul journeys can be uncomfortable and are slower than air.

Passengers boarding a long-haul coach

PRAGUE'S MAJOR RAIL AND COACH STATIONS

*The major points of arrival by train and coach are all
fairly central and easily accessible by metro – the nearest
metro to each terminal is shown in the boxes
along with more detailed travel information.*

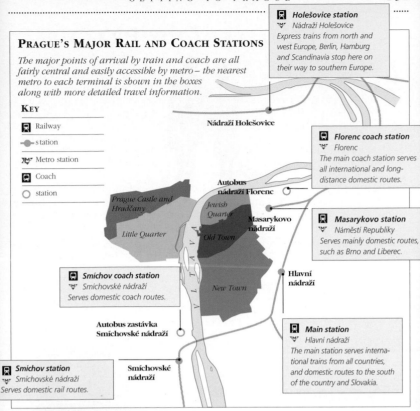

KEY

🚉 Railway

● station

Ⓜ Metro station

🚌 Coach

○ station

Holešovice station
Nádraží Holešovice
Express trains from north and
west Europe, Berlin, Hamburg
and Scandinavia stop here on
their way to southern Europe.

Nádraží Holešovice

Florenc coach station
Florenc
The main coach station serves
all international and long-
distance domestic routes.

Autobus
nádraží Florenc

Masarykovo station
Náměstí Republiky
Serves mainly domestic routes,
such as Brno and Liberec.

Smichov coach station
Smíchovské nádraží
Serves domestic coach routes.

Masarykovo
nádraží

Hlavní
nádraží

Main station
Hlavní nádraží
The main station serves international trains from all countries,
and domestic routes to the south
of the country and Slovakia.

Autobus zastávka
Smíchovské nádraží

Smichov station
Smíchovské nádraží
Serves domestic rail routes.

Smíchovské
nádraží

Prague Castle and
Hradčany / Jewish Quarter / Little Quarter / Old Town / New Town / VLTAVA

A Czech motorway sign

TRAVELLING BY CAR

TO DRIVE A CAR in the Czech Republic you must be at least 18. Most foreign driving licences, including Canadian, US and EC ones, are honoured – New Zealand and Australian drivers should get an International Driving Licence. If you bring your own car to Prague, by law you must carry the following with you at all times: a valid driver's licence, vehicle registration card, a hire certificate or, if you are borrowing the car, a letter signed by the owner and authorized by a recognized body, such as the AA or RAC, giving you permission to drive it and a Green Card (an international motoring certificate for insurance). If you drive on the motorway, you will also need to display a special card available at the border, petrol stations and post offices. Other items you have to carry at all times are a set of replacement bulbs, red warning triangles and a first-aid kit. You also have to display a national identification sticker. Headlights must be used even during daylight hours between November and April, and whenever visibility is poor. It is compulsory to wear seatbelts if fitted, and children under 12 are not allowed in the front seat. When you are driving it is strictly forbidden to have any alcohol in your blood and to use a mobile phone.

There are now good connections to all the major cities in the Czech Republic, including Bratislava and Brno, and many more are currently under construction.

Road signs are clear and easy to follow. The speed limit on motorways is 130 km/h (81 mph); on dual and single carriageways 90 km/h (56 mph) and in urban areas 50 km/h (31 mph). The traffic police patrolling the roads are very vigilant, and any infringements are dealt with harshly. There are also occasional road blocks to catch drunken drivers.

The popular, Czech-made Skoda car

GETTING AROUND PRAGUE

THE CENTRE OF PRAGUE is conveniently small and most of the sights can be reached comfortably on foot. But to cross the city quickly or visit a more remote sight, the public transport is efficient, clean and cheap. It is based on trams, buses and the underground (metro) system, all of which are run by the Prague Transport Corporation (Dopravní-podnik). Throughout this guide, the best method of transport

Walking around the city

is given for each sight. The metro and trams serve the city centre, while buses are used to reach the suburbs. The entire system is simple to use – only one ticket is needed for all three forms of transport. Bus, tram and metro routes are found on city maps, available at most city centre tabáks, bookshops and newsagents; or refer to the map on the inside back cover of this guide.

DRIVING A CAR

MOST VISITORS ARE better off not driving around the centre of Prague. The city's complex web of one-way streets, the large number of pedestrianized areas around the historic core of the city and a very severe shortage of parking spaces make driving very difficult. Prague's public transport system is a much more efficient way of travelling around the city centre.

If you do decide to use a car, remember that on-the-spot fines for traffic violations are common, especially if you are caught driving in one of the city's restricted areas, such as Wenceslas Square. Prague's motorists have become less disciplined and caution is often needed, You must drive on the right and the law states that both driver and front- and back-seat passengers should wear seat belts, if they are fitted. The speed limit in the city is 50 km/h (31 mph) unless a sign indicates otherwise. Traffic signs are similar

One-way traffic and No stopping except for supply lorries

to those in Western Europe. Cars can be useful for seeing sights outside the city. Car rental is inexpensive, but public transport is almost as efficient getting out of the city as in it (see pp228–31).

PARKING

CAR PARKING SPACES in the city centre are scarce and the penalties for illegal parking, harsh. Many parking areas are restricted and the only places to park legally on

PRAGUE ON FOOT

Pedestrian zone

Pedestrian crossing

Street or square name and Prague district

Walking around Prague is the most enjoyable way to see the city. Some pedestrian crossings are controlled by traffic lights, but be sure to cross only when the green man is flashing, and even then, check the road carefully. It is now illegal for drivers to ignore pedestrian crossings, but for years they were allowed to do so, and old habits die hard. Those crossings without lights are still ignored by drivers. Remember that trams run in the centre of the road and go in both directions, which can be confusing. They also travel at high speeds, occasionally coming upon you with little warning. With the uneven cobbled streets, steep hills and a mass of tram lines, flat comfortable shoes are strongly recommended.

Street number   **City registration number**

Brown street signs with tourist information

the street are in front of the New Town Hall in Karlovo náměstí, in Na Florenci and at Hlavní station. Unfortunately, car theft is rife, and expensive Western cars are a favourite target. It is safer to park in an official – preferably underground – car park *(see the Street Finder pp244–9)*. But these are expensive and tend to get full early on in the morning. Many parking spaces are reserved for office workers and disabled drivers. Parking at central hotels is limited, with only a few spaces allocated. It is better to park at one of the guarded car parks at the edge of the city and use public transport. Parking meters are rare in Prague but traffic wardens are not.

Parking sign

TOWING AND CLAMPING

Many prague locals park on the pavement. But ignoring *No Parking* signs may well mean that you find your car has been towed away or clamped. Both the municipal and the private firms that patrol the city are vigilant and ruthless with illegally parked cars, especially with foreign cars. If your car has disappeared, ring 158 to find out if it has been towed away or stolen. To reclaim your towed-away car, you have to go to one of the parking lots (the police will tell you which one) and pay a hefty fine before the car is released. Wheel clamping is becoming very

Prague's colourful clamp, also known as the Denver Boot

popular. You must pay a fine of several hundred crowns at a police station (the ticket on your windscreen will tell you the address) and return to your car to wait for the clamp to be removed.

THE TRANSPORT SYSTEM

The best way to get around the city centre is by metro or tram. Prague's rush hours are between 6am and 8am and 3pm and 5pm, Monday to Friday. But more trains, trams and buses run at these times, so crowding is not a problem. Some bus routes to the suburbs only run during peak hours. From 1 July to 31 August a summer timetable operates and the entire transport system is reduced. There are information offices at Muzeum and Karlovo nám metro stations (7am–9pm daily) and at Ruzyně Airport (7am–10pm daily); English is spoken.

One of the many newsstands in Wenceslas Square

TICKETS

Paying on the transport system relies on the honour system, with periodic checks by plain-clothes ticket inspectors who levy an on-the-spot and large fine if you don't have a valid ticket. There is one ticket for use on the entire system – bus, tram and metro. Buy the ticket before you travel and stamp or punch it yourself in the machines provided, or you will be travelling illegally. You can buy single ride tickets, from tabák stores and metro stations, or from the driver on buses, with exact change. There are automatic ticket machines in the metros *(see p234)*. Charges vary according to type of journey: up to 15 minutes with no changes (or 30 minutes and four stops on the metro), or up to 60 minutes with the possibility of changing your route. Children under six travel free and 6- to 15-year-olds travel half price.

You can also buy network tickets *(síť'ová jízdenka)*. These offer unlimited rides on buses, trams and metro for periods ranging from 24 hours to 30 days.

One-day pass

15-day pass

Travelling by Metro

T HE UNDERGROUND RAILWAY, known as the metro, is the
quickest and most comfortable form of transport in
Prague. Managed by the Prague Transport Corporation
(see p232), its construction began in 1967. It has three
lines, A, B and C, and 55 stations. The straightforward
layout and clear signs make finding your way around the
system very easy. Trains run between 5am and midnight.

**The metro sign for
Můstek metro station**

FINDING YOUR WAY
AROUND THE METRO

M ETRO ENTRANCES are not
always easy to spot.
Look for a sign displaying
the 'M' within an upside-
down triangle *(see right).*
The street entrance will
normally lead you down a
flight of steps. A high-
pitched bleep (for the blind)
at some entrances can also
help to guide you.

Once you have purchased
your ticket and passed
through the unmanned ticket
barriers, continue down the
fast-moving escalators to the
trains. At the bottom of each
escalator is a long central
corridor with a platform on
either side for trains
travelling in either direction.
Signs suspended from the
ceiling indicate the direction
of the trains *(see opposite
page).* The edges of the

platforms are marked with a
white, broken line which
should not be crossed until
the train stops. The metro
doors open and close automatically, giving a recorded
message when they are
about to close. During the
journey the name of the next
station is announced in
Czech.

Maps of the underground
system can be found above
each metro door.

Line A is the most useful
for tourists, because it covers
all the main areas of the city
centre – Prague Castle, the
Little Quarter, the Old Town
and the New Town – as well
as the main shopping area
around Wenceslas Square.

Displayed above some
seats are disabled signs.
These seats should be given
up for the elderly, disabled,
and those with small
children.

The spacious interior of Můstek metro station

AUTOMATIC
TICKET MACHINES

You can buy transport
tickets at designated
ticket sellers *(see p233)*
or at the automatic
ticket machines in the
metro station. The ticket
machines, and tickets
themselves, may vary in
design and colour, but
they are still applicable
to all forms of transport.
The machine offers a
choice of tickets at
varying prices, for adults,
children, bicycles and
other bulky items. Once
it has been validated, a
single-journey ticket is
valid for an hour.

1 Check which
price band is the
right one to meet
your requirements,
then press the
appropriately
labelled button.

3 If you are happy
that you have
selected the right
type of ticket, then
press the *výdej*
button to confirm
your choice. (If you
are unsure, press the
button labelled
storno and start the
process again.)

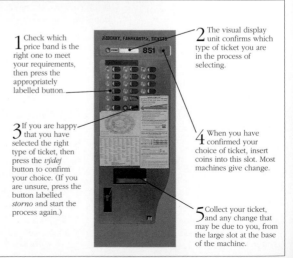

2 The visual display
unit confirms which
type of ticket you are
in the process of
selecting.

4 When you have
confirmed your
choice of ticket, insert
coins into this slot. Most
machines give change.

5 Collect your ticket,
and any change that
may be due to you, from
the large slot at the base
of the machine.

MAKING A JOURNEY BY METRO

1 The letters, each in a different colour, indicate the three metro lines. The number above the letter is the time it takes to get from one end of the line to the other.

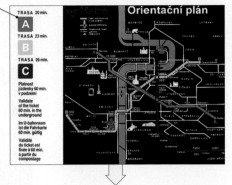

This metro map can be bought from most metro stations, tabáks and newsagents. A metro map has also been included at the end of this book.

2 To decide which line to take, find your destination on the *Street Finder (see pp244–9)*, its nearest metro station and then plot your route on a metro map.

3 You can use single-journey tickets *(left)*, or a network ticket *(below)* which give you unlimited travel for a set period of time, and are also valid for buses and trams *(see p233)*. Generally, a child's ticket costs half that of an adult's.

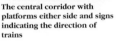

The central corridor with platforms either side and signs indicating the direction of trains

4 Before going down the escalators, you must stamp a single-journey ticket in one of these machines. If the ticket has not been stamped, it is not valid and you will have to pay a fine if caught. Do not stamp tourist tickets.

5 This sign, hanging from the ceiling, is visible when you come down the escalator. It shows the direction of the trains on each platform. This one says that the train's final station *(Stanice)* on the left is Háje, so from the metro map you know the train is travelling south.

"Stanice" means station

"Směr" means direction

Name of station

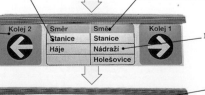

6 This sign along the central platform indicates the station on line C where you are (white circle) and those stations where you can transfer to the other lines (A and B). For stations to the left of the white circle follow the arrow to the left, and vice-versa for stations to the right.

The white circle indicates which station you are in

7 Once you are at your stop, follow the exit signs *(Výstup)* leading out of the metro system.

Travelling by Tram

TRAMS ARE PRAGUE'S oldest method of public transport. Horse-drawn trams appeared on the streets in 1879, but by 1891 the first electric tram was in operation. After the metro, the tram system is the fastest and most efficient way of getting around the city. Some lines only operate in the rush hour and there are a number of night trams, all of which pass by Lazarská in the New Town.

TRAM TICKETS

THE TRAM SYSTEM is run by the Prague Transport Corporation (see p230). Tram tickets are also valid for the metro and buses (see p233).

You have to buy your ticket before you board a tram. Once you have entered, you will see two or three small punching machines on metal poles just inside the door. Insert your ticket and it will be stamped automatically.

If you do not punch your ticket it is not valid and, if you are caught by a ticket inspector, you will have to pay an on-the-spot fine (see

p233). A single-journey ticket is valid for one journey only (see p233), however long.

Each tram stop has a time-table – the stop underlined is where you are standing. The stops below that line indicate where that tram is heading.

Trams run every 10 to 20 minutes. The doors open and close automatically and each stop is announced in Czech. After the metro closes, a small number of night trams run every 30 minutes or so. These trams (numbers 51 to 58) are marked by blue numbers at the tram stop. For more information see www.dp-praha.cz.

Tram Signs
These are found at every tram stop and tell you which trams stop there, and in what direction each tram is going.

Name of the tram stop   **Tram logo**

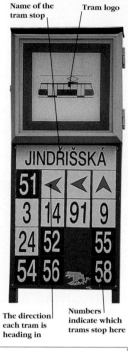

The direction each tram is heading in

Numbers indicate which trams stop here

One of the new trams on the streets of Prague

USEFUL TRAM ROUTES

These three tram routes are the most useful for getting around the centre of Prague. They pass many of the major sights on both sides of the Vltava, so are also a cheap, pleasant way of sightseeing.

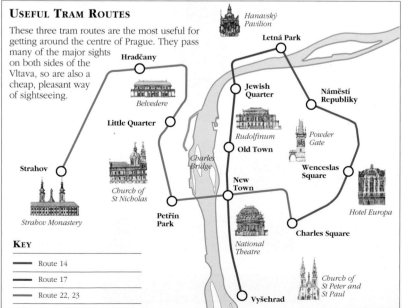

KEY

— Route 14

— Route 17

— Route 22, 23

Travelling by Bus

Y OU ARE UNLIKELY to use a bus unless you want to visit the outer suburbs. By law, buses are not allowed in the city centre (they produce noxious fumes and the streets are too narrow), so they transport people from the suburbs to tram and metro stops outside the centre.

Bus stop logo

BUS TICKETS

A typical public bus in Prague

U NLESS YOU HAVE small change, you must buy a ticket before you board a bus. Tickets are available from all the usual agents *(see p233)*.

Again, you must validate your ticket in the punching machine on the bus. If you buy a single-journey ticket, it is only valid for one journey. Each time you change bus, you will have to buy a new ticket, unless you have a tourist ticket *(see p233)*. The doors open and close automatically and the end of the boarding period is signalled by a high-pitched signal. You are expected to give up your seat for the elderly and disabled.

Bus timetables are located at every stop. They have the numbers of all the buses that stop there and the timetable for each route. The frequency of buses varies considerably. In the rush hour there may be 12 to 15 buses an hour, at other times as few as three.

Throughout the night there are 12 buses which go to the outer areas not served by the tram and metro system. For more information see www.dp-praha.cz.

Travelling by Taxi

F OR VISITORS TO PRAGUE taxis are a useful but often frustrating form of transport. After decades of public ownership, all taxis are now privately owned, but there are many unscrupulous drivers who are out to charge as much as they can get away with. For this reason it's worth taking a few simple precautions. For a start, find out how much a fare should cost.

An illuminated taxi sign

TAXI FARES

One of the many taxi ranks in the centre of the town

A S SOON AS you enter a taxi there is a minimum charge. After that, by law the fare should increase at a set rate per kilometre. However, this set charge is rarely, if ever, adhered to and taxis can be a very expensive way of getting around the city. Taxi meters can be set at four different rates but for journeys in the city it should be set at one (the cheapest). However, rather than depend on the meters –

they are often rigged – it is a wise move to negotiate a fare you think is reasonable before you enter the cab. Vigorous bargaining can often bring the price down. Few taxi drivers speak more than the most rudimentary English, so communication can be difficult. Unless your Czech pronunciation is good, write down your destination for them in Czech. At night, charges will increase, sometimes by 200 or even 300 per

Taxi receipts, if requested, are required to be given by law.

The distance travelled	Amount charged

eb
us european business solutions

cent. Be sure surcharges are included in the figure you negotiate beforehand. If problems do arise at the end of the journey, ask for a receipt before you pay. This will normally deter drivers from trying to overcharge you. Avoid taxis around the main tourist sights, these can often be the worst offenders. Despite occasional problems, taxis are a safe form of transport and women should feel comfortable alone in them.

The meter displays your fare and surcharges.

Fare	Surcharges	Rate

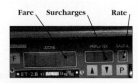

STREET FINDER

THE MAP REFERENCES given for all the sights, hotels, restaurants, bars, shops and entertainment venues described in this book refer to the maps in this section. A complete index of street names and all the places of interest marked, can be found on the following pages. The key map (right) shows the area of Prague covered by the *Street Finder*. This map includes sightseeing areas, as well as districts for hotels, restaurants, pubs and entertainment venues.

In keeping with Czech maps, none of the street names in the index or on the Street Finder have the Czech word for street, *ulice*, included (though you may see it on the city's street signs). For instance, Celetná ulice appears as Celetná in both the index and the Street Finder. The numbers preceding some street names are dates. In our index we ignore the numbers, so that 17. listopadu (17 November), is listed under 'L'.

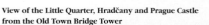

EVROPSKÁ

PATOČKOVA

MYSLBEKOVA

Prague Castle and Hradčany

VANÍČKOVA

KEY TO STREET FINDER

	Major sight
	Places of interest
	Other building
ⓜ	Metro station
🚆	Train station
🚌	Coach station
🚊	Tram stop
🚠	Funicular railway
🚢	River boat boarding point
🚕	Taxi rank
P	Car park
ℹ	Tourist information office
✚	Hospital with casualty unit
🏢	Police station
✝	Church
✡	Synagogue
⊠	Post office
══	Railway line
→	One-way street
	City wall
	Pedestrian street

SCALE OF MAP PAGES

0 metres   200
                       1:10,000
0 yards   200

View of the Little Quarter, Hradčany and Prague Castle from the Old Town Bridge Tower

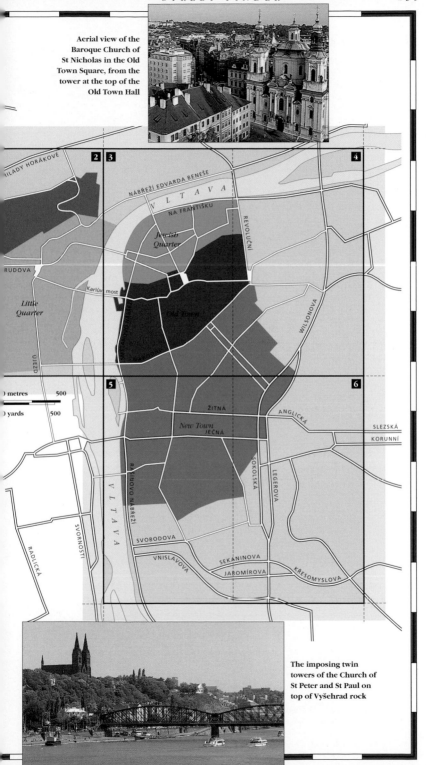

Aerial view of the
Baroque Church of
St Nicholas in the Old
Town Square, from the
tower at the top of the
Old Town Hall

2 **3**

MILADY HORÁKOVÉ

NÁBŘEŽÍ EDVARDA BENEŠE

V L T A V A

NA FRANTIŠKU

REVOLUČNÍ

*Jewish
Quarter*

4

RUDOVA

Karlův most

*Little
Quarter*

Old Town

WILSONOVA

ÚJEZD

0 metres   500

0 yards   500

5

ŽITNÁ

ANGLICKÁ

New Town

JEČNÁ

SLEZSKÁ

KORUNNÍ

6

RAŠÍNOVO NÁBŘEŽÍ

SOKOLSKÁ

LEGEROVA

V L T A V A

SVOBODOVA

VNISLAVOVA

SEKANINOVA

KŘESOMYSLOVA

RADLICKÁ

SVORNOSTI

JAROMÍROVA

The imposing twin
towers of the Church of
St Peter and St Paul on
top of Vyšehrad rock

Street Finder Index

THE ORDER OF THE NAMES in the index is affected by the *háček*, the accent like an inverted circumflex (*háček* means "little hook"). In the Czech alphabet, **č**, **ř**, **š** and **ž** are treated as separate letters. Street names beginning with **ř**, for example, are listed after those beginning with **r** without an accent.

Churches, buildings, museums and monuments are marked on the Street Finder maps with their English and Czech names. In the index, both forms are listed. However, English names for streets and squares, such as Wenceslas Square, do not appear on the maps. Where they are listed in the index, the Czech name is given in brackets in the form that appears on the map.

USEFUL WORDS	
dům	house
hrad	castle
kostel	church
klášter	convent, monastery
most	bridge
nábřeží	embankment
nádraží	station
náměstí	square
sady	park
schody	steps
třída	avenue
ulice	street
ulička	lane
zahrada	garden

A

Albertov	5 C4
Alšovo nábřeží	3 A3
Americká	6 F3
Anenská	3 A4
Anenské náměstí	3 A4
Anežská	3 C2
Anglická	6 E2
Anny Letenské	6 F1
Apolinářská	5 C4
Archbishop's Palace	2 D3
Arcibiskupský palác	2 D3
At St Thomas's	2 E3
At the Three Ostriches	2 F3
autobusové nádraži Praha, Florenc	4 F3
autobusová zast. Hradčanská	2 D1

B

Badeniho	2 F1
Balbínova	6 E2
Bartolomějská	3 B5
Barvířská	4 E2
Bazilika sv. Jiří	2 E2
Bělehradská	6 E2
Belgická	6 F3
Bělohorská	1 A4
Belvedér	2 E1
Belvedere	2 E1
Benátská	5 B3
Benediktská	4 D3
Besední	2 E5
Bethlehem Chapel	3 B4
Betlémská	3 A5
Betlémská kaple	3 B4
Betlémské náměstí	3 B4
Bílkova	3 B2
Biskupská	4 E2
Biskupský dvůr	4 E2
Blanická	6 F2

Bolzanova	4 E4
Boršov	3 A4
Botanical Gardens	5 B3
Botanická zahrada	5 B3
Botič	6 D5
Botičská	5 B4
Boženy Němcové	6 D4
Bridge Street (Mostecká)	2 E3
Bruselská	6 E3
Brusnice	1 C2
Břehová	3 A2
Břetislavova	2 D3

C

Capuchin Monastery	1 B2
Carolinum	3 C4
Celetná	3 C3
Chaloupeckého	1 B5
Chalice Restaurant	6 D3
Charles Bridge (Karlův most)	2 F4
continues	3 A4
Charles Square (Karlovo náměstí)	5 B2
Charles Street (Karlova)	2 A4
continues	3 B4
Charvátova	3 B5
Chodecká	1 A5
Chotkova	2 E1
Chotkovy sady	2 F1
Chrám sv. Víta	2 D2
Church of Our Lady before Týn	3 C3
Church of Our Lady beneath the Chain	2 E4
Church of Our Lady of the Snows	3 C5
Church of Our Lady Victorious	2 D4
Church of St Castullus	3 C2

Church of St Catherine	5 C3
Church of St Cyril and St Methodius	5 B2
Church of St Gall	3 C4
Church of St Giles	3 B4
Church of St Ignatius	5 C2
Church of St James	3 C3
Church of St John on the Rock	5 B3
Church of St Lawrence	1 C5
Church of St Martin in the Wall	3 B5
Church of St Nicholas (Little Quarter)	2 D3
Church of St Nicholas (Old Town)	3 B3
Church of St Simon and St Jude	3 B2
Church of St Stephen	5 C2
Church of St Thomas	2 E3
Church of St Ursula	3 A5
Church of the Holy Ghost	3 B3
Cihelná	2 F3
Clam-Gallas Palace	3 B4
Clam-Gallasův palác	3 B4
Clementinum	3 A4
Cubist Houses	3 B2
Cukrovarnická	1 A1

Č

Čechův most	3 B2
Čelakovského sady	6 E1
continues	6 D1
Černá	5 B1
Černín Palace	1 B3
Černínská	1 B2
Černínský palác	1 B3
Čertovka	2 F4
Červená	3 B3

D

Dalibor Tower	2 E2
Daliborka	2 E2
Dělostřelecká	1 A1
Diskařská	1 A5
Dittrichova	5 A2
Divadelní	3 A5
Dlabačov	1 A4
Dlážděná	4 E4
Dlouhá	3 C3
Dražického	2 F3
Dražického náměstí	2 E3
Dřevná	5 A3
Dům pánů z Kunštátu	3 B4
Dům U Dvou zlatých medvědů	3 B4
Dušní	3 B2
Dvořák Museum	6 D2
Dvořákovo nábřeží	3 A2

E

Elišky Krásnohorské	3 B2
Estates Theatre	3 C4

F

Faust House	5 B3
Faustův dům	5 B3
Florenc (metro)	4 F3
Franciscan Garden	3 C5
Francouzská	6 F2
Františkánská zahrada	3 C5
Fügnerovo náměstí	6 D3
Funicular Railway	2 D5

G

Gogolova	2 F1
Golden Lane (Zlatá ulička)	2 E2
Golz-Kinský Palace	3 C3

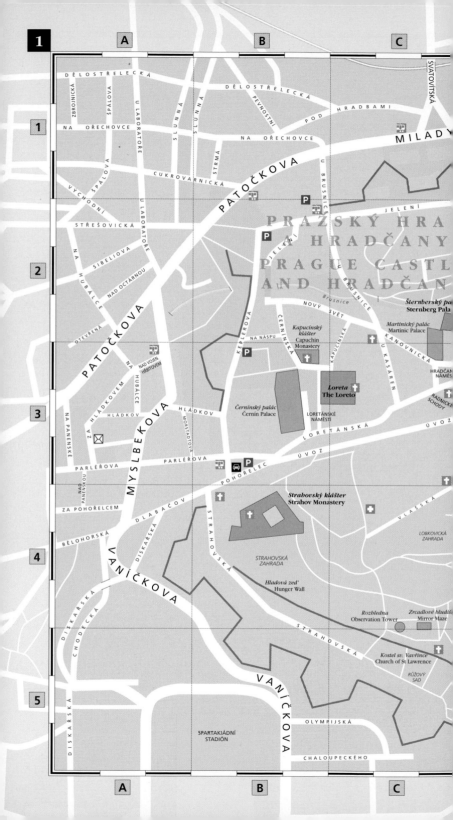

A B C

1

DĚLOSTŘELECKÁ
ZBROJNICKÁ
ŠPALOVA
U LABORATOŘE
SLUNNÁ
SLUNNÁ
DĚLOSTŘELECKÁ
PEVNOSTNÍ
POD HRADBAMI

SVATOVÍTSKÁ

NA OŘECHOVCE
NA OŘECHOVCE
STRMÁ

MILADY

VÝCHODNÍ
SPALOVA
CUKROVARNICKÁ
PATOČKOVA
U BRUSNICE
JELENÍ

STŘEŠOVICKÁ
U LABORATOŘE

PRAŽSKÝ HRA

NA HUBALCE
SIBELIOVA
NAD OCTÁRNOU
JELENÍ
Brusnice

A HRADČANY

2

PATOČKOVA
OTEVŘENÁ

NOVÝ SVĚT
Brusnice
U KASÁREN

PRAGUE CASTL

AND HRADČAN

KELLEROVA
NA NÁSPU
ČERNÍNSKÁ
Kapucínský klášter
Capuchin Monastery
KAPUCÍNSKÁ
KANOVNICKÁ

Šternberský pa
Sternberg Pala

Martinický palác
Martinic Palace

NA HLÁDKOVEM
ZA HLÁDKOVEM
NAD VOJEN. HŘBITOVEM
NA HUBALCE

Loreta
The Loreto

HRADČAN
NÁMĚS

3

NA PANENSKÉ
PATOČKOVA
HLÁDKOV
HLÁDKOV
MORSTADTOVA
Černínský palác
Černín Palace
LORETÁNSKÉ
NÁMĚSTÍ
LORETÁNSKÁ
ÚVOZ

RADNICKÉ
SCHODY

PARLÉŘOVA
MYSLBEKOVA
PARLÉŘOVA
POHOŘELEC
ÚVOZ

NAD PANENSKOU
ZA POHOŘELCEM
DLABAČOV
STRAHOVSKÁ
Strabovský klášter
Strahov Monastery

VLAŠSKÁ

LOBKOVICKÁ
ZAHRADA

4

BĚLOHORSKÁ
DISKAŘSKÁ
VANÍČKOVA
STRAHOVSKÁ ZAHRADA

Hladová zeď'
Hunger Wall
STRAHOVSKÁ

Rozhledna
Observation Tower
Zrcadlové bludiš
Mirror Maze

DISKAŘSKÁ
CHODECKÁ

VANÍČKOVA
Kostel sv. Vavřince
Church of St Lawrence

RŮŽOVÝ
SAD

5

DISKAŘSKÁ
SPARTAKIÁDNÍ STADIÓN
OLYMPIJSKÁ

CHALOUPECKÉHO

A B C

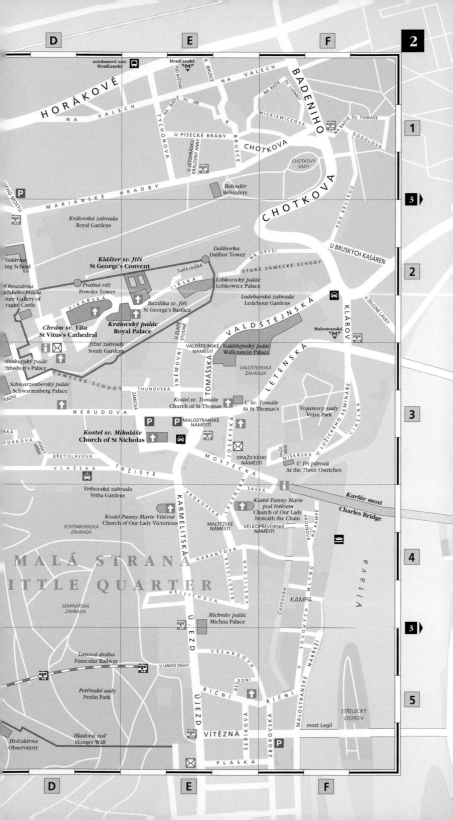

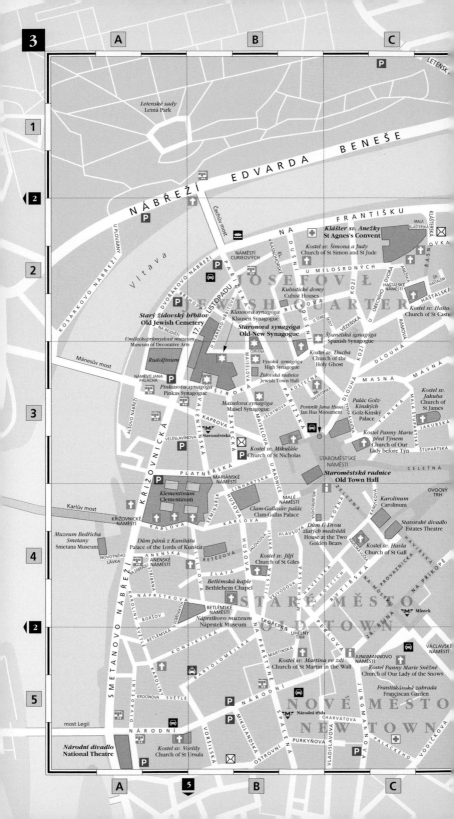

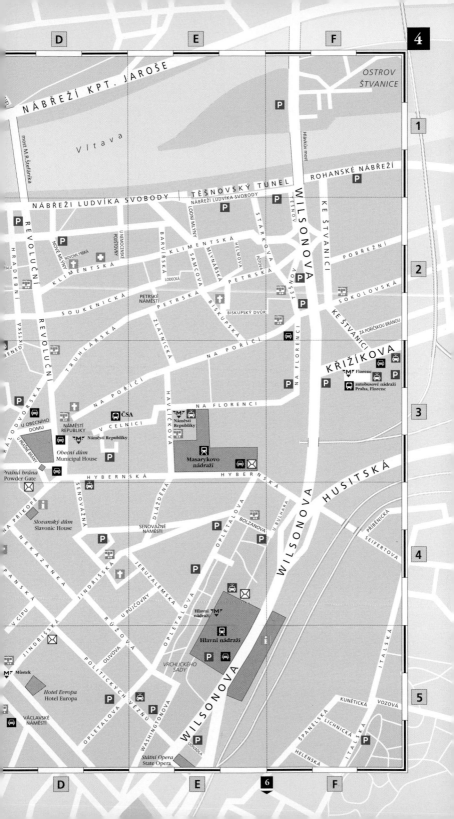

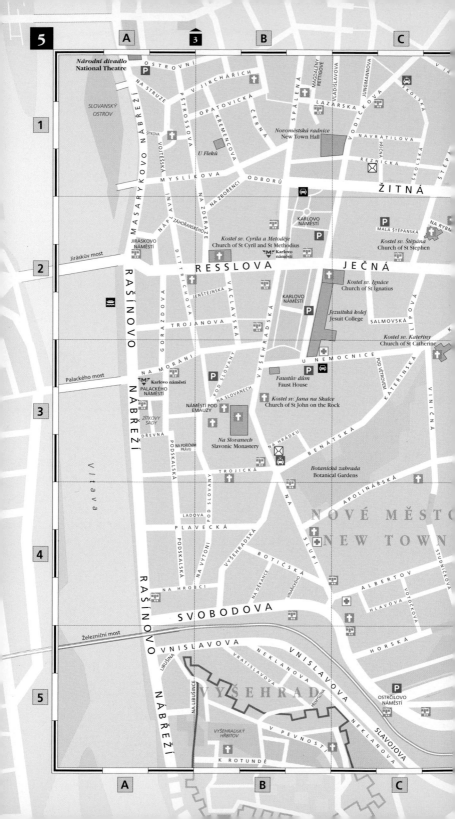

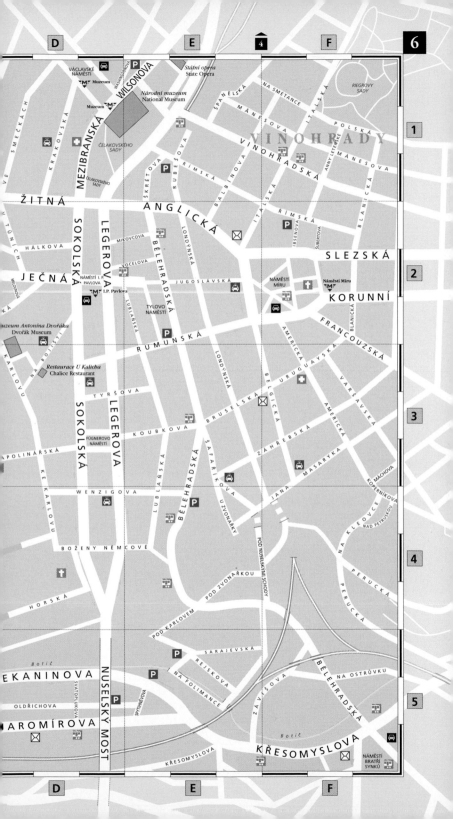

General Index

Acknowledgments

DORLING KINDERSLEY wishes to thank the following people who contributed to the preparation of this book.

MAIN CONTRIBUTOR

Vladimír Soukup was born in Prague in 1949. He worked for the daily newpaper, *Evening Prague*, for 20 years, eventually becoming Deputy Chief Editor. He has written a wide range of popular guides to Prague.

ADDITIONAL CONTRIBUTORS

Ben Sullivan, Lynn Reich.

EDITORIAL AND DESIGN

MANAGING EDITOR Carolyn Ryden; MANAGING ART EDITOR Steve Knowlden; SENIOR EDITOR Georgina Matthews; SENIOR ART EDITOR Vanessa Courtier; EDITORIAL DIRECTOR David Lamb; ART DIRECTOR Anne-Marie Bulat; PRODUCTION CONTROLLER Hilary Stephens; PICTURE RESEARCH Ellen Root; DTP DESIGNER Salim Qurashi; CONSULTANT Helena Svojsikova; MAPS Caroline Bowie, Simon Farbrother, James Mills-Hicks, David Pugh (DKCartography).

Tessa Bindloss, Lucinda Cooke, Michelle Crane, Russell Davies, Stephanie Driver, Fay Franklin, Alistair Gunn, Elaine Harries, Charlie Hawkings, Jan Kaplan, Dr Tomáš Kleisner, Susannah Marriott, Sam Merrell, Robert Purnell, Marian Sucha, Helen Townsend, Daphne Trotter, Conrad Van Dyk, Christopher Vinz.

ADDITIONAL PHOTOGRAPHY

DK Studio/Steve Gorton, Otto Palan, M Soskova, Clive Streeter, Alan Williams.

t = top; tl = top left; tc = top centre; tr = top right; cla = centre left above; ca = centre above; cra = centre right above; cl = centre left; c = centre; cr = centre right; clb = centre left below; cb = centre below; crb = centre right below; bl = bottom left; b = bottom; bc = bottom centre; br = bottom right; d = detail.

Works of art on the pages detailed above have been reproduced with the permission of the following copyright holders: Aristide Maillol *Pomona* 1910 © ADAG, Paris, and DACS, London, 1998: 164cr. Gustav Makarius Tauc (An der Aulenkaut 31, Wiesbaden, Germany) under commission of the Minorite Order in Rome: 35br.

The publishers are grateful to the following individuals, companies and picture libraries for permission to reproduce photographs or to photograph at their establishments: ARCHEOLOGICKÝ ÚSTAV ČESKÉ AKADEMIE VĚD: 20t; ARCHIV FÜR KUNST UND GESCHICHTE, BERLIN: 17b, 18tl (d), 18tr, 18bc(d), 18br(d), 19tl(d), 19tc(d), 19tr(d), 19c(d), 19bc(d), 20clr, 20bl, 23cb(d), 29cla(d), 32t(d), 32bl, 34ca(d), 35ca(d), 35bl, 43tl, 50b(d), 105cr, 118t, Erich Lessing 28ca(d), 31bl(d), 88c, 89cb; ARCHÍV HLAVNIHO MESTA. PRAHY (CLAM-GALLASÜV PALÁC): 23cl, 24bl, 28bl, 28br, 30b, 33clb, 33bc, 72t, 136br, 137br(d), 138ca, 168c. BILDARCHIV PREUSSISCHER KULTURBESITZ: 4t(d), 19bl(d), 29br, 34bc, 68tr, 104bl(d); BRIDGEMAN ART LIBRARY, London: Prado, Madrid 29t; Rosegarten Museum, Constance 26ca. ČESKÁ TISKOVÁ KANCELÁŘ: 19br, 35cbr, 195cr; ČSA: 228t;

JEAN-LOUP CHARMET: 18bl(d), 21c, 31br, 33t, 33bl, 33br(d), 34tr(d), 34bl, 62c, 69tc; ZDENEK CHRAPPEK: 50c; COM-STOCK: Georg Gerster: 10; JOE CORNISH: 58–9, 60, 148br; CZECH NATIONAL BANK: 223. MARY EVANS PICTURE LIBRARY: 9, 59, 138cb, 181, 217. GRAFOPRINT NEUBERT: 31clb, 38clb, 116c. ROBERT HARDING PICTURE LIBRARY: Michael Jenner 128tl; Christopher Rennie 24ca, 103tr; Peter Scholey 30t, 129tl; HUTCHISON LIBRARY: Libuše Taylor 51b, 52t, 175tl, 197c. THE IMAGE BANK: Andrea Pistolesi 14b; Courtesy of ISIC, UK: 226c. KANCELÁŘ PREZIDENTA REPUBLIKY: 20–1, 21tr, 21bl, 21br, 22c; KAPLAN PRODUCTIONS: 117t; OLDRICH KARASEK: 56cb, 62tr, 101crb, 134t, 176t, 197c, 211t, 225cl, 233bc; KARLŠTEJN: 25tl; Vladimír Hyhlík 24–5, Oldrich Karasek 135b; KAREL KESTNER: 35cbl; KLEMENTINUM: 23tl; Prokop Paul 22t; THE KOBAL COLLECTION: 35tl; DALIBOR KUSÁK: 164bl, 166–7 all, 16–9 all. IVAN MALÝ: 210t, 210c; MUZEUM HLAVNÍHO MĚSTA PRAHY 32–3; MUZEUM POŠTOVNÍ ZNÁMKY: 149cl. NÁRODNÍ FILMOVÝ ARCHIV: 34br; NÁRODNÍ GALERIE V PRAZE: 24br, 40b; Grafická sbírka 26t, 27bl, 31t, 67b, 69c, 100t, 102b, 121t, 125cb, 129br, 138b, 157cb, 175b, 178b; Klášter sv. Anežky 39tr, 83t, 92–3 all, 133b; Klášter sv. Jiří 16, 37br, 38t, 39tr, 97clb, 106–7 all, 108 –9 all, Šternberský palác 38ca, 112–3 all, 114–5 all, Veletržni Palac 164–5 all; Zbraslav 40b; NÁRODNÍ MUZEUM, PRAHA: 147b; NÁRODNÍ MUZEUM V PRAZE: Vlasta Dvořáková 20clb, 26–7, 26bl, 26bc, 26br, 27t, 27cl, 27cr, 27br, 29bl, 39cb, 75b, 72b, Jarmila Kutová 20c, 22bl, Dagmar Landová 28bc, 126c, Muzeum Antonína Dvořáka 39b, Muzeum Bedřicha Smetany 32ca, Prokop Paul 75b, Tyršovo Muzeum; 34cb, 149bl; NÁRODNÍ TECHNICKÉ MUZEUM: Gabriel Urbánek 41t. OBRAZÁRNA PRAŽSKEHO HRADU: 98b; ÖSTERREICHISCHE NATIONALBIBLIOTHEK, WIEN: 25clb, 26cb. PIVOVARSKÉ MUZEUM: 190c, 196c; BOHUMÍR PROKŮPEK: 25bl, 30t, 120c, 121c, 121bl, 163b. REX FEATURES LTD: Alfred 35tr, Richard Gardener 232t. SCIENCE PHOTO LIBRARY: Geospace 11, 38crb; SOTHEBY'S/ THAMES AND HUDSON: 104c; STÁTNÍ ÚSTREDNI ARCHIV: 23b; STÁTNÍ ÚSTAV PAMÁTKOVÉ PÉČE: 23tc; STÁTNÍ ŽIDOVSKÉ MUZEUM: 39ca, 85t, 85c, 90t; LUBOMÍR STIBUREK, www.czfoto.cz: 55b, 132c, 145ca, 163t, 176c, 234c, 235cl, 235cba, 235bca, 236cr; MARIAN SUCHA: front endpaper Lbl, 55t, 56cb, 94, 127b, 174t, 197bl, 197t, 225b, 229tr, 229c; SVATOVÍTSKÝ POKLAD, PRAŽSKÝ HRAD: 14t, 21tl, 24t, 24cb, 28t, 40tr. UMĚLECKOPRÚMYS-LOVÉ MUZEUM V PRAZE: 39tl, 40tl, 149c, 149br, Gabriel Urbánek 28clb, 41b; UNIVERZITA KARLOVA: 25tr. PETER WILSON: 4b, 191t, 216–7, 238. ZEFA: 33cra. Front endpaper: all special or additional photography except (centre) JOE CORNISH. JACKET: Front - DK PICTURE LIBRARY: Clive Streeter bc; Stanislav Tereba cbl; Vladimir Kozlik crb; GETTY IMAGES: Joe Cornish main image. Back - DK PICTURE LIBRARY: Peter Wilson t, b. Spine - GETTY IMAGES: Joe Cornish.

All other images © Dorling Kindersley.

For further information, see: www.dkimages.com

Phrase Book

IN EMERGENCY

Help!	**Pomoc!**	*po-mots*
Stop!	**Zastavte!**	*za-stav-te*
Call a	**Zavolejte**	*za-vo-ley-te*
doctor!	**doktora!**	*dok-to-ra!*
Call an	**Zavolejte**	*za-vo-ley-te*
ambulance!	**sanitku!**	*sa-nit-ku!*
Call the	**Zavolejte**	*za-vo-ley-te*
police!	**policii!**	*poli-tsi-yi!*
Call the fire	**Zavolejte**	*za-vol-ey-te*
brigade!	**hasiče**	*ha-si-che*
Where is the	**Kde je**	*gde ye*
telephone?	**telefón?**	*tele-fohn?*
the nearest	**nejbližší**	*ney-blish-ee*
hospital?	**nemocnice?**	*ne-mots-nyitse?*

COMMUNICATION ESSENTIALS

Yes/No	**Ano/Ne**	*ano/ne*
Please	**Prosím**	*pro-seem*
Thank you	**Děkuji vám**	*dye-ku-ji vahm*
Excuse me	**Prosím vás**	*pro-seem vahs*
Hello	**Dobrý den**	*do-bree den*
Goodbye	**Na shledanou**	*na s-hle-da-no*
Good evening	**Dobrý večer**	*dob-ree vech-er*
morning	**ráno**	*rah-no*
afternoon	**odpoledne**	*od-po-led-ne*
evening	**večer**	*ve-cher*
yesterday	**včera**	*vche-ra*
today	**dnes**	*dnes*
tomorrow	**zítra**	*zeet-ra*
here	**tady**	*ta-di*
there	**tam**	*tam*
What?	**Co?**	*tso?*
When?	**Kdy?**	*gdi?*
Why?	**Proč?**	*proch?*
Where?	**Kde?**	*gde?*

USEFUL PHRASES

How are you?	**Jak se máte?**	*yak-se mah-te?*
Very well,	**Velmi dobře**	*vel-mí dob-rzhe*
thank you.	**děkuji.**	*dye kuyi*
Pleased to meet you.	**Těší mě.**	*tyesh-ee mye*
See you soon.	**Uvidíme se**	*u-vi-dyee-me-se-*
	brzy.	*br-zi*
That's fine.	**To je v**	*to ye vpo-*
	pořádku.	*rzhahdku*
Where is/are...?	**Kde je/jsou ...?**	*gde ye/yso ...?*
How long does	**Jak dlouho trvá**	*yak dlo ho to tr-va*
it take to get to..?	**se dostat do..?**	*se do-stat do...?*
How do I get to...?	**Jak se**	*yak se*
	dostanu k ..?	*do-sta-nu k ..?*
Do you speak	**Mluvíte**	*mlu-vee-te*
English?	**anglicky?**	*an-glits-ki?*
I don't understand.	**Nerozumím.**	*ne-ro-zu-meem*
Could you speak	**Mohl(a)* byste**	*mohl- (a) bis-te*
more slowly?	**mluvit trochu**	*mlu-vit tro-khu*
	pomaleji?	*po-maley?*
Pardon?	**Prosím?**	*pro-seem?*
I'm lost.	**Ztratil(a)***	*stra-tyil (a)*
	jsem se.	*ysem se.*

USEFUL WORDS

big	**velký**	*vel-kee*
small	**malý**	*mul-ee*
hot	**horký**	*hor-kee*
cold	**studený**	*stu-den-ee*
good	**dobrý**	*dob-ree*
bad	**špatný**	*shpat-nee*
well	**dobře**	*dob-rzhe*
open	**otevřeno**	*ot-ev-rzhe-no*
closed	**zavřeno**	*zav-rzhe-no*
left	**do leva**	*do le-va*
right	**do prava**	*do pra-va*
straight on	**rovně**	*rov-nye*
near	**blízko**	*blee-sko*
far	**daleko**	*da-le-ko*
up	**nahoru**	*na-ho-ru*
down	**dolů**	*do-loo*
early	**brzy**	*br-zi*
late	**pozdě**	*poz-dye*
entrance	**vchod**	*vkhod*
exit	**východ**	*vee-khod*
toilets	**toalety**	*toa-leti*
free, unoccupied	**volný**	*vol-nee*
free, no charge	**zdarma**	*zdar-ma*

MAKING A TELEPHONE CALL

I'd like to place a	**Chtěl(a)* bych**	*khtyel(a) bikh*
call.	**volat**	*vo-lat*
I'd like to make a	**Chtěl(a)* bych**	*khtyel(a) bikh*
reverse-charge call.	**volat na účet**	*volat na oo-chet*
	volaného.	*volan-eh-ho*
I'll try again later.	**Zkusím to**	*skus-eem to*
	později.	*poz-dyey*
Can I leave	**Mohu nechat**	*mo-hu ne-khat*
a message?	**zprávu?**	*sprah-vu?*
Hold on.	**Počkejte.**	*poch-key-te*
Could you speak	**Mohl(a)* byste**	*mo-hl (a) bis-te*
up a little, please?	**mluvit hlasitěji?**	*mluvit hla-si-tyey?*
local call	**místní hovor**	*meest-nyee hov-or*

SIGHTSEEING

art gallery	**galerie**	*ga-ler-riye*
bus stop	**autobusová**	*au-to-bus-o-vah*
	zastávka	*za-stah-vka*
church	**kostel**	*kos-tel*
garden	**zahrada**	*za hra-da*
library	**knihovna**	*knyi-hov-na*
museum	**muzeum**	*muz-e-um*
railway station	**nádraží**	*nah-dra-zhee*
tourist	**turistické**	*tooristi-tske*
information	**informace**	*in-for-ma-tse*
closed for the	**státní**	*staht-nyee*
public holiday	**svátek**	*svah-tek*

SHOPPING

How much does	**Co to stojí?**	*tso to sto-yee?*
this cost?		
I would like ...	**Chtěl(a)* bych ...**	*khtyel(a) bikh...*
Do you have ...?	**Máte ...?**	*maa-te ...?*
I'm just looking.	**Jenom se dívám.**	*ye-nom se*
		dyee-vahm
Do you take	**Berete kreditní**	*be-re-te kred-it*
credit cards?	**karty?**	*nyee kartí?*
What time do	**V kolik**	*v ko-lik*
you open/	**otevíráte/**	*o-te-vee-rah-te/*
close?	**zavíráte?**	*za vee rah-te?*
this one	**tento**	*ten-to*
that one	**tamten**	*tam-ten*
expensive	**drahý**	*dra-hee*
cheap	**levný**	*lev-nee*
size	**velikost**	*vel-ih-kost*
white	**bílý**	*bee-lee*
black	**černý**	*cher-nee*
red	**červený**	*cher-ven-ee*
yellow	**žlutý**	*zhlu-tee*
green	**zelený**	*zel-en-ee*
blue	**modrý**	*mod-ree*
brown	**hnědý**	*hnyed-ee*

TYPES OF SHOP

antique shop	**starožitnictví**	*sta-ro zhit--*
		nyits-tvee
bank	**banka**	*banka*
bakery	**pekárna**	*pe-kahr-na*
bookstore	**knihkupectví**	*knih-kupets-tvee*
butcher	**řeznictví**	*rzhez-nyits-tvee*
camera shop	**obchod**	*op-khot*
	s fotoaparáty	*sfoto-aparahti*
chemist		
(prescriptions etc)	**lékárna**	*leb-kah-rna*
chemist (cosmetics,		
toiletries etc)	**drogerie**	*drog-erye*
delicatessen	**lahůdky**	*la-boo-dki*
department store	**obchodní dům**	*op-khod-nyee doom*
grocery	**potraviny**	*pot-ra-vini*
glass	**sklo**	*sklo*
hairdresser		
(ladies)	**kadeřnictví**	*ka-derzh-nyits-tvee*
(mens)	**holič**	*ho-lich*
market	**trh**	*trkh*
newsstand	**novinový**	*no-vi-novee*
	stánek	*stah-nek*
post office	**pošta**	*posh-ta*
supermarket	**samoobsluha**	*sa-mo-ob-slu-ha*
tobacconist	**tabák**	*ta-bahk*
travel	**cestovní**	*tses-tov-nyi*
agency	**kancelář**	*kantse-laarzh*

STAYING IN A HOTEL

Do you have a vacant room?	Máte volný pokoj?	*mah-te vol-nee po-koy?*
double room	dvoulůžkový pokoj	*dvo-loozh-kovee po-koy*
with double bed	s dvojitou postelí	*sdvoy-to pos-telee*
twin room	pokoj s dvěma postelemi	*po-koy sdvye-ma pos-tel-emi*
room with a bath	pokoj s koupelnou	*po-koy s ko-pel-no*
porter	vrátný	*vraht-nee*
hall porter	nosič	*nos-ich*
key	klíč	*kleech*
I have a reservation.	Mám reservaci.	*mahm rez-ervatsi*

EATING OUT

Have you got a table for ...?	Máte stůl pro ...?	*mah-te stool pro ...?*
I'd like to reserve a table.	Chtěl(a)* bych rezervovat stůl.	*khtyel(a) bikh rez-er-vov-at stool*
breakfast	snídaně	*snyee-danye*
lunch	oběd	*ob-yed*
dinner	večeře	*vech e-rzhe*
The bill, please.	Prosím, účet.	*pro-seem oo-chet*
I am a vegetarian.	Jsem vegetarián(ka)*.	*ysem veghe-tariahn(ka)*
waitress!	slečno	*slech-no*
waiter!	pane vrchní!	*pane vrkh-nyee!*
fixed price menu	standardní menu	*stan-dard-nyee men-u*
dish of the day	nabídka dne	*nab-eed-ka dne*
starter	předkrm	*przhed-krm*
main course	hlavní jídlo	*hlav-nyee yeed-lo*
vegetables	zelenina	*zel-en-yin-a*
dessert	zákusek	*zah-kusek*
cover charge	poplatek	*pop-la-tek*
wine list	nápojový lístek	*nah-po-yo-vee lee-stek*
rare (steak)	krvavý	*kr-va-vee*
medium	středně udělaný	*strzhed-nye ud-yel-an-ee*
well done	dobře udělaný	*dobrzhe- ud-yel-an-ee*
glass	sklenice	*sklen-yitse*
bottle	láhev	*lah-hev*
knife	nůž	*noozh*
fork	vidlička	*vid-lich-ka*
spoon	lžíce	*lzhee-tse*

MENU DECODER

biftek	*bif-tek*	steak
bílé víno	*bee-leh vee-no*	white wine
bramborové knedlíky	*bram-bo-ro-veh kne-dleeki*	potato dumplings
brambory	*bram-bo-ri*	potatoes
chléb	*khlehb*	bread
cibule	*tsi-bu-le*	onion
citrónový džus	*tsi-tron-o-vee dzhuus*	lemon juice
cukr	*tsukr*	sugar
čaj	*chay*	tea
čerstvé ovoce	*cher-stveh-o-vo-ce*	fresh fruit
červené víno	*cher-ven-eh vee-no*	red wine
česnek	*ches-nek*	garlic
dort	*dort*	cake
fazole	*fa-zo-le*	beans
grilované	*gril-ov-a-neh*	grilled
houby	*ho-bi*	mushrooms
houska	*hous-ka*	roll
houskové knedlíky	*ho-sko-veh kne-dleeki*	bread dumplings
hovězí	*hov-ye-zee*	beef
hranolky	*hran-ol-ki*	chips
husa	*hu-sa*	goose
jablko	*ya-bl-ko*	apple
jahody	*ya-ho-di*	strawberries
jehněčí	*ye-hnye-chee*	lamb
kachna	*kakh-na*	duck
kapr	*ka-pr*	carp
káva	*kah-va*	coffee
krevety	*krev-et-i*	prawns
kuře	*ku-rzhe*	chicken
kyselé zelí	*kis-el-eh zel-ee*	sauerkraut
maso	*ma-so*	meat
máslo	*mah-slo*	butter
minerálka	*min-er-ahl-ka*	mineral water
šumivá/ nešumivá	*shum-i-vah/ ne-shum i-vah*	fizzy/ still

mléko	*mleh-ko*	milk
mořská jídla	*morzh-skah-yeed-la-*	seafood
ocet	*ots-et*	vinegar
okurka	*o-ku-rka*	cucumber
olej	*oley*	oil
párek	*paa-rek*	sausage/frankfurter
pečené	*petsh-en-eh*	baked
pečené	*pech-en-eh*	roast
pepř	*peprzh*	pepper
polévka	*pol-eh-vka*	soup
pomeranč	*po-me-ranch*	orange
pomerančový džus	*po-me-ran-ch-- o-vee dzhuus*	orange juice
pivo	*pi-vo*	beer
rajské	*rayskeh*	tomato
ryba	*rib-a*	fish
rýže	*ree-zhe*	rice
salát	*sal-at*	salad
sůl	*sool*	salt
sýr	*seer*	cheese
šunka	*shun-ka*	ham
vařená/ uzená	*varzh-enah u-zenah*	cooked smoked
telecí	*te-le-tsee*	veal
tuna	*tu-na*	tuna
vajíčko	*va-yee-chko*	egg
vařené	*varzh-en-eh*	boiled
vepřové	*vep-rzho-veh*	pork
voda	*vo-da*	water
vývar	*vee-var*	broth
zelí	*zel-ee*	cabbage
zelenina	*zel-enyina*	vegetables
zmrzlina	*zmrz-lin-a*	ice cream

NUMBERS

1	jedna	*yed-na*
2	dvě	*dvye*
3	tři	*trzhi*
4	čtyři	*chti-rzhi*
5	pět	*pyet*
6	šest	*shest*
7	sedm	*sedm*
8	osm	*osm*
9	devět	*dev-yet*
10	deset	*des-et*
11	jedenáct	*ye-de-nahtst*
12	dvanáct	*dva-nahtst*
13	třináct	*trzhi-nahtst*
14	čtrnáct	*chtr-nahtst*
15	patnáct	*pat-nahtst*
16	šestnáct	*shest-nahtst*
17	sedmnáct	*sedm-nahtst*
18	osmnáct	*osm-nahtst*
19	devatenáct	*de-va-te-nahtst*
20	dvacet	*dva-tset*
21	dvacet jedna	*dva-tset yed-na*
22	dvacet dva	*dva-tset dva*
23	dvacet tři	*dva-tset-trzhi*
24	dvacet čtyři	*dva-tset chti-rzhi*
25	dvacet pět	*dva-tset pyet*
30	třicet	*trzhi-tset*
40	čtyřicet	*chti-rzhi-tset*
50	padesát	*pa-de-saht*
60	šedesát	*she-de-saht*
70	sedmdesát	*sedm-de-saht*
80	osmdesát	*osm-de-saht*
90	devadesát	*de-va-de-saht*
100	sto	*sto*
1,000	tisíc	*tyi-seets*
2,000	dva tisíce	*dva tyi-see-tse*
5,000	pět tisíc	*pyet tyi-seets*
1,000,000	milión	*mi-li-ohn*

TIME

one minute	jedna minuta	*yed-na min-uta*
one hour	jedna hodina	*yed-na hod-yin-a*
half an hour	půl hodiny	*pool hod-yin-i*
day	den	*den*
week	týden	*tee-den*
Monday	pondělí	*pon-dye-lee*
Tuesday	úterý	*oo-ter-ee*
Wednesday	středa	*strzhe-da*
Thursday	čtvrtek	*chtvr-tek*
Friday	pátek	*pah-tek*
Saturday	sobota	*so-bo-ta*
Sunday	neděle	*ned-yel-e*

Alternatives for a female speaker are shown in brackets.

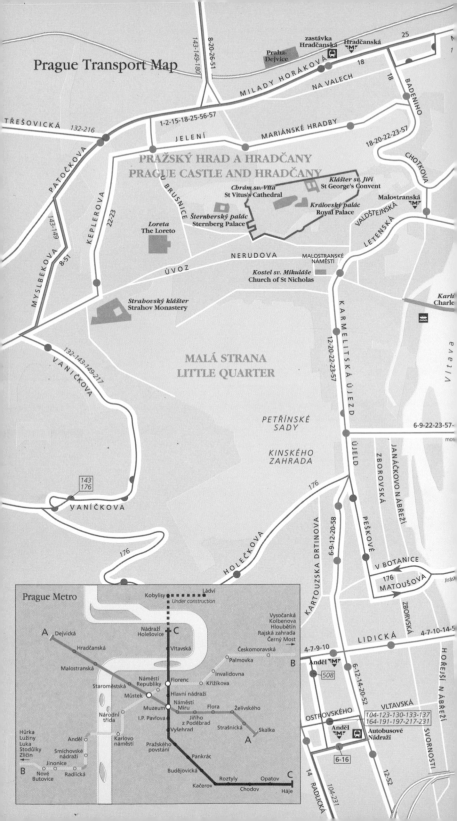